COLORADO
ON GLASS

02927

Solomon N. Carvalho

Adventurer in the West

Solomon Nunes Carvalho — daguerreo-typist on the 1853 Fremont expedition across Colorado — is portrayed here in a self portrait, painted shortly before the expedition set forth into the "Great American Desert."   SHSC

COLORADO ON GLASS

Colorado's First Half Century As Seen by the Camera

By

Terry Wm. Mangan

With a Directory of Early Colorado
Photographers by Opal Murry Harber

SUNDANCE *Limited*
100 KALAMATH STREET
DENVER, COLORADO 80223

COLORADO ON GLASS

Colorado's First Half Century As Seen by the Camera

By

Terry Wm. Mangan

To Charles Edward Rowbotham
without whose initial encouragement and constant
support over a period of five years, this book
would not have been written

Printing by Sundance Limited
Denver, Colorado, U.S.A.

Binding by Mountain States Bindery
Salt Lake City, Utah

FIRST EDITION — FIRST PRINTING

Foreword

Photographs are coming more and more to be recognized as important resources for historical research. Along with the manuscripts, official records, newspapers, and other materials routinely consulted by historians, photographs can add a wealth of information to be found nowhere else. In the burgeoning field of historic preservation, for example, what source surpasses a photograph for showing exactly how a structure looked at a specific time? If a series of photographs of a building, taken over a period of years, is available, even minor changes and alterations soon become evident. In restoring the Baca House in Trinidad, for example, the State Historical Society of Colorado found that photographs were among the most important sources of information to aid staff members in reconstructing features such as the "widow's walk" and the shutters, which had disappeared since Don Felipe Baca and his family lived in the adobe house, built in 1869.

Photographs truly provide a "window into the past," stopping the clock for one instant and allowing a glimpse of life in a particular place and time. Especially prized by historians are the relatively rare photographs of building interiors. One photograph of a Nineteenth-Century parlor can speak volumes about the Victorian way of life, showing exactly how the pictures were hung and just where they ever-present ferns and greenery were placed.

Coloradans are fortunate in having rich photographic resources in the Documentary Resources Department of the State Historical Society. Preeminent among the society's holdings are the negatives of the renowned William Henry Jackson taken west of the Mississippi River (his Eastern and foreign views are in the Library of Congress in Washington, D.C.). Ranging in size from 5 x 7 inches to 16 x 20 inches, Jackson's photographs cover almost all aspects of Colorado and the West, from the Indian antiquities at Mesa Verde to panoramic views of the bustling city of Denver.

Another major collection comprises the approximately 35,000 glass-plate negatives created from 1889 to 1920 by the Aultman Studio, a well-known Trinidad photographic house. Along with a vast number of portraits, the plates include views of streets, businesses, homes, schools and mining

Photographs used in the restoration of the Baca house were: left, the original porch, and center, the porch about 1950. The view at right is of the restored porch.   SHSC

camps, as well as scenic views of southern Colorado and northern New Mexico. Frank Dean, H. H. Buckwalter, Ola Garrison and Laura Gilpin are a few of the other prominent photographers represented among the society's holdings, together with the vast numbers of anonymous picture-takers who made their contributions to the history of Colorado.

Coloradans also are fortunate to have recorded now a history of the first half-century of photography in the Centennial State. Beginning with Solomon Carvalho, those who played some part in preserving the Colorado scene can be found in the following pages, coating their plates, loading their cameras and uncapping their lenses in *Colorado on Glass.*

Maxine Benson, Curator of
Documentary Resources

State Historical Society of Colorado

Table of Contents

———— ∙◦∙ ————

Acknowledgments

This book came together over several years spent gathering material from many locations, and with the cooperation of many generous people—both well-known to me and ones I have never met. All of these people have contributed to the final product and all have my sincere thanks. Richard Ronzio I would like to mention especially; who, along with his associate, Charles Ryland, initially arranged to have the manuscript published and who have shared their vast photographic collections so generously.

Among the other people who have spent much valuable time locating obscure material, I should like to especially mention Opal Harber and the entire staff of the Western History Department of the Denver Public Library; Dr. Maxine Benson and my collegues at the State Historical Society of Colorado. I should also like to thank Harry J. Mooney Jr., Robert Huddleston, Allan Culpin and Virginia McConnell-Simmons for reading and commenting on portions of the manuscript. Special thanks goes to Charles Edward Rowbotham, my roommate, who typed the manuscript both in rough draft and in finished form, and whose care and attention in spelling and a thousand other details has contributed materially to the finished book.

Terry Wm. Mangan

Illustrations

The majority of the photographs in this book are in the collection of the State Historical Society of Colorado (SHSC) and the private collections of Richard Ronzio and Charles Ryland (Q-BAR), publishers. These two sources represent the major holdings of Colorado photographic collections and contain many prints and negatives never before published. Additional prints used to supplement these two major collections were obtained from; Beaumont Newhall (NEWHALL), who is as generous with his print collection as with his information; the Western History Department of the Denver Public Library (DPL), which maintains a fine collection of prints and negatives; the Cincinatti Art Museum, which supplied the Carvalho oil painting; Donald McCloud, who supplied the Jackson oil painting; Mrs. Delano Shreve, for the Sabine Ambrotype; the National Park Service, for the Kinetoscope print; the United States Geological Survey (USGS); Sally Osgood Lawrence and Robert Lawrence for the picture of the CF&I mill (OSGOOD); and Glenn Aultman (whose friendship and cooperation were highly appreciated) who supplied Autochromes from the Aultman Collection (AC).

All of the photographic illustrations in this book are credited by showing the initials or surnames of the institutions or individuals listed above. Photographs without credit came from the author's collection.

Introduction

From the Colorado gold rush of 1859—when miners posed before the hooded cameras of itinerant "Ambrotypists"—until the early part of this century—when flexible plastic film provided an unbreakable support for photographic emulsions—the visual record of the history of the state was preserved on fragile, ephemeral sheets of plate glass. From the plush surroundings of the Victorian photographic galleries to the rugged terrain of the Rocky Mountains, the plates were transported, sensitized, exposed, developed and stabilized—to capture on glass the image of the rapidly changing face of the Centennial State. From this media, the photographs in this book have been taken; they are, perhaps, typical of Colorado photography during the pioneer age.

A sense of what it was like to be alive in another age cannot be conveyed so accurately by any other means. The horsecar rattling down Larimer Street in Denver, or the first train into Aspen, are as real as the Eiffel Tower to those of us who have never seen either for ourselves. We have almost as much contact with places far removed in time as we do with places far removed in distance. This great accessibility into the past is a product of photography, and the recent increase of interest in this media as a channel into the Victorian Age, had brought the art/science into the center of our attention.

The chemical and mechanical limitations of photographic processes as they evolved during this period had a marked effect on the nature of the subjects photographed. Interiors were rarely photographed at first, but became more common as the century drew to a close. Casual photographs increased in number as the length of exposure needed to make a negative became shorter, and every-day life situations began to appear. The austere expressions and glassy stares of the 1860-vintage portraits began to disappear, and groups of people gathered around a picnic blanket set the stage.

Equipment does not make photography, however—photographers do! Men and women; who, while trying to eke out a living for themselves and their loved ones, unknowingly left us in the process, a rich, exciting and unequaled record of the past. It is in these people and their work that our interest lies.

The best way to find out about photographers is to look at their photographs. What subjects did they choose to shoot? And from what perspective? The choice of subject is often more revealing than the photographer would feel comfortable admitting. But as important as their works are in learning about them, what they had to say about themselves and their efforts is immensely revealing. To read William H. Jackson's own account of the discoveries in Mesa Verde, or George Wakely's carping defense of his refusal to donate to charity, says more about these men than any second-hand account. If enough photographers had written of their work, no history of photography in Colorado would be needed; one would need only to collect what they said and publish it. Unfortunately, the story as told in their own words is sketchy and must be augmented by a considerable amount of additional material. Wherever possible, however, the photographers' own accounts have been included in the text of this book, with as little tampering as possible.

Terry Wm. Mangan
State Historical Society of Colorado
Denver, Colorado
May, 1975

In the Beginning

PHOTOGRAPHY came to Colorado in 1853, fourteen years after news of the process reached the United States from France. The area which is now Colorado was crossed that year by an expedition headed by John Charles Fremont. Traveling across the continent between the thirty-eighth and thirty-ninth degree of latitude, the party crossed the southern part of the state during mid-winter. Among the baggage of the party was the first camera in the area. And accompanying the expedition was a daguerreotypist—Solomon N. Carvalho, the first photographer to set foot in Colorado.

An interesting account of why Fremont undertook the expedition, and what made him decide to cart a bulky daguerreotype apparatus along, comes from the pen of his wife, Jessie Benton Fremont, the daughter of the influential senator from Missouri, Thomas Hart Benton:

> In 1853 we were living in Paris, where Mr. Fremont was having his first leisure and rest, and his plan was repose and congenial study for a year or more longer, when there came from my father the information that Congress had ordered three lines to be surveyed with a view to select the best for overland travel and ultimately a railway; that it had been intended that he, Mr. Fremont, should lead one, but as Congress had not inserted any name in the bill, the then Secretary of War, Mr. Jefferson Davis, had not named Mr. Fremont to any of the three. Captain Gunnison, who had been given the command of the line of surveys intended for Mr. Fremont, was killed by the Indians in the earlier part of his work.
>
> Of the four journeys of exploration already made by Mr. Fremont, three had been under orders of the Government, and one, that of 1848-1849, was at his own cost. Finding himself omitted from this culminating work which was based on his own labors, Mr. Fremont organized and made a fifth journey at his own expense.
>
> The intruments were selected in Paris, and on the way through London to his steamer at Liverpool, he found the just published volume of *Cosmos,* in which Humboldt, speaking of photography, hopes it will be applied in travel,* as securing "the truth in Nature." In New York, the daguerre apparatus was bought, and a good artist secured, Mr. Carvalho. [1]

Solomon Nunes Carvalho was the daguerreotypist referred to by Mrs. Fremont. He was 38 years old in 1853 when asked to join the expedition. [2] Carvalho was primarily a portrait artist. Like many other men in his profession, he saw the photographic art taking clients away from the portrait painters and decided to learn the trade. Between 1845 and 1850, he learned to make daguerreotypes and in the latter year he opened a gallery in Baltimore, Maryland. [3] He was already established as an artist and became well-known as a photographer, especially after 1852, when he patented a new process for protecting the delicate mercury image of the daguerreotype. [4] In 1853, he was working for one of the major chains of galleries in the United States, that of Jeremiah Gurney. [5] He met Fremont in New York and accepted an offer to join the projected exploring party from Kansas to California.

Carvalho left New York on the fifth of September, 1853, and headed west. At St. Louis, Missouri, he joined several other members of the expedition which was forming. Among these was a Mr. Bomar, a "photographist" who took pictures using the newly developing positive and negative process. Carvalho used the older daguerreotype method. By this process, the image is recorded on a silver-coated copper plate which has been made

1

This is a view of the Arkansas River below Bent's Fort, probably from a daguerreotype by Carvalho.   SHSC

light sensitive by the fumes of iodine and bromine. Once the plate is exposed in the camera, it is suspended above a container of mercury which is heated to drive off the vapor, which adheres to those portions of the plate affected by the light which was allowed into the camera. Although this sounds as if it might be rather more trouble than one would reasonably want on a transcontinental horseback trip, the process was probably the best available for this kind of job in 1853.

Carvalho could "fume" several of his plates with iodine and bromine before they were needed and store them all day in light-tight boxes until used. After being exposed, they could be developed on the spot by using an alcohol burner to heat the mercury in the bottom of a developing box. After the print had been fumed with mercury, it could be examined under red light to make sure it was properly made, and then it was stored in a light-tight box—along with other developed prints —until the operator was able to "fix" them in hyposulphate of soda.

The disadvantage of the daguerreotype process was that each metal plate was a unique picture. The only way to make duplicates was to make a picture of the picture. The process which Mr. Bomar proposed to use, however, was similar to the modern practice in that a negative image was produced in the camera and any number of positive prints could be obtained from these in a darkroom at some later time. Carvalho objected to this method, perhaps feeling it was some "newfangled" idea that had yet to be perfected,

or perhaps he did not want any competition. He told Colonel Fremont that he did not think that the process was practical on such a trip. He proposed that a contest be held and that the results would determine which process—and which photographer—would be used on the trip. Carvalho described the event:

Col. Fremont requested that daguerreotypes and photographs should be made. In half an hour from the time the word was given, my daguerreotype was made; but the photograph could not be seen until the next day, as it had to remain in water all night, which was absolutely necessary to develop it. Query, where was water to be had on the mountains, with a temperature of 20° below zero? [6]

Carvalho may have been unduly pessimistic about the negative-positive process which Bomar planned to use, but he probably saved Fremont a lot of trouble by discouraging him from taking Bomar along. Bomar obviously was not well-acquainted with the process he was using, as it was not necessary to leave the negatives overnight in water! [7]

Carvalho's chances of succeeding were not considered good by many expert daguerreotypists of the day. Probably his foresight and careful planning were responsible for his success. He writes:

The preparation for my journey occupied about ten days, during which time I purchased all the necessary materials for making a panorama of the country, by the daguerreotype process, over which we had to pass. To make daguerreotypes 30 degrees below zero, requires different manipulation from the process by which pictures are made in a warm room. My professional friends were all of the opinion that the elements would be against my success. Buffing and coating plates and materializing them on the summits of the Rocky Mountains, standing at times up to one's middle in snow, with no covering above save the arched vault of heaven, seemed to our city friends one of the impossibilities, knowing as they did that iodine will not give out its fumes except at a temperature of 70 to 80 degrees Farenheit.

I shall not appear egotistical if I say that I encountered many difficulties, but I was well prepared to meet them by having previously acquired a scientific and practical knowledge of the chemicals I used, as well as of the theory of light. A firm determination to succeed also aided me in producing results which, to my knowledge, have never been accomplished under similar circumstances. While suffering from frozen hands and feet, without food for twenty-four hours, traveling on foot over mountains of snow, I have stopped on the trail, made pictures of the country, repacked my materials and found myself frequently, with my friend, Egloffstein, who generally remained with me to make barometric observations, and a muleteer, five or six miles behind camp, which was only reached with great expense of bodily as well as mental suffering.[8]

An excellent account of the journey has been left by Carvalho in his book, *Incidents of Travel and Adventure in the Far West* [1857]. As the only full-length account of the expedition, it is of great historical interest.

Soon after beginning the trip from Kansas City, Carvalho made a short side trip into one of the last frontier villages they were to pass:

My ride into the town was for the purpose of having strong boxes made to carry my daguerreotype apparatus. The baskets in which they had been packed being broken and unfit for use. There was not a carpenter, nor any tools to be had in town. There was a blacksmith's about ten miles from town, where it was likely I could procure them. It being absolutely necessary that I should have the boxes, I induced one of the Delawares to accompany me, carrying on our horses a sufficient quantity of dry goods box covers and sides to manufacture them. When we arrived at the blacksmith's house, the proprietor was absent. His wife, an amiable woman, prepared dinner for us, and gave us the run of the workshop, where I found a saw and hatchet; with these instruments I made the boxes myself, and by the time they were finished, the blacksmith returned. He refused to receive pay for my dinner, but charged for the nails, raw hide, &c., I covered the boxes with, and

the use of his tools. The lady told me I was the first white man she had seen, except her husband, in three years. I gave some silver to the children, and mounting our horses, with a huge box before us on our saddles, we slowly retraced our way to camp, where we arrived at dark. Nobody in camp knew my errand to town, and I never shall forget the deep mortification and astonishment of our muleteers when they saw my boxes. All their bright hopes that the apparatus would have to be left, were suddenly dissipated . . . I have every reason to believe that my baskets were purposely destroyed; and but for my watchful and unceasing care, they would have been rendered useless. The packing of the apparatus was attended with considerable trouble to the muleteers, and also to the officer whose duty it was to superintend the loading and unloading of the mules; and they all wanted to be rid of the labor. Hence the persecution to which I was subjected on this account. Complaints were continually being made to Col. Fremont, during the journey, that the

INCIDENTS

OF

TRAVEL AND ADVENTURE

IN THE

FAR WEST;

WITH

COL. FREMONT'S LAST EXPEDITION

ACROSS THE ROCKY MOUNTAINS : INCLUDING THREE MONTHS' RESIDENCE IN UTAH, AND A PERILOUS TRIP ACROSS THE

GREAT AMERICAN DESERT,

TO THE PACIFIC.

BY S. N. CARVALHO,

ARTIST TO THE EXPEDITION.

NEW YORK:
DERBY & JACKSON, 119 NASSAU ST.
CINCINNATI :—H. W. DERBY & CO.
1857.

The view of Pikes Peak as it was seen by Colonel Fremont and his expedition before entering the vast expanse of the Colorado Rockies.   SHSC

weights of the boxes were not equalized. Twice I picked up on the road the tin case containing my buff, &c., which had slipped off the mules, from careless packing—done purposely; for if they had not been fortunately found by me, the rest of the apparatus would have been useless. On one occasion, the keg containing alcohol was missing; Col. Fremont sent back after it, and it was found half emptied on the road.

I am induced to make these remarks to show the perserverance and watchfulness I had to exercise to prevent the destruction of the apparatus by our own men. 9

As the party traveleled across Kansas, Carvalho made numerous daguerreotypes of the territory. His attempts to photograph the herds of buffalo on the open prairie were only partially successful. He was able to get photographs of distant herds grazing quietly, but was not able to get any pictures of the animals running. The long exposures necessary to make a daguerreotype precluded taking pictures of anything which was not still. While on the far-western plains of Kansas, near the present Colorado border, the party discovered a large Cheyenne Indian village. Carvalho took the opportunity to introduce the Indians to photography:

I went into the village to take daguerreotype views of their lodges, and succeeded in obtaining likenesses of an Indian princess—a very aged woman, with a papoose, in a cradle or basket, and several of the chiefs. I had great difficulty in getting them to sit still, or even to submit to have themselves daguerreotyped. I made a picture, first, of their lodges, which I showed them. I then made one of the old woman and papoose. When they saw it, they thought I was a "supernatural being"; and, before I left camp, they were satisfied I was more than human.

The squaws are very fond of ornaments; their arms are encircled with bracelets made of thick brass wire—sometimes of silver beaten out as thin as pasteboard. The princess, or daughter of the Great Chief, was a beautiful Indian girl. She attired herself in her most costly robes, ornamented with elk teeth, beads, and colored porcupine quills—expressly to have her likeness taken. I made a beautiful picture of her.

The bracelets of the princess were of brass; silver ones are considered invaluable, and but few possess them.

After I had made the likeness of the princess, I made signs to her to let me have one of her brass bracelets. She very reluctantly gave me one. I wiped it very clean, and touched it with "quicksilver." It instantly became bright and glittering as polished silver. I then presented her with it. Her delight and astonishment knew no bounds. She slipped it over her arm, and danced about in ecstacy. As for me, she thought I was a great "Magician." 10

Carvalho may have been a favorite with the Indians—but not so with the mule-skinners. They disliked his heavy equipment and perhaps they resented his foresight in equipping his baggage with so many things which they had either forgotten or had run short of through careless use earlier:

In his book, *Incidents of Travel and Adventure in the Far West,* Carvalho wrote of this scene: "After crossing the Huerfano River, we saw the immense pile of granite rock, which rises perpendicularly to the height of four or five hundred feet, from a perfectly level valley. It appeared like a mammoth sugar loaf (called the Huerfano Butte). Col. Fremont expressed a desire to have several views of it . . . To make a daguerreotype view, generally occupied from one to two hours, the principal part of that time, however, was spent in packing, and reloading the animals. . . ." SHSC

Previous to leaving New York, I had two tin flasks made, to contain about a quart each, which I intended to have filled with alcohol for daguerreotype purposes. At Westport, I purchased a quart of the best quality of old cognac, filled one of them for medicinal purposes, and carefully packed my flask in my daguerreotype boxes. One day during our camp at Salt Creek, one of our Indians being ill, I opened my flask, and pouring out about an ounce, replaced it. I noticed, however, that a chemical action had taken place, turning the brandy exactly the color of ink. One of our mess saw me open my box and appropriate a portion of the contents of the bottle; I am not certain but that I tasted it myself.

The next day I had the occasion to go to my box, when to my utter astonishment, my flask of brandy was gone. I immediately suspected the very person who afterwards proved to be the thief. Keeping my loss a secret, at dinner I carefully watched the countenances and actions of the whole party, and the effects of liquor were plainly visible on the person of this man.

"How excellent," said I, "would a bottle of old cognac be as a digester to our tough old buffalo bull. — Gentlemen, how would you like a drop?" "Bring it forward by all means, Carvalho. You have, I verily believe, Pandora's box; for you can produce everything and anything at a moment's

notice, from a choice Havana to old brandy."

"With your leave, gentlemen, I will procure it. I have two flasks exactly alike; one contains poison, a mixture of alcohol, and some poisonous chemicals for making daguerreotypes; the other contains the best brandy to be had on the Kansas River."

I went to my box, and turning up my hands with an exclamation of surprise, announced to the mess that the "bottle containing the poison, and which I laid on the top of my box last night, is missing." Like Hamlet I looked into the face of the delinquent, and I never shall forget his expression when I remarked that "the liquid in the purloined flask was poison, and perfectly black, and although it would not kill immediately, an ounce will produce certain death in 48 hours."

"Gentlemen! I shall, in consequence, have to reserve the brandy to make another similar mixture, to substitute for alcohol; therefore I am sorry I cannot treat you as intended."

Of course the innocent parties felt indignant that my flask had been stolen, and that one of their party was suspected.

The thief was discovered, although neither he nor any one else knew that I detected him. The next day I went to my box again, and in its proper place, I found my brandy flask about half full. Our friend had taken several strong pulls during the night and morning, and likely enough

The deep snows of the Rocky Mountains close in on Colonel Fremont and his men.   SHSC

he looked at the contents, and finding them black as ink, believed all about the poison, and fearing to die, replaced the flask, without detection. When I discovered it, I showed it around and also the color of the contents, and told them it was not poison, but "good old brandy." I tasted a little, and divided it among the party.

The man that took it knew I suspected him, and his whole conduct to me during the journey, was influenced by that event, although I never taxed him with it.[11]

There was much to be learned by an Eastern photographer about the resources of the prairie:

I was busily engaged making my daguerreotype views of the country, over which I had to travel the next day. On looking through my camera I observed two of our men approaching over a slope, holding between them a blanket filled with something; curious to know what it was, I hailed them, and found they had been gathering "dried buffalo chips," to build a fire with. This material burns like peat, and makes a very hot fire, without much smoke, and keeps the heat a long time; a peculiar smell exhales from it while burning, not at all unpleasant. But for this material, it would be impossible to travel over certain parts of this immense country. It served us very often, not only for cooking purposes, but also to warm our half frozen limbs. I have seen chips of a large size—one I had the curiosity to measure, was two feet in diameter.[12]

The first major landmark which the party met after entering what is now Colorado was Bent's new fort on the Arkansas River. Old Fort Bent, a few miles away, had been destroyed a short while earlier. Carvalho penned the following description of Bent's Fort:

Bent's house is built of adobes, or unburnt brick, one story high, in form of a hollow square, with a courtyard in the centre. One side is appropriated as his sleeping apartments, the front as a store-house, while the others are occupied by the different persons in his employ. He has a large number of horses and mules . . .

I breakfasted with Mr. Bent and Doctor Ober, on baked bread, made from maize ground, dried buffalo meat, venison steaks, and hot coffee; a treat that I had not enjoyed for a very long time . . .

The weather continuing so cold I found it inconvenient to use my oil colors and brushes; accordingly I left my tin case with the doctor, who promised to take charge of them for me to the States.

When the weather is very clear, you can see the snowy peaks of the Rocky Mountains from Bent's house, which is seventy miles distant. Our friend the doctor wanted to obtain a nearer view of them, and proposed that I should accompany him. We started on a clear morning, for that purpose. I took my apparatus along; we rode thirty miles, but the weather becoming hazy, it entirely shut out our view of the mountains. We returned to camp late at night, after a tiresome day's ride.[13]

Had Carvalho succeeded in taking a daguerreotype of the mountains, this would have been the first photograph of Pikes Peak, easily seen from this area when the weather is clear.

After leaving Bent's Fort, the party continued up the Arkansas River to the mouth of the Huerfano River and thence up the Huerfano:

> After crossing the Huerfano River, we saw the immense pile of granite rock, which rises perpendicularly to the height of four or five hundred feet, from a perfectly level valley. It appeared like a mammoth sugar loaf (called the Huerfano Butte). Col. Fremont expressed a desire to have several views of it from different distances.
>
> The main party proceeded on the journey, leaving under my charge the mules which carried our apparatus . . .
>
> To make a daguerreotype view, generally occupied from one to two hours, the principal part of that time, however, was spent in packing and reloading the animals. When we came up to the Butte, Mr. Fuller made barometrical observations at its base, and also ascended to the top to make observations, in order to ascertain its exact height. The calculations have not yet been worked out. [14]

As the party advanced farther into the Rocky Mountains, travel became increasingly difficult. Snow began to slow the pace of the days' marches and to make the nights bitterly cold. Photographing the terrain, which had been relatively easy up to this point, now became increasingly difficult. One afternoon, the party camped near the summit of Cochotopa Pass:

> Near by our camp, a rugged mountain, barren of trees, and thickly covered with snow, reared its lofty head high in the blue vault above us. The approach to it was inaccessible by even our surefooted mules. From its summit, the surrounding country could be seen for hundreds of miles. Col. Fremont regretted that such important views as might be made from that point, should be lost, and gave up the idea as impracticable from its dangerous character. I told him that if he would allow two men to assist me in carrying my apparatus up the mountain, I would attempt the ascent on foot, and make the pictures; he pointed out the difficulties, I insisted. He then told me if I was determined to go he would accompany me; this was an unusual thing for him and it proved to me, that he considered the ascent difficult and dangerous, and that his superior judgment might be required to pick the way, for a misstep would have precipitated us on to the rugged rocks at its base; and it also proved that he would not allow his men or officers to encounter perils or dangers in which he did not participate.
>
> After three hours' hard toil we reached the summit and beheld a panorama of unspeakable sublimity spread out before us; continuous chains of mountains reared their snowy peaks far away in the distance, while the Grand River [now the Colorado] plunging along in awful sublimity through its rocky bed, was seen for the first time. Above us the cerulean heaven, without a single cloud to mar its beauty, was sublime in its calmness . . .
>
> Plunged up to my middle in snow, I made a panorama of the continuous ranges of mountains around us. Col. Fremont made barometrical and thermometrical observations, and occupied a part of this time in geological examinations. We descended safely, and with a keen appetite, discussed the merits of our dried buffalo and deer meat. [15]

The expedition continued pushing west through snow, down the Gunnison River to the Colorado River. Following that stream, they passed out of Colorado and into Utah. Food ran out and they were forced to shoot and eat several of their horses. Even this did not stave off hunger and the loss of the horses further slowed their progress. One night after returning from his watch, Carvalho relates:

> Cold, tired and hungry, I rested myself before the fire, and warmed my frozen limbs.
>
> Some little distance from the fire, now covered with snow, lay the frozen meat of the horse we had killed the night before; all in the camp were fast wrapped in sleep. I was the only one awake. Taking out my jackknife, I approached the pile of meat intended for the men's breakfast, and cutting about a half pound of the liver from it, I returned to the fire, and without waiting to cook it, I consumed it raw—the finer feelings of my nature were superseded by the grosser animal propensities, induced most probably from the character of the food we had been living upon for the last forty days. [16]

When the situation became even more desperate, Fremont ordered that all excess baggage be cached in the snow and the remaining pack animals be pressed into service to carry the men. The daguerreotype apparatus was left, along with the astronomical instruments and surplus buffalo robes. The pictures which Carvalho had made were saved, however, as were the journals and other records of the trip. The night before the instruments were abandoned in the frozen mountains, Colonel Fremont and Carvalho made observations of the stars through the sextant. By these observations, Fremont decided to head in a certain direction, which he hoped would bring the party to the Mormon outpost of Parowan, a few buildings and several families, which represented the outer limits of the Mormon empire in Utah. One of the party had already died of starvation and exposure, and most of the rest were in desperate straits:

The original caption for this view reads: "Col. Fremont came out to us, and after referring to the dreadful necessities to which his men had been reduced on a previous expedition, of eating each other, he begged us to swear that in no extremity of hunger would any of his men lift his hand against or attempt to prey upon a comrade; sooner let him die with them than live upon them." SHSC

I was riding side by side with Egloffstein after Mr. Fuller's death, sad and dejected. Turning my eyes on the waste of snow before me, I remarked to my companion that I thought we had struck a travelled road. He shook his head despondingly, replying "that the marks I observed, were the trails from Col. Fremont's lodge poles." Feeling satisfied that I saw certain indications, I stopped my mule, and with very great difficulty alighted, and thrust my hand into the snow, when to my great delight I distinctly felt the ruts caused by wagon wheels. I was then perfectly satisfied that we were "saved!" The great revulsion of feeling from intense despair to a reasonable hope, is impossible to be described; from that moment, however, my strength perceptibly left me, and I felt myself gradually breaking up. The nearer I approached the settlement, the less energy I had at my command; and I felt so totally incapable of continuing, that I told Col. Fremont, half an hour before we reached Parowan, that he would have to leave me there; when I was actually in the town, and surrounded with white men, women and children, paroxysms of tears followed each other, and I fell down on the snow perfectly overcome.17

Carvalho was completely worn out by his ordeal and was not able to continue with Fremont on the rest of the trip to California. He developed scurvy and spent some time recuperating in Parowan before he could be transferred by wagon to Salt Lake City, where he eventually recovered.

Fremont continued west and arrived in California sometime later with the daguerreotypes. These were shipped by sea via Panama to New York. As Mrs. Fremont writes:

...Their long journeying by mule through storms and snows across the Sierras, then the searching tropical damp of the sea voyage back across the Isthmus, left them unharmed and surprisingly clear, and, so far as it is known, give the first connected series of views by daguerre of an unknown country, in pictures as truthful as they are beautiful.

During the winter of '55 - '56 Mr. Fremont worked constantly at Mr. Brady's* studio aiding to fix these daguerre pictures in their more permanent form of photographs. Then at our own house I made a studio of the north drawing-room, where a large bayed window gave the proper light. Here for some months Hamilton† worked on these views, reproducing many in oil; he was a pupil of Turner and had great joy in the true cloud effects as well as in the stern mountains and castellated rock formations. The engravings on wood were also made under our home supervision; by an artist young then, a namesake and grandson of Frank Key, the author of *The Star Spangled Banner*. From these artists their work was passed to artist-engravers of the best school of their art. Darley also contributed his talent.

* Matthew Brady, the photographer.
† An artist.

Some pictures he enlarged into india-ink sketches, and from his hand came the figures in many of the plates.* This work progressed through the busy year to us of 1856.

. . . The time for writing did not seem to come. Private affairs in California, then our war,† and again private business until now. During these thirty years, the boxes containing the material for this book were so carefully guarded by me, that all understood that they must be saved first in case of fire. When we were leaving for Arizona in '78 the boxes containing the steel plates and wood blocks were placed in Morrell's "Fire-Proof" warehouse, which was destroyed by fire in October of '81. We lost much that was stored in that warehouse, choice books, pictures, and other treasured things, but these materials for the book we had had placed for greater security in the safes below the pavement, where the great fire passed over them and left them completely unharmed.[18]

Carvalho was probably disappointed by the failure of Fremont in not using his daguerreotypes as illustrations for an account of the expedition. The book which Mrs. Fremont mentions was the first volume of Fremont's memoirs, which was published in 1887. It is all too apparent that the original plates did not survive the fire in 1881—but what of the copy prints made by Brady? Several attempts have been made to locate the Brady negatives or prints, but none of them have come to light. It is quite possible that they may still be found among the Brady material in the National Archives in Washington, D.C.[19] Those who saw the daguerreotypes state that they were quite clear and that the photographer had succeeded in his mission. Fremont briefly mentions the views in a short article which appeared in a leading Washington newspaper:

Along all this line the elevation was carefully determined by frequent barometrical observations, and its character exhibited by a series of daguerreotype views, comprehending the face of the country almost continuously, or at least sufficiently so to give a thoroughly correct impression of the whole.[20]

* The illustrations for John Charles Fremont's *Memoirs of My Life* (New York; Belford, Clarke & Co., 1887).

† The Civil War.

The night before they abandoned their daguerreotype equipment and other non-essential supplies, Colonel Fremont and Solomon N. Carvalho tried to fix their location with the use of a sextant. The next morning they began a desperate march through the snow toward a Morman village in what is now the State of Utah.   SHSC

The photographic mission was certainly not a failure, even though none of the prints have been found. Many of the illustrations used in the Fremont memoirs were more accurate for their having been copied from daguerreotypes. The two views of Huerfano Butte will serve to show the difference between a "cut" reproduced from a rough field sketch and one copied from a photograph. It is a great misfortune, however, that none of the original photographs have been found. After enduring the hardships of the trip, it must have been a blow to Carvalho when the daguerreotypes he risked his life to produce were burned in the fire of 1881.

9

James Sabine's ambrotype of William Maine is Colorado's oldest-known photograph and the first portrait taken in the gold fields — in 1859. SHSC

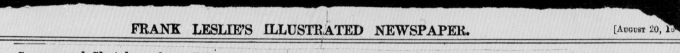

Scenes and Sketches about Pike's Peak.—From Photographs by our own Correspondent.

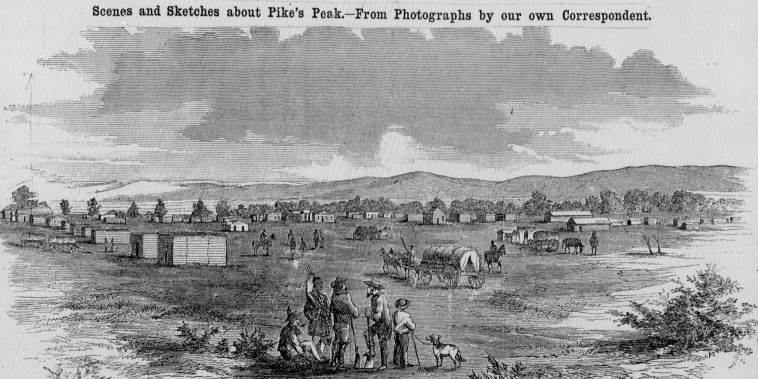

"Scenes and Sketches about Pike's Peak." This wood engraving of Denver was published in *Frank Leslie's Illustrated Newspaper* in August of 1859. Their photographer, a "Mr. Welch," probably was in the gold fields as early as any other photographer. However, none of his photographs have come to light. SHSC

Gold Rush

II

OR SIX YEARS after Solomon N. Carvalho's trek across the West, no photographers came to the Rocky Mountains. The mountains were regarded as an obstacle on the road to the gold fields of California — little else. Interest in the region increased greatly, however, during the summer of 1858. By July of that year, gold had been found along Cherry Creek. Because they knew of no landmark closer, the gold seekers referred to the new *Eldorado* as the "Pikes Peak Country." Ox carts, wagons, buckboards, handdrawn carts, anything with wheels was used to get there—some even walked the entire distance.

Among the hopeful thousands who arrived that fall and winter to search for gold was Rufus E. Cable, a photographer from Kansas City. He had not come to the Pikes Peak Country to make pictures, however; he was there to seek his fortune. Although he had not found any gold, he was not easily discouraged. As he wrote his brother:

South Platte, January 28, 1859.
Dear Brother:
 . . . There have been no mines discovered yet which are worth working. Any place here one can get small quantities, but will not pay more than $2 or $3 per day, and the ground is frozen so that no person tries to make anything. When spring opens I think we will find good mines . . .

Yesterday I went to Auraria, to witness a feast given by the whites to the Arapahoe Indians. There were assembled some 500 warriors, and 300 or 400 women and children. Two oxen were roasted, and piles of dried apples heaped up on blankets, coffee, bread, etc. I have never seen men eat till now. I have heard that one man could eat an antelope at one meal, and I verily believe one Indian, called, "Heap of Whips," could eat a whole ox. It is worth one year's travel to witness such a scene.

When I come from the Cassa la Poudre, which will be in ten or twelve days, I will write you.

I have sixteen lots in El Paso, at the base of Pike's Peak; and if I do not find any gold, I shall go there and build houses. . . .

Some of the boys have frozen their feet and have all their toes cut off. But, so far, I am safe, and enjoy better health than ever I did in my life, and am not at all disheartened, for I think I will make money here by next fall, if I live.

We are expecting 500 Mexicans here in two weeks, and am cultivating my Spanish.
Yours, ever,
RUFUS E. CABLE. [1]

Four months later, optimism had been replaced by determination. It was becoming clear that there must be easier ways to make a living than by digging for gold:

Denver City, May 14th, 1859.
I wrote you about two weeks ago, and was then starting for the South Park—and have just returned. It proved a failure. The rivers there are frozen 4 and 5 feet, with no indication that summer ever makes its appearance in that quarter. The air is so light that one cannot breathe freely. Located at the base of the "Snowy range," and some 5,000 feet [2] above the level of the ocean, it is not very probable that any one will ever attempt to work there.

Coarse gold has been found, but not in sufficient quantities to justify working. I saw, last evening, some very good specimens of gold taken out 25 miles from here, and will start for that place the day after tomorrow. We will very likely stop there and work until October, when I go home, for I would not spend another winter here for any amount of money. Those sentimentalists, who sigh for a "lodge in some vast wilderness," can find several by coming to this place.

During the Colorado gold rush, many miners had photographs taken of themselves to send back to "the States" to show the folks at home what they looked like as miners. Here, William Slater — who came to the Pikes Peak country in 1858 and later became the chief justice of the extra-legal Territory of Jefferson — is shown as he was photographed by an unknown daguerreotypist while chewing on his cigar.   SHSC

I suppose by the time you receive this 'twill be pretty generally known in the states that Pike's Peak is a humbug. Every day crowds are starting for home, cursing the country and those who wrote letters from here last fall . . .

There are now some twelve or fourteen hundred men out here; a great many of them have started within a day or two to the mines, which I think will pay, at least enough to justify out here.

There is a great deal of sickness here at present, confined principally to those who came here last fall; as the breaking up of the winter has commenced, they have the pleurisy and some fever, but generally speaking, I think the country remarkably healthy. I have not been ill an hour since I left home.

The next letter you get from me I will be able to inform you whether or not the mines will pay. If they do I will be home next fall; if not, ho! for Arizona or Sonora.

Yours truly,
RUFUS CABLE.[2]

Photographs of the 1859 gold rush are quite rare. In this tintype copy of an earlier paper print, a gold seeker posed with exactly the same props — shovel, pick and ''gold'' — which the photographer used in several other portraits taken during 1859. Whether produced by Sabine, Cable or one of their contemporaries, this print gives us a rare look at one of the men who made the Colorado gold rush.   SHSC

The earliest-known photographs of Colorado mining operations . . . Among the most unusual photographs of Colorado is this series, taken before October of 1860 by Rufus E. Cable. Probably the earliest photographs of mining operations and camps during the height of the gold rush, this series shows the very beginning of Colorado's mining industry. The negatives of these views were acquired by the Denver Public Library some years ago. Their authorship has not been established beyond all doubt; however, they came as part of a collection which contained a print of Larimer Street in 1860, which was signed "REC." This strongly suggests, therefore, that since they are all easily that early, they are the work of Cable.

Frontier enterprise in the gold camps — already the owner of Graham's Drug Store had added a wooden false front to the original log building. Perhaps the important-looking gentleman in the left foreground is Graham himself? Photographed in 1860 by Rufus E. Cable. The structure was in Central City.   DPL

Probably the earliest photograph of mining in Colorado, eager Easterners were tearing up Gilpin County in search of "color." DPL

The first two full years of the Colorado gold rush — 1859 and 1860 — saw mining operations started on an unbelievable scale. This view, made in Gilpin County not later than October of 1860, shows some of the devastation brought about by mining during these first two years. The few remaining trees on the hillside would soon provide lumber and fuel for the growing population.   SHSC

Here we see the main street of Nevadaville during the first full year of this wide-open gold camp — 1860. DPL

Three miners paused beside their sluce long enough for Rufus Cable to expose this plate — from the series produced during 1859-1860.   DPL

This is the earliest-known photograph of Central City.   DPL

Another view taken by Rufus E. Cable is this picture showing a mill near Blackhawk. In the left foreground is Cable's portable darkroom on wheels. This cart probably was brought into Colorado by James Sabine and later was sold to Cable. DPL

The earliest photographers reaching the Colorado gold fields had to carry every piece of equipment with them. James E. Sabine set up Colorado's first portrait business with a tent similar to this one during the summer of 1859.

Waterfalls at Montgomery C.T.

Entered according to Act of Congress in the year 1864, by G. D. WAKELY, Photographer, in the Clerk's Office of the District Court, Denver City, C. T.

18

Apparently the idea of going south had come from Cable's old friend, James E. Sabine, who arrived from Las Vegas, New Mexico,[3] sometime before August of 1859.[4]

Sabine knew it was easier to get gold out of the pockets of miners than out of the good Colorado earth, so he brought his camera. He was the first photographer to set up business in the gold field.[5]

The first day Sabine set up his camera, William H. Maine, 21 years of age, from Mansfield, Ohio, was first in line. The photograph made on this occasion probably is the first portrait taken in Colorado. Recently rediscovered, it is the only Colorado photographic portrait from the 1850's which is completely documented.[6]

Rufus Cable was quick to follow Sabine's example and their hometown newspaper reported in August that he had joined Sabine's watch-making and ambrotype business in Denver.[7]

An ambrotype is an underexposed glass negative backed with black velvet or painted on the reverse side with dark varnish. This produces a positive picture with great contrast and usually reversed from left to right, as were daguerreotypes.

Sabine did not stay long in Denver. In June, 1860, Cable opened "Cable's Pioneer Ambrotype Gallery" on the second floor of the Denver Herald Building.[8] No mention is made of Sabine in the notice of the new gallery, so it is safe to assume that he had left the area. Quite probably, Cable was using equipment obtained from Sabine to open his gallery, although this is not definitely known. Associated with Cable in his new gallery was another disgruntled miner, Oliver Case. Case had been in Denver City long enough to be discouraged with mining by April, 1859.[9] He may well have known Cable and Sabine in Kansas City, as a paper from that city printed letters from both Cable and Case.

Cable was quick to realize that more money was to be had from selling mountain views than in the portrait business. *The Western Mountaineer* of Golden City, Colorado, noted on August 30, 1860:

> Last week, in a stroll among the environs of Colorado City, we found R. E. Cable, Esq., the accomplished artist, busy in photographing the fine scenery near that metropolis. The Soda

Springs, Red Rocks from several points of view, "ye Peak," Colorado City, the Mountains and other beautiful pictures familiar to the frequenters of that region, he has transferred to paper. Mr. Cable can be found at his rooms in the *Herald* building and will take pleasure in exhibiting his photographs to visitors.

Cable and Case apparently decided two winters in the gold fields were enough and they left in October of 1860.[10] Only one photograph is known to remain from the many which Cable must have taken. It is a paper print of Larimer Street in Denver, 1860.*

Although Sabine took the first picture, a 37-year-old Englishman,[11] George Wakely, gets the credit for the first gallery. Sabine probably operated out of a tent or the back of a wagon, but Wakely was more permanent. The *Rocky Mountain News* for October 20, 1859, carried the following notice:

> G. Wakely, a talented artist, from Chicago, Ill., has opened an Ambrotype gallery opposite the Theatre, on Larimer street, in Denver.

In the first business directory of Denver, Wakely's name appears under the heading of Ambrotypist. As only businesses with a permanent location were listed, it is not surprising that he was the only photographer to appear in the directory. It is also possible that Sabine was no longer in the area by late 1859 when the directory was published.[12]

Wakely had been in Denver for some time before opening his gallery. He was a member of Charles Thorne's Theatrical Company which had arrived in Denver on September 27, 1859, to perform in Apollo Hall.[13] Wakely soon decided to abandon the stage in favor of the Ambrotype business. An advertisement which he inserted in the *Rocky Mountain News,* during October of 1859 announced that he was prepared to make pictures on leather:

> . . . which can be sent to any part of the world for the cost of a letter only . . .[14]

The idea was that the miners would rush to have their likenesses made on leather so that the folks back in the States could see them "way out here" in the west end of what was then Kansas Territory. But Wakely was not one to simply sit back and wait for his customers.

In early July, 1861, the *Rocky Mountain News* ran the following article:

Opposite, below: By 1864, when George Wakely visited the town, Buckskin Joe's main street had assumed a less sparse appearance — reproduced from a 5 x 7-inch original.   Q-BAR

* This photograph is in the Western History Collection of the Denver Public Library, Denver, Colorado.

LANTERN SLIDES . . .

Among the earliest uses for photographs of the gold rush was for publicity. *Leslies* published woodcuts from photographs in their story about gold discoveries. Reproduced here are the lantern slides painted in oil, from photographs taken in the gold fields during the summer of 1859. The original photographs probably the work of J. H. Young, a New York photographer. SHSC

Auraria

General William Larimer in front of his Denver cabin

Denver

Confluence of South Platte River and Cherry Creek

Golden

Golden

Golden City

Golden Gate

Atkins Toll Gate on Clear Creek

Apparently the idea of going south had come from Cable's old friend, James E. Sabine, who arrived from Las Vegas, New Mexico,[3] sometime before August of 1859.[4]

Sabine knew it was easier to get gold out of the pockets of miners than out of the good Colorado earth, so he brought his camera. He was the first photographer to set up business in the gold field.[5]

The first day Sabine set up his camera, William H. Maine, 21 years of age, from Mansfield, Ohio, was first in line. The photograph made on this occasion probably is the first portrait taken in Colorado. Recently rediscovered, it is the only Colorado photographic portrait from the 1850's which is completely documented.[6]

Rufus Cable was quick to follow Sabine's example and their hometown newspaper reported in August that he had joined Sabine's watch-making and ambrotype business in Denver.[7]

An ambrotype is an underexposed glass negative backed with black velvet or painted on the reverse side with dark varnish. This produces a positive picture with great contrast and usually reversed from left to right, as were daguerreotypes.

Sabine did not stay long in Denver. In June, 1860, Cable opened "Cable's Pioneer Ambrotype Gallery" on the second floor of the Denver Herald Building.[8] No mention is made of Sabine in the notice of the new gallery, so it is safe to assume that he had left the area. Quite probably, Cable was using equipment obtained from Sabine to open his gallery, although this is not definitely known. Associated with Cable in his new gallery was another disgruntled miner, Oliver Case. Case had been in Denver City long enough to be discouraged with mining by April, 1859.[9] He may well have known Cable and Sabine in Kansas City, as a paper from that city printed letters from both Cable and Case.

Cable was quick to realize that more money was to be had from selling mountain views than in the portrait business. *The Western Mountaineer* of Golden City, Colorado, noted on August 30, 1860:

> Last week, in a stroll among the environs of Colorado City, we found R. E. Cable, Esq., the accomplished artist, busy in photographing the fine scenery near that metropolis. The Soda

Springs, Red Rocks from several points of view, "ye Peak," Colorado City, the Mountains and other beautiful pictures familiar to the frequenters of that region, he has transferred to paper. Mr. Cable can be found at his rooms in the *Herald* building and will take pleasure in exhibiting his photographs to visitors.

Cable and Case apparently decided two winters in the gold fields were enough and they left in October of 1860.[10] Only one photograph is known to remain from the many which Cable must have taken. It is a paper print of Larimer Street in Denver, 1860.*

Although Sabine took the first picture, a 37-year-old Englishman,[11] George Wakely, gets the credit for the first gallery. Sabine probably operated out of a tent or the back of a wagon, but Wakely was more permanent. The *Rocky Mountain News* for October 20, 1859, carried the following notice:

> G. Wakely, a talented artist, from Chicago, Ill., has opened an Ambrotype gallery opposite the Theatre, on Larimer street, in Denver.

In the first business directory of Denver, Wakely's name appears under the heading of Ambrotypist. As only businesses with a permanent location were listed, it is not surprising that he was the only photographer to appear in the directory. It is also possible that Sabine was no longer in the area by late 1859 when the directory was published.[12]

Wakely had been in Denver for some time before opening his gallery. He was a member of Charles Thorne's Theatrical Company which had arrived in Denver on September 27, 1859, to perform in Apollo Hall.[13] Wakely soon decided to abandon the stage in favor of the Ambrotype business. An advertisement which he inserted in the *Rocky Mountain News,* during October of 1859 announced that he was prepared to make pictures on leather:

> . . . which can be sent to any part of the world for the cost of a letter only . . .[14]

The idea was that the miners would rush to have their likenesses made on leather so that the folks back in the States could see them "way out here" in the west end of what was then Kansas Territory. But Wakely was not one to simply sit back and wait for his customers.

In early July, 1861, the *Rocky Mountain News* ran the following article:

Opposite, below: By **1864**, when George Wakely visited the town, Buckskin Joe's main street had assumed a less sparse appearance — reproduced from a 5 x 7-inch original.   Q-BAR

---

* This photograph is in the Western History Collection of the Denver Public Library, Denver, Colorado.

LANTERN SLIDES . . .

Among the earliest uses for photographs of the gold rush was for publicity. *Leslies* published woodcuts from photographs in their story about gold discoveries. Reproduced here are the lantern slides painted in oil, from photographs taken in the gold fields during the summer of 1859. The original photographs probably the work of J. H. Young, a New York photographer.   SHSC

Auraria

General William Larimer in front of his Denver cabin

Denver

Confluence of South Platte River and Cherry Creek

Golden

Golden

Golden City

Golden Gate

Atkins Toll Gate on Clear Creek

Atkins Toll Gate on Clear Creek

Gregory Diggings ⟶

Gregory Diggings ⟶

Gregory Diggings

Russell Gulch ⟶

Russell Gulch ⟶

GRAND TIGHT ROPE ASCENSION —

Gus. Shaw, the agent of M'lle Caralista, has called upon us to state that a subscription is now in circulation, which if sufficiently endorsed, will secure a *Grand Tight Rope Ascension* in this city about the 15 inst. The ascension will be made from some high points . . .15

Shortly after this announcement, Denverites had raised $170.00 for the performance and the forthcoming event was advertised:

On Thursday next M'lle Carolista is to take a tight rope walk in this city. The rope is to be stretched from the New York Store to Graham's Drug Store over which she will pass, stopping by the way for the purpose of balancing, posing, &c. This daring feat will no doubt call a large concourse of people to the city. 16

It is probably more than coincidence that her journey across the street was to be interrupted at mid-point for the purpose of "balancing, posing, etc." Not only was this a good way to publicize Carolista's act at the Criterion, where she walked a rope between the stage and the balcony railing,17 but Wakely received some free publicity as well. He was waiting with his camera when she stopped at mid-point. The next day the *Daily Colorado Republican and Rocky Mountain Herald* carried the following account:

Mr. Wakely, Daguerrean and Ambrotypist on Larimer street; showed us some beautiful views taken of the crowd assembled yesterday to see M'lle Carolista in her daring feat of rope walking. These are valuable not only on account of representing that interesting affair, but they also present a grand view of Larimer street, the plains, etc. Call at Wakely's and see those pretty representations. 18

Although the paper spoke of "views," only one has survived. It is an Ambrotype measuring 4.25 x 6.5 inches, a "half-plate" Ambrotype.*

Apparently it paid to advertise, for Wakely began to construct a new brick studio during the spring of 1862.19 This building, finished in June of the same year, was located just opposite the post office on Larimer Street. The same month during which he completed his new studio, he announced that he was about to modernize his methods. Ambrotypes on glass, which were very fragile and visually quite flat, were becoming less fashionable in the East. Photographs on paper were the thing—and not just any paper photograph would do, either: *cartes de visite*—

that's what was really "in." As the name implies, they were visiting cards with the photograph instead of the name of the visitor, although as time went by, it became fairly common for the visiting card to be used as a standard size for inexpensive photographs. They were usually about 2.5 x 3.5 inches. The equipment needed to produce these small prints was considered quite unusual out on the Western frontier. Once again, Wakely had a good press:

GREAT NOVELTY COMING — Wakely isn't done yet. Not satisfied with fitting up the most showy and pleasant picture gallery West of the Missouri River, he has actually purchased the apparatus, which is now on the way out here, to take those exquisite little *cartes de visite* photographs which are so much in fashion in the *beau monde* of the states. There is no better artist than Wakely in the country. Like any man who studies his business and attends to it, he excels. His rooms are commodious, well lighted, cleanly and well furnished. On the walls around are to be seen the faces of most of our celebrities, both white and aboriginal. Go and see. 20

To make a *carte de visite*, a negative on glass was first made in the camera. The exposure varied from 5 to 30 seconds, depending on how bright the sun shone through the glass roof of the gallery. From the glass negative, dozens of prints could be made on albumin paper for less than the cost of one daguerreotype or of a good ambrotype, both of which produced but one print.

In August, the apparatus finally arrived and Wakely inserted an advertisement in the *Denver Weekly Commonwealth:*

WAKELY'S
NEW PHOTOGRAPHIC GALLERY!

Larimer Street Opposite the Post Office.

The undersigned would respectfully inform his patrons, and the inhabitants of Colorado Territory, that he has just received from New York the apparatus, chemicals, etc., for taking those exquisite pictures, *Carte de Visite* or Card Photographs, now so fashionable in Eastern cities. Having re-fitted my Rooms on the Eastern style, and having ten years experience in the business, I feel confident of success, and am now prepared to take

Cartes de Visites,
Photographs,
Ambrotypes,
Ferrotypes,
Ivorytypes,
&c., &c.,
At reasonable prices, for cash only.
G. Wakely. 21

---

* In the museum of the State Historical Society of Colorado.

This print is from George Wakely's ambrotype of Carolista walking a tightrope across Larimer Street in Denver.   SHSC

Montgomery, a mining camp near Alma, as it appeared when George D. Wakely visited the town, C. 1863. The mill at center was powered by water taken out of the headwaters of the South Platte River.
Q-BAR

This Wakely view of Blackhawk, C. 1864, shows a town of remarkable stature for one which was less than five years old. SHSC

Fairplay looked like this at the beginning of its colorful life as a mining town. This scene was recorded in 1866 by George Wakely. Prospectors first settled here in 1859, after being driven out of Tarryall, another South Park mining camp. They named their new camp, "Fairplay," to belittle their rivals at Tarryall. SHSC

On the first of April, 1864, Wakely advertised his photographic business for sale because of poor health.[22] The idea was to teach the art of photography to the purchaser.[23] But a purchaser did not immediately materialize and Wakely was still behind his camera in the early morning hours of May 20 to record the devastating Cherry Creek flood which had occured during the previous night. The alarm had been given during the night that the creek was flooding the many houses and businesses which had been built along its course. Men sleeping in the *Rocky Mountain News* building had been awakened when the water shifted the building (which had been built in the "dry" bed of the creek) off its foundation. The men narrowly escaped drowning and the entire contents of the building—and the building itself— were lost. At sun-up that morning, the waters were receding rapidly. Wakely was waiting on the west side of the creek, however, and began to record the event. He climbed to the tops of several

On the morning of May 20, 1864, George Wakely climbed to the rooftops of several buildings to capture scenes of the Cherry Creek flood — such as this one — where so many buildings had been standing the night before. New residents had to learn about "flash" floods in the Rocky Mountain West the hard way. **SHSC**

buildings, from which he made his exposures.

Wakely was long believed to be the only photographer to record the event. He made six views of the flood. Although there are many prints still in evidence which bear the names of other photographers, they are nearly all pirated copies from Wakely.

The flood marked the end of Wakely's particularly good press coverage, at least with one editor:

> We were told to-day of a photographic institution on Larimer street, which realized considerable from pictures of the flood, the proprietor of which refused to give anything towards constructing a foot-bridge and road-way, that the Creek might be forded, or crossed on foot.[24]

Wakely responded to the indirect criticism and wrote to the editor, who in turn took him publicly to task:

> We received the following letter through the Denver Post Office a few days since.
>
> Denver, C.T., May 25, 1864.
> Charles M. Ferrell—Local Editor Commonwealth.
> If you enter my Rooms again, or make any disrespectful allusions to me in your Local Columns, I will whip you publicly on the streets.
> G. D. Wakely,
> Photographer.

By 1863, Denver was becoming a city of brick. H. J. Brendlinger's building at Fifteenth and Blake streets boasted of a complete stock of "tobacco, cigars, snuff, pipes, &c." — from a 5 x 7-inch print by Wakely.   SHSC

The absence of any regular issue of our paper since its reception is the reason we have not paid our respects to the insulting document before this. *We stand on our own bottom and do not fear the ruffian threats of any one.* We do not court an affray with any man, nor is our disposition quarrelsome, but when a man sends us such an epistle, with the threat that he will "whip us publicly on the streets," we will flatly inform him that we shall not allow him to do anything of the kind, not if we can help it . . .

If there is a word embodied in the above which warrants Mr. Wakely in "whipping us publicly on the streets" we don't see it. His name is not mentioned, nor any reference made to him. There are two photographic institutions on Larimer street. The parties who requested the notice to be put in, did not mention the name, nor did they request us to. We have never had any desire to injure the business of Mr. Wakely or any one else. That is not our nature. — So far as entering his house goes we are satisfied to stay out of it; but we are not to be muzzled as to what we shall write. If an article of ours injures any person, it is not intentional; we are always ready to repair a wrong when requested in a decent way.[25]

This was about the end of Wakely's career in Denver. Shortly thereafter he disappeared from view and was only heard of again when he returned to Colorado—probably from New York—to work for a short time in the new mining town of Leadville, in 1879. [26]

By September, 1860, Central City had a photographer of its own. Charles Hopping opened an ambrotype gallery in that boom town. He stayed in Central City for at least three years, photographing miners so that their families back in the States could see what a frontier miner looked like. The town was too rich a field for any one man to have all to himself for long. In April of 1861 Hopping, was competing with another "Daguerrean Artist,"* Henry Faul.

Faul opened his first Central City gallery with a man named Mark Allyn. One month after the gallery opened, Mr. Allyn traveled down to

_____
* Neither of these men used the daguerreotype process. The phrase, "daguerrean artist," was by this time an anacronism.

William Byers, founder of the *Rocky Mountain News,* posed with his family in front of their home along the banks of Cherry Creek in Denver, about 1863. The Byers home and the *Rocky Mountain News* were both lost in the flood of 1864 — from an ambrotype, probably by George Wakely. DPL

Denver to spend some time taking views of the city and making portraits. The *Rocky Mountain News* ran the following article under the heading:

BEAUTIFUL PICTURES

Messrs. Mark Allyn and Faul, Daguerrean Artists from Central City and Spring Gulch, are now in our city, taking most exccelent ambrotypes and melainotypes of our streets, stores and private buildings. Those here, or in the Mountains, who may want to have a true likeness taken of themselves, their stores or dwelling, their mills or their stock yards, to forward to their friends East, had better call on Mr. Allyn, while sojourning here, or on Mr. Faul, in Central City, and have them — "secure the shadow, ere the substance perish."[27]

Faul had a long succession of partners in the Central City gallery. Presumably they were left to the portrait trade while Faul traveled around the mountains and gold camps, taking views which could be sold—rather like picture postcards are today.

The photographic process being most widely used at this time is commonly called the "wet process." The reason this process is called the wet process is because the glass plate was photosensitive only so long as the chemicals on it were damp. When the plate dried, it was not useable in the camera. Each photographer had to be his own chemist and prepare his own plates. Usually 45 minutes to an hour were as long as one could wait between making the plates and exposing them in the camera. For this reason, mountain picture-taking trips required that a darkroom be taken along! Usually these darkrooms were tents lined with orange cloth (orange light would not easily harm this type of plate). Some of the more ingenious photographers used the back of a covered wagon. Considering that the photographer had to haul tremendous numbers of glass plates for long journeys over difficult terrain, pitch a tent and prepare the plate, set up the tripod and camera, make a one or two-second exposure, return to the tent and develop the picture—it is a wonder that any pictures were made away from the gallery.

George Wakely had traveled as far south as the Garden of the Gods with his camera and darkroom, but Faul went at it on a larger scale. In June, 1862, the *Rocky Mountain News* carried the following article describing Faul's views of the mountains:

> PHOTOGRAPHIC VIEWS — We are indebted to Mr. Faul, of Central City, for several fine views of the mountains around Central City, Black Hawk Point and vicinity, for which he has our thanks. Mr. F., we believe, is the only artist of his profession now in the mountains, and that he is a master in the art, none will deny who have patronized him. Get your "counterpart presentment" taken and send it to your friends and sweethearts at home. Mr. F. informs us that he intends soon to go over the snowy range for the purpose of taking some fine views.[28]

The effort which Faul expended in securing his photographs seems to have been sufficiently rewarded. Late in 1862, he opened a new Central City gallery:

AMBROTYPES AND PHOTOGRAPHS

> Mr. Faul has just completed his ambrotype and photographic gallery, and has everything in complete order. His building is in itself an ornament. The lower story is occupied as a grocery and provision store. Mr. Faul is a fine artist, as his work plainly shows; his views of mountain scenery are particularly fine. These last he is ready to copy for his customers on the shortest notice. Those who want a good picture, cannot do better than to call on him.[29]

Faul was always looking for opportunities to expand his business. In October, 1863, he reached an agreement with George Wakely of Denver for the sale of Faul's views of mountains and mining towns at Wakely's gallery opposite the post office on Larimer street.[30] These were described as:

> The nicest, newest works of Photographic art, showing mountain sceneries, mining views, and beautiful pictures of mountain cities, streets, gulch and quartz mining, that we have ever seen . . .[31]

As the Cherry Creek flood had proved to be a boon to George Wakely, a murder did the same for Henry Faul. Late in 1863, William S. Van Horn was convicted of murder in Central City.

The citizens of the town were so incensed over the affair that Van Horn had to be transferred to the Denver jail for safety. While awaiting the execution of the death sentence in Denver, he very nearly escaped the gallows by attempting to take his own life. It is a curious sidelight to the history of photography that the weapon he used was a photograph! Had he succeeded, his death certificate might have listed the cause as "death by daguerreotype":

WM. S. VAN HORN.

> Van Horn attempted, yesterday afternoon, to commit suicide, by opening a vein with a fragment of glass. After his conviction and sentence, whilst still remaining in the jail at Central City, he was given, at his solicitation, Daguerreotypes of some of his friends—his Father, Mother and Sister we believe—which he retained until his removal to Denver. After finding the knife concealed upon his person, and hearing his reiterated threats to commit suicide, Marshal Hunt very judiciously took everything from him, that could in any way be used as a means to destroy life. Since then he has not been allowed to have even a pin.
>
> Yesterday afternoon he requested to again see the miniatures of his relatives, and they were given him. Some hours later, the jailor entered his cell and found him drenched with blood. An examination revealed a horrible gash in his left arm, from which the blood was flowing. Further search was rewarded by finding the instrument with which the wound had been made—a triangular fragment of very thick glass, broken from the front of one of the miniatures. A physician was called and the wound bound up. Still greater care has since been taken to prevent his suicide.[32]

The precautions taken to guard Van Horn were successful and he was taken to the place of execution in satisfactory condition. Because of the extreme interest in the case in Central City, Faul was there with his camera to record the event. The photograph he made on this occasion was later being offered for sale out of his Central City gallery. This is believed to be the first photograph taken of a hanging in Colorado.[33] Unfortunately, Faul's big photographic moment was not as permanent as Wakely's had been. His photograph of the hanging has not come to light. At the time, he was making *cartes de visite*[34] and it is quite likely that he may have issued a good number of these small, cheap pictures of the hanging. If this is the case, there is a good chance that at least one of them has survived—tucked away in some family album or in an old book—perhaps someday to be rediscovered. Henry Faul remained in business in Central City and Denver until 1864, when he disappeared from the Colorado scene.

Ceremonies welcoming the Arapahoe and Cheyenne Indian delegations to Denver were conducted outside Governor John Evans' house (left of view) during the 1864 Camp Weld conference. Photographed by either Chamberlain or Wakely.   SHSC

Fifteenth Street in Denver as it looked in the mid-1860's. The Denver Theatre at Sixteenth and Lawrence streets can be seen to the right, over the top of Dr. Cunningham's offices — from a *carte de visite* made by William Chamberlain.   SHSC

As the 1860's came to a close, iron rails relentlessly drew Denver nearer to connections with the outside world. After the coming of the railroads this six-horse team and coach of Wells Fargo & Company would no longer ply its route. Photographed in Denver.   SHSC

William Gunnison Chamberlain

ROBABLY the photographer who gave Wakely and other Colorado photographers of the early period the greatest amount of competition was William Gunnison Chamberlain. He produced more paper photographs during the 1870's than anyone else in the territory: Seemingly, he produced more than all of his contemporaries combined, with the exception of William H. Jackson, who arrived 10 years later. Chamberlain was not really as prolific as all his rivals combined, but the number of his prints which have survived is enormous. Unlike many of his contemporaries, Chamberlain's career can be followed with some detail, as much information has been preserved.

After spending his boyhood in Boston, Chamberlain went to Peru in 1839 at the age of 24. While in Peru he engaged in the manufacture of silk and other speculations. He prospered in Peru and by 1847 he had a good deal of leisure. It was at this time that he first saw a camera in operation and he immediately took up daguerreotyping as a hobby to fill his spare moments. As he wrote years later:

> . . . Early in '47 two young men had made a tour through Chili and Peru with a daguerreotype outfit and on their return to the U.S. stopped off in Lima to take daguerreotype pictures; at this early date the sun picture was a marvel and I became interested in the process. Having much leisure from the nature of the business on which I was then occupied, I was induced to purchase an outfit from them, with some instructions and a little practice for all of which I paid them $300. So I became possessor of this art and as a recreation improved many leisure hours in its practice and became quite proficient in its manipulation. [1]

Chamberlain moved back to the United States in 1855 and established himself in the daguerreotype business in Chicago. [2] Unfortunately the mercury and bromine vapors used in the production of daguerreotypes were extremely noxious to many who were exposed to them for long periods. Chamberlain found that the additional time spent around the chemicals as a professional caused such a severe reaction that he was forced to give up photography as a career shortly after he had really gotten started. He turned to other means of livelihood.

In 1859, Chamberlain headed for the Colorado gold fields. After he had started the trip, he heard of the "Pikes Peak Humbug"—the story told by the thousands of prospectors who returned East empty-handed during the months before the large discoveries were made by Gregory and others. Discouraged by the bad reports about Colorado, he went instead to California. Satisfied that California would make a good home, he returned to the East in 1860 to bring his family out. His wife's health was so delicate, however, that she could not stand the trip all the way to California, so it was decided to make only half the trip the first year. The plan was to stay over the winter in Denver and continue on to California the following spring; however, Mrs. Chamberlain's health improved so greatly during her stay in Denver that it was decided to remain permanently.

Although it is not certain when, Chamberlain had acquired skill in making ambrotypes and tintypes sometime before coming to Denver. He began taking pictures in Denver the first week of June, 1861. He was located across the street from Tappan and Company at the corner of F. and McGaa (now Fifteenth Street and Market). At this time, he styled himself a "traveling artist" and urged his customers to get their pictures made soon, before he left for a trip to photograph the mountains. [3] This was the first of Chamberlain's

A portrait of the early-day Denver photographer, William G. Chamberlain, taken about 1880. **SHSC**

One of the things which Chamberlain did to decorate his new gallery was to put an American flag on the outside of the building. Whether he did so for patriotic reasons or for some other purpose, we do not know, but the gesture was cause for no small amount of comment about town. With the Civil War raging and a large number of Southerners in Colorado, there was great interest in Union flags flying over Colorado. The *Weekly Commonwealth and Republican* wrote:

> We have a kind of respect for a man who displays the good old flag which has stood the wear and tear of years, which has never been trailed in the dust at the heels of an oppressor, or decorated the triumphal car of a despot; we say, we like a man who shows his devotion to his country by displaying the ever-glorious flag of our fathers, which they fought so long and so stoutly to plant in that azure field. And for that reason we who'd ask those of our readers who wish to

annual summer trips to make collodion negatives from which any number of prints could be made later for sale in his gallery. He spent all of the summer of 1861 in the mountains and did not return to Denver until fall.

In August of the following year, he moved into quarters above Florman's Confectionery and Ice Cream Saloon on Larimer,[4] across the street from George Wakely's gallery. In addition to the wet collodion negatives and ambrotypes, he was still doing at least a limited daguerreotype business at this time.[5] His new quarters must have rivaled Wakely's as they had a marked effect upon one local editor:

> . . . He has an elegant room for taking pictures, a side room which is fitted up as a laboratory, a neat little parlour as retiring room and a petite lady's sanctum. The suite of rooms is tastefully arranged and fitted up, and in every way qualified for the business for which it is devoted. From the window is a beautiful view of the mountains and the eastern part of town.[6]

This small-format print of Mrs. William Chamberlain is believed to have been made during the late 1870's by her photographer husband. **SHSC**

In 1862, William G. Chamberlain moved into the second floor of Florman's ice cream saloon between Fourteenth and Fifteenth streets on Larimer Street in Denver. Next door was Apollo Hall, the city's pioneer theater. The *Rocky Mountain News* building, under construction at the time, can be seen at right. This view is from a *carte de visite* made by the photographer, circa 1864.   SHSC

send their features and forms down to an appreciative posterity by means of Photography, to call at the saloon of Professor Chamberlain, who has thrown the American Flag across Larimer street, and floated its ample folds to the western breeze. His motto is "A good picture or no pay." If the doctors would but use a parallel motto, and say "no cure no pay," we would think some of patronizing them occasionally ourselves. [7]

This print shows a wagon train pulling into Denver, C. 1860 — from a *carte de visite* copy of an earlier photograph copied in 1861 by Chamberlain.   SHSC

The *Rocky Mountain News* office in 1864 was located in what was considered the "dry" bed of Cherry Creek. This building, and everything else built in the water course, was swept away by the floodwaters of May 19, 1864.   SHSC

The sole Chamberlain view of the Cherry Creek flood, this recently identified *carte de visite* was taken from an almost identical location as the view of the *Rocky Mountain News* building shown above. Notice the Tremont House in both scenes (at left).   SHSC

Streams of water under high pressure ripped into the earth to wash away the soil, leaving behind rocks and — hopefully — free gold, C. 1869.   SHSC

William Barth and his brother were John Fink's principal rivals. His elegant book parlor, located on Fifteenth Street, between Blake and Market, is seen in this card photograph by Chamberlain, produced about 1865.   SHSC

By the second half of the 1860's, Central City was expanding out of the creek bed and beginning to spread up the slopes of the hills. This view was photographed about 1867 by William Chamberlain. SHSC

This card photograph shows part of Denver's residential section at the close of the 1860's. Photographed by Chamberlain. SHSC

Business seems to have been good for Chamberlain during these early years. He was selling views of mountain scenery and towns as far west as Salt Lake City, Utah. These views he obtained during his annual summer trips. He was also making *cartes de visite* by the dozens at this time.[8] A large variety of Chamberlain's views of mountain scenery were issued on the small, cheap *cartes de visite*, as well as on stereographic cards and later, the more expensive "cabinet" photographs, prints approximately 5 x 9 inches in size. During January, 1864, Chamberlain opened a branch gallery in Central City. This gallery was to be operated by Frank M. Danielson, a photographer recently arrived from New York City.[9]

One of the most puzzling questions about Chamberlain's career has been why he did not take any views of the Cherry Creek flood of May, 1864. In 1957, the Library of Congress published a guide to an exhibit prepared by the library in which they give George Wakely credit for being the first American photographer to record a flood. They mention his six views of the flood and state that they were later copyrighted by Wakely.[10] Recently, however, there was found a seventh view of the flood. The photograph is a *carte de visite* and bears Chamberlain's name. It was printed before September, 1864.* The glass negative was in some way broken soon after it was made and very few prints were made from it, thus accounting for the fact that it has only recently come to light—over a century later. None of the contemporary newspaper accounts which mention Wakely's six pictures say anything about Chamberlain having made any. One paper, the *Daily Mining Journal* of Blackhawk, criticized Chamberlain's operator in Central City for not taking any pictures.[11] It is apparent from this criticism that at least one member of Chamberlain's staff, if not Chamberlain himself, was in Denver and could have taken the photograph. Whether it was Chamberlain or his assistant who took the picture is not certain; but one thing is sure, George Wakely will have to share the credit for being the first American photographer to photograph a flood, if not with Chamberlain, then with his assistant, Frank M. Danielson.†

Saint John's in the Wilderness — located at Fourteenth and Arapahoe streets in Denver — mirrors the boomtown growth of the early days of the Mile High City. The original brick church — incorporated in 1865 — was almost lost behind the later wooden additions by the time Chamberlain made this *carte de visite* late in the 1860's.

When George Wakely closed his gallery in 1863, a large number of his clients went to Chamberlain;[12] who, by the closing months of 1864, had outgrown his old quarters over the ice cream saloon on Market Street. In November of that year, he moved into the second story of a brick building, still on Larimer Street:

> . . . Mr. Chamberlain, the eminent artist of the camera, will open his capacious, splendid suite of rooms, over Graham's drug store, corner of Larimer and F street,* tomorrow morning. A visit to the elegant establishment, lately, convinced us that his place will be the nicest in this western country, while his arrangements and facilities of adjusting light, and controlling the chemicals, are according to the latest approved improvements, and will, no doubt at all, result in making photographs equal to those executed in the highest style of the art back east. His sitting room, ladies' dressing room, salon, laboratory, etc., are models of arrangement, taste and comfort.[13]

Chamberlain—like many other photographers in the Rocky Mountain Region—took full advantage of the opportunities afforded by the mountains to supplement their portrait business by the sale of scenic views. Each summer he would leave his gallery in the hands of an assistant capable of meeting the usual demand for portraits, and head for the mountains. During the early 1870's, Chamberlain's son, Walter, accom-

---

* To be correct, three copies of the photograph were found. One — in excellent condition — has no identification on the back. The second — faded yellow — has Chamberlain's hallmark on the back. The third — printed from a badly craked glass plate — has a tax stamp on the back, thus proving that the other two earlier prints were made before September 1, 1864, when the stamp was required.

† Chamberlain also sold some other views of the flood, but they are pirated copies of one or another of the Wakely views mentioned earlier.

Fifteenth Street.

The sign on the corner of this building reads, "Colorado National Bank, dealers in Gold Dust, Coin Exchange, Government Vouchers, Script, Land Warranty, &c., &c." — something for everyone. This is the way the corner of Fifteenth and Larimer streets looked in the late 1860's when it was part of the commercial heart of the Colorado capital — from a *carte de visite* by William Chamberlain. SHSC

This portrait of Chief Ouray of the Ute tribe in southwestern Colorado was produced by William Chamberlain in the 1870's. It was pirated by William Henry Jackson in the years immediately following Ouray's death in 1880, and was circulated over his name for 20 years. SHSC

Opposite: An early view of placer diggings in Illinois Gulch, C. 1860. Facing the camera in the lower foreground is David Henderson, owner of the mining claim, who made a fortune from this operation. When he died in 1909, he left his relatives in Scotland $150,000 — mostly in gold nuggets that he had stashed away under carpets, in closets and dishes, and wherever there was a likely hiding place. SHSC

38

panied his father on these trips. During the summer of 1871, a third man joined the party. He was George Kirkland, a young photographer recently arrived from Wyoming. Kirkland was to become an excellent photographer in his own right and some of his portraits of Indians, as well as his few extant scenic views, are among the best of the period. Kirkland's brother, Charles, had come to Denver three years earlier and had worked for the Chamberlain gallery. Charles Kirkland was left at the Denver gallery to: ". . .sustain the good reputation of the gallery, and guarantee satisfaction to all. . . ." [14]

George Kirkland wrote an interesting account of the trip they made during the summer of 1871, which is so typical of the annual summer trips made by many Colorado photographers as to merit being quoted at length:

My trip extended four weeks, in company with Mr. Chamberlain and Son Walter. Object— pleasure, recreation, and taking photographic views. So imagine us fairly "outfitted" (a word signifying many things "in these parts") and prepared to do our own cooking, washing, etc., etc. For a month or two previous I had worked hard and faithfully in order to get ahead of my work enough to last till my return, and at the expiration of that time my desire to cultivate a closer acquaintance with the grand old hills, cañons, rivulets, and lakes of the Rockies, was all fomenting, "sizzling" and "billing over," and with a loving good-bye kiss to my other half and

Members of William Chamberlain's party at Hot Sulphur Springs are shown in this 1871 stereo card view which was photographed by either Chamberlain or his associate, George Kirkland. SHSC

George Kirkland — an early-day photographer in Colorado — is shown above in his Civil War uniform. From the Neal Fisk Collection, Silver Plume Museum.

The picture at left is one of the few-known prints by George Kirkland. It is a stereographic portrait of a Ute named Nic-a-a-gat Achgat and was produced about 1871. SHSC

The Fillmore Block at Fifteenth and Blake streets, Denver, as it looked in 1865. William Chamberlain captured the spirit of what is now the lower downtown section of the city — with boys and men lounging along Blake Street on a now-forgotten day of long ago. Wherever the tripod and black cloth of the photographer appeared, the curious always gathered.   SHSC

accumulated wealth, I bade good-bye to care and toil and gave myself full away to enjoyment and all appurtenances thereunto belonging. It was August the first that our "outfit" might have been seen wending its way slowly (for reasons which I will hereafter explain) on the Golden City road, to the mountains twelve miles distant. At eve we entered the cañon of Clear Creek, and then commenced the initial step to ascend. The grade is easy, and scenery enchanting; the road being so crooked and winding that you can see about one block ahead from each point. The next day we reached the Gray Hills known to all. Tourists "pass" and make a "go" for the South Boulder, through a delightful portion of the mountains, passing rich ranches in the miniature valleys, producing all kinds of substantials, necessary to good healthy living and comfort.

From the little city of South Boulder, our path is a troublesome one, following up the Boulder River, over an *imitation* road; the river is correctly named, as it is completely lined with huge rocks and drift wood. After following it six miles we enter the Boulder Park, where we are bro't in closer contact with the range. Our destination is "over the range" into Middle Park, via Boulder Pass. We see a trail, leading up a tremendous steep hill, which in point of *degrees* would discount forty-five degrees all to pieces, and it was hard for us to persuade ourselves that it was our route, but alas for human expectations, for by the time we had fully made up our minds to it we were at the base, and occular demonstrations said plainly that *our load* must be divided. Just then one of the natives came up; we asked him how far it was to the summit of the range. He said it was *Fifteen* to the top of timber line, then we would have Two to go to the top, but "allowed" that we

In 1867, Georgetown was little more than a smelter-town — as the smokestack in this view indicates. There were signs of permanence, however. Just below the smelter (left side of view) can be seen what is now considered a splendid example of Victorian Gothic architecture, the Hamill house — now a museum. This was one of the many views sold by William G. Chamberlain in Colorado Territory.

would have hard "pegging" with those critters to make it. We started up with half the load; Mr. C. at the brake and lines; Walter and I at each hind wheel with huge blockers, as extra brakemen and motive power. It was like playing cribbage, pegging one hole at a time till finally we worried up; then going down again we cut down a tree nine inches through, and hitched it on behind the wagon, branches forward, and dragged it down; yet withall that, and wheels locked, it was as much a bargain that the ponies kept the wagon from running on them. After a "double run of two" we were safely landed over the first pitch, and as we then thought the worst; but, alas, again—delusion.

We camped by a clear running brook, amid pines so tall and densely packed together that you might look up, down, this way, or that way, and not see daylight unobstructed. Taking up our line of march we encountered some of the *worst* roads that mortal or *immortal* could think of inventing and call it a road; and all day over rough boulders, fallen trees, high stumps, and the devil knows what we travelled at snail pace, through dense forests, up, on, up the endless hills, as it seemed, with the roaring creek below, way down, thro' mud-holes, caused by springs and quaggy places, till finally, after many *trials* and *tribulations* (for one of our ponies *mutinied* on the *upslope* of a terrible rocky hill and "swore off" on this up-hill business, and would not *budge* an inch, except that he *kicked* remarkably well for a *tired* (?) horse, when being persuaded by a gad and blacksnake simultaneously to "get up!!") we came in sight of "timber line." *Timber line* is that point of altitude where timber ceases to grow, and above it is snow line, or all barren and rocky. After two or three steep pulls, unloading, packing up, unloading again, we arrived at the top of "timber line," only to see a still worse road to the summit of the Pass. Here, at timber line, we stop near a large snowbank; the melting snow forms a pretty lake about a quarter of a mile long, clear as crystal, and cold as ice; the name of it Jennie

The railroad — which was rapidly advancing toward Denver — would soon put cross-country wagon trains like this one out of business. Williams & McDonald captured this freight outfit on glass, after it had circled on Larimer Street on June 20, 1868. Shortly after this picture was taken, the train headed south from Denver where the mules were lost to hostile Indians.   SHSC

Lake; also from this point James Peak forms a pretty view. There is something that fills one with feelings indescribable as they stand near these huge snowbanks, as they are, near the crest of the grand old mountains overhanging cliffs and deep chasms below; it fills one with such thoughts as "now if this melting snow should suddenly 'slide,' what would become of me;" and "it's a wonder the July and August sun won't melt it all away, &c., but no! snow remains on them the year 'round;" we stopped at this point two days, and in the mean time the clouds hung over and below; and at one time mist so thick one could almost cut it. Seeing the work we had before us to get our load up the summit we *divided* again and packed the most, and with the empty wagon we found it "nip and tuck" to get up; the road, if such it could be called, was terribly steep, rocky and sideling; we took to the top of one rise thinking when we reach it the worst will be over, but when we reach it we see a still higher point ahead, and so on till finally Walter, who is ahead of us, waves us and cries Excelsior!! It is amusing, at this altitude of 12,100 feet, to see the antic actions of the natives; said natives being *Coneys* or Rocky Mountain dogs; they are nearly as large as a prairie dog, with

actions the same; no tail to speak of, and their heads have some resemblance to the monkey (Darwin may possibly have passed here and seen them); their "chet, chit, cheo," is amusing to listen to as they "scollop 'round" from one boulder to another. How they subsist is a mystery to me, as the range affords no food except *stone in large quantities* . . .

After travelling along the top of the range, and descending for four or five miles, we came to timber line, on the Middle Park side. The view of the Park affords wide scope for the eye of the tourist. We had thought that the worst of the travelling would be ended, after reaching the top; but some of the steep hills we had to descend, and ascend also, and the ugly, muddy, mucky, swampy places; then a strip of good road where . . . we would abruptly "strike a torrent" and be compelled to drive along down the middle of its course over rocky boulders and driftwood, landing places to cross some ugly streams, and cutting away fallen timber to make the road passable; over sideling places that required "funeral like" driving to keep from upsetting; again through timber so close that in trying to escape locking against trees on one side would bring us chuck

McCUNE. KASSERMAN. TRITCH. MAYOR BRENDLINGER. MALONEY. BOWEN. GAFFNEY.

CITY COUNCIL _ DENVER _ 1864 _ 5.

These seven stern Victorian gentlemen comprised the city council of Denver (including the mayor) during the last two years of the War Between the States — photographed either in 1864 or 1865 by William Chamberlain.

against a stump on the other.

One place I remember vividly; to talk about a man walking on the ceiling; it would be quite as great an undertaking to keep a wagon from upsetting going over the place. Walter had a rope attached to the top of the bows and on the up side of the hill, "heaving on it." Mr. C. and I both making drag anchors of ourselves by clinging to the brake beam and hind wheel, and for all that we could feel the wagon surging; so unloading again for about the twentieth time, and getting a pole for a lever we managed to run the blockade.

At one place, coming down the range, night overtook us before we came to feed, and we had to go three miles for feed for the horses. The road is narrow, and in places not wide enough for teams to pass each other.

The Park is about fifty by seventy miles in extent, possessing good grazing land, but is principally hilly; it is surrounded by snowy peaks, and the range hems it in like a ring; it is, so to speak, a large amphitheatre. Crooked Creek is a novelty in itself and was correctly named, and I can best compare it, in point of direction and sources, as a lot of "S'es," and if it was much "crookeder," it couldn't run. Next comes Frazer River, abounding in trout and sand-hill cranes, ducks and geese. After twenty miles travel we reach the *Grand** River and Hot Sulphur Springs, the resort of the health-seeking ones.[15]

* Colorado River

George H. Fryer posed with his horse and buggy for Chamberlain in 1863. Fryer was the discoverer of the famous gold-bearing hill near Leadville, which was named for him. Meckling & Shallcross' drugstore on Larimer Street is in the background.   SHSC

The Pacific House and the Denver Theatre, two pre-eminent pioneer institutions of the Mile High City, were recorded in this view about 1867 by an unknown artist.   SHSC

The First National Bank of Denver was photographed 10 years apart — as shown in these two views by William Chamberlain. In the first one (above) the building was under construction in 1865, while in the second one (opposite) — photographed in 1875 — a third story had been added. This building still stands at the corner of Fifteenth and Blake streets, at the bottom of the Fifteen Street Viaduct.   SHSC

Traveling on, the party saw indications of a band of Indians in the area. Kirkland, who vehemately hated and despised the Indians, was on edge:

Well, with Indians in my mind, and my extreme dislike for them was not a pleasant feeling for one to carry along with him when looking after the ponies; nevertheless I had been looking after them and had just entered the tall willow, along the bank of the Grand, when suddenly I heard the bushes crack and an UNEARTHLY yell of "ah-eh ah! eh-ah! eh-ah ooooh!!" In an instant my hand was on my revolver, and a whole possee of "wild *live* inguns" I fancied ready to "whip" me; but after the first prolonged "ah-eh" I knew the *gentle voice*, and immediately grew brave and laughed at myself, and wondered what earthly use a revolver was in my hands. It needed no one to say "God save the mark" for my reputation as a marksman would save the side of a mountain twenty paces—for a fact.

Well, lets go back to the springs. I told no one of my scare, but went to the springs and cooled my excited nerves with a good tin cup (glasses a novelty here) of warm water, and after that I felt ashamed to look a donkey in the face.

Before we left the springs, a band of about fifty Utes pitched their "teepes" on the opposite bank of the Grand; there were about fifteen whites at the springs, and in case of any demonstration we felt safe. But they were peaceably inclined toward us, although the knowledge of whites inhabiting the Middle Park was not liked by them—the Park is *not* in their reservation, and they have no right whatever to insist on the whites abandoning it. They came over and took free baths, (always allowed them to keep peace of course) and it was amusing to see their actions and hear their chattering. . . .

The little papooses, and older ones too, with bare ideas of dress, felt it a treat to take off a "little of the loose dirt" in nature's warm bath. But I seriously think, had the bath been a cold one, that dirt might have been allowed to accumulate till they would have been *portable* and living plantation ranches, or small-sized farms; even as it was, with such cheap and pleasant facilities for cleansing, some of them "passed" the opportunity from knowledge that it would *reduce* their weight, and also open a way for catching *death* colds by removing too much covering at a time; and I suppose the prominent reason was that they removed the coating of filth and dirt, that the vermin, which abound plentifully on them, would have much fairer show, and it would be a continual "You scratch my back. I'll scratch yours."

Poor Walter; with his young, generous

disposition, he robbed himself of fishing tackle and caps. One burley Ute saw a fish hook in his coat and in his accumulated English said "bish hook you, me." Walter wasn't posted in character of speech, but when Mr. Ute, who spells his name *Wanchech* (or Antelope) took it from his coat, he felt sensible of what was wanted, and parted with it. Soon another came up, "bish hook, you, me." Walter went down into his pocket and brought up two and "go" they did. He soon had a dozen applications, for an Indian is a *thoroughbred*

beggar—"dyed in the wool" and "stamped." I was next interviewed on the "bish hook you, me" question. I didn't bite, had no *bish*, etc., to give away to the Ute Company.

Desiring to get a view of their camp, we packed up tent* and apparatus, and crossed over; they closely watched movements with suspicious eyes,

* The portable darkroom tent used to prepare the glass plates for the camera.

Blake Street, Denver, C. 1864 — where H. Burton had just received a wagon-train loaded with necessities from "back East." Every nail, every piece of glass, every bolt of cloth, most staple foods, and everything else which had to be imported into the Rocky Mountain country during the 1860's, had to be laboriously hauled across the continent in wagons, often drawn by teams of oxen.   SHSC

Denver's famous Tremont House was a leading hostelry during the 1860's. As early as 1859, this hotel had been a community center; and, in October of that year, a crowd had assembled in front of the hotel to vote *en masse* on the guilt or innocence of an accused murderer. After the voice vote was taken, the judge stood on the balcony to announce the verdict to the prisoner and crowd below. This view was made by Chamberlain, C. 1865.   SHSC

In 1865, Chamberlain produced this *carte de visite* view of the home of Colorado's second territorial governor, John Evans. This building was at the corner of Fourteenth and Arapahoe streets in Denver. This reproduction and the one above have been printed the same size as the original card, including the borders.

In this *carte de visite* by William Chamberlain, a group of children posed proudly in front of a residence on Arapahoe Street — near Fourteenth — in Denver, C. 1864.   SHSC

The City Bakery and Occidental Billiard Hall at the southwest corner of Fifteenth and Blake streets in Denver — as they appeared in 1863 — from a card photograph produced by William Chamberlain.   SHSC

and when Mr. C. said "take picture Ute house?" they all said "no *pickure*; make Ute sick; heap headache, etc., etc." Not wishing to rush matters, on dangerous grounds, we layed on our oars a couple of hours coaxing, I had fancied I was proficent in coaxing, but I found I was weak . . .

When coaxing failed, the photographers decided to try to obtain the photographs any way they could:

> . . . taking the main portion of the *teepes*, Mr. C. leveled his camera on two others, that were off to one side, around which were a lot of squaws, tanning beaver, elk and antelope skins.
>
> The moment they saw the camera directed toward them it created a great panic among them . . . and they struck a bee line for the inside of the *teepes* "to all *in tents* and purposes" and the next scene was a shriveled weather-beaten, caved-in buck Chimingin maneuvering to Mr. C. to the tune of ". . . Ute wanted no pickur, maket Ute heap tsick," meaning "hello there, go away, not good; Ute wants no pictures, as it brings sickness, etc., etc."
>
> I stood by witnessing the affair with minglings of *ticklishness*, amused, and yet fearing an outbreak, and as Mr. C. raised his head from under the "dark cloth," just catching the last few words and gesticulations of Mr. Ute's speech, and inquiringly asked "Eh!?" amusement with me at the seeming farce, got in the ascendency . . .

We troted off thenceforthly, and I found out that I had to take part in the melodramas which followed as Mr. C. had patronizingly told four of the "Chief muckey mucks" that he would give them a free lunch, if they preserved peace, and I was assigned [the] part of chief caterer, or boss hasher.

From the Hot Springs we traveled the trail up the Grand River to Grand Lake, twenty-eight miles distant and the head of Grand River. The route is a pleasant one, being a continual change of scenery, and the greater portion of it magnificently grand. . . .

The atmosphere was quite hazy, and not so clear as is usual to the clear, rarified mountain air, in consequence of the Indians setting fire to the woods, all through the mountains, to scare out the game, and it was quite detrimental to our success in getting views, as sometimes the atmosphere was so dense and foggy that we could not see the mountains on the opposite side of the lake—three miles distant; and in order to get a view of them we waited nearly a week longer than would have been necessary had it been pleasant, waiting for a rain or snow storm to purify the atmosphere. Mr. C., after three or four days waiting, solicited my prayers in behalf of rain. I begged an excuse that if I attempted such a novelty that I would be sure to overdo the thing, so he thought best to take chances, and run them for luck. Luck won, to my astonishment, for all afternoon the clouds began to congregate and showed signs of restlessness as though something was up and about to come down. And after we had crowded into our nests, and Morpheus getting the best of us, I was aroused by a gentle, undertoned yet withal a husky voice, of "Kirkland——it's come!!" —— "What?" (with minglings of fear and pleasure) "The rain." So with more confidence in my ability than previous, I wrapped myself again in sleep.

Morning found the air clear and pure; we succeeded in getting views and next day bidding good by to the lake and its grand surroundings . . .[16]

Largely from the sale of mountain views obtained during the summer trips, the Chamberlain gallery prospered during the 1870's.

This view is inscribed, "Libbie Payne, daughter of Rev. Jno. Payne, aged 3 Years, 1863." Keeping children still long enough to get their pictures taken was a problem during the days of slow photographic emulsions. Judging by her facial expression, threats had been employed to keep little Libbie from moving — except for her left hand, which shook slightly as the hooded camera lens was opened and the seconds were counted out loud. The base of the headrest can be seen on the floor in back of the girl's feet.   SHSC

The beginning of the most important single event in Colorado since the gold rush was the ground-breaking ceremony for Denver's first railway, the Denver Pacific, which took place on May 18, 1868, at what is now Blake Street and Fortieth Avenue. All the "best citizens" of Denver turned out *en masse* to watch Mrs. Frederick Stanton and Miss Nettie Clark handle the plow, as Governor Gilpin spoke. It is interesting to note that every one of the buggies in this view, as well as elsewhere in and around Denver at this time, had either been hauled into town on wagons or driven over the wide-open spaces of the prairie from "back East." SHSC

Chamberlain was recognized as the leading photographer in Colorado during this period. His views of mountain scenery were widely circulated and the gallery turned out a large number of portraits of the famous and the obscure of Colorado. In June of 1872, a third story was added to the gallery to accomodate the expanding business. The newly remodeled gallery was described briefly by the *Rocky Mountain News*:

The reception room with ladies' dressing room adjoining, is situated on the second floor, and is fitted up in a convenient and tasteful manner, exactly adapted to the exhibition of portraits and mountain views. Here may be found pictures of the various grades, from the cheapest to the most expensive kinds, which will enable the patron to make his selection, especially of mountain views, without the trouble of expenditure of time required to visit other extablishments. The operating room or glass house, size 24 x 50, is on the third floor, and is admirably arranged, having a convenient system of sliding curtains. Back-grounds, of a variety of shades and sizes, adapted to all contingencies, and erected on castors, are here. On this floor are ladies' and gentlemen's dressing rooms. Mr. Chamberlain operates seven cameras, one of which, wrought in exquisite form [is] valued at $125 . . .[17]

The gallery caught fire two years after it was remodeled. During a severe windstorm, sparks from a nearby chimney lighted on the roof of the third story. The fire bell echoed across the town and the firemen formed a bucket brigade to get water to the roof. Although the fire was quickly extinguished, the wind was blowing so hard that the wooden shingles were still in danger of rekindling. A section of the roof had to be cut and chopped away in order to prevent the wind from whipping up a blaze that would consume the rest of the roof and the neighboring buildings as well.[18] Chamberlain repaired the damage and remained at this location until he sold his business in 1881.

The teaching staff of Wolf Hall in Denver was photographed by
William G. Chamberlain in 1870.   SHSC

The Photographic Album.

NEW YORK,

D. APPLETON & C?, 443 & 445 BROADWAY.

1862.

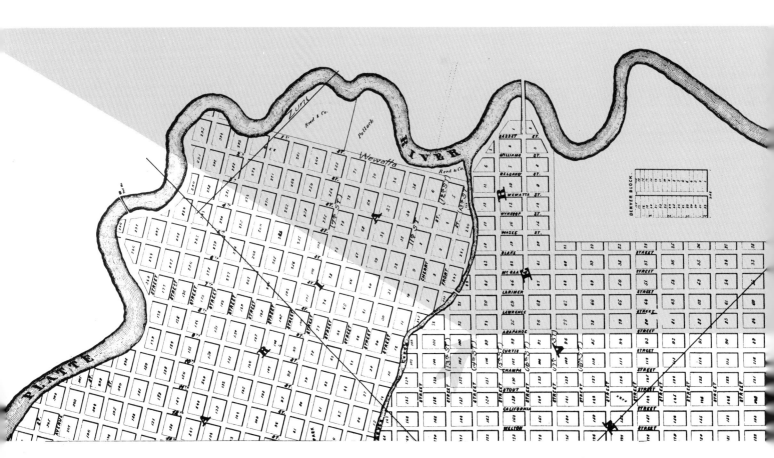

54

The Photographic Album.

NEW YORK,

D. APPLETON & C?, 443 & 445 BROADWAY.

1862.

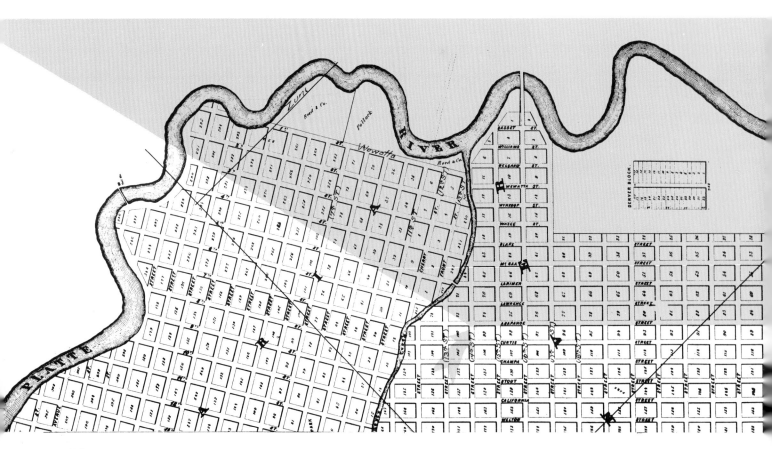

at the corner of Fourteenth and Arapahoe
oking northward. The rooftop below the
ey in the third section belongs to the house
John Evans on Fourteenth Street, between
and Lawrence. The Methodist Episcopal
on Fourteenth and Lawrence. To the right
h, cottonwood trees can be seen outlining
latte River. The main business section of
town can be located in this view by the tower of the
mint at Sixteenth and Market streets, rising in the
center of the fourth section. The square false front of
the Denver Theatre can be seen in the far right section.
This panorama was in Chamberlain's private collection,
which was donated to the State of Colorado in 1954 by
Chamberlain's granddaughter, Helen Chamberlain
Tedman.   SHSC

o at the corner of Fourteenth and Arapahoe
ᵬking northward. The rooftop below the
ᵥy in the third section belongs to the house
᠇ John Evans on Fourteenth Street, between
₃nd Lawrence. The Methodist Episcopal
₅ on Fourteenth and Lawrence. To the right
᠌h, cottonwood trees can be seen outlining
ᵱlatte River. The main business section of

town can be located in this view by the tower of the
mint at Sixteenth and Market streets, rising in the
center of the fourth section. The square false front of
the Denver Theatre can be seen in the far right section.
This panorama was in Chamberlain's private collection,
which was donated to the State of Colorado in 1954 by
Chamberlain's granddaughter, Helen Chamberlain
Tedman.   SHSC

With the outbreak of the Civil War in the East, many Coloradans rushed to enlist in the armed services. Here, a group of volunteers from the First Colorado Cavalry Detachment, Company G, is seen in drill formation at Empire in 1862 — photographer unknown. SHSC

Among the men of the Colorado gold rush, none is so well known perhaps as William Green Russell, the man for whom Russell Gulch was named. This tintype was taken shortly after the gold rush by an unknown photographer. SHSC

As the Civil War was drawing to its close in 1864-'65, an immigrant photographer, Henry Garbanati, made this view of a slow day in Central City.   SHSC

Cristopher "Kit" Carson, scout, guide and commander of Colorado's Fort Garland — in the eastern part of the San Luis Valley — is shown here in his military uniform in a view which is believed to be an ambrotype.   SHSC

Officers of the Colorado Volunteers came to an unknown photographer's studio before marching off to fight in the Union Army during the Civil War. SHSC

An 1869 street scene in Trinidad, showing Main Street as it looked at that time, is reproduced above. On the right is Davis & Barraclough's store — dealers in general merchandise — located at the corner of Main and A streets. Trinidad was on the Mountain Branch of the Santa Fe Trail and was an important supply town. SHSC

L.N. GREENLEAF, S.W.   WM. PORTER, W.M.   A. McCUNE, J.W.

DENVER LODGE, NO. 5, A.F. & A.M. A.L. 5865.

The view above is another rare photograph of a street in early-day Trinidad. This scene was photographed the year after W. A. Bell visited this commercial trading center in southern Colorado — in 1868. However, the photographer is unknown.   SHSC

People were quick to institute organizations in Colorado which they had known in their Eastern homes. Here, we see the senior warden, worshipful master and junior warden of Denver Lodge No. 5, A.F. & A.M. A.L. 5865 (the Masonic Lodge) in the year 1865. SHSC

Early-day street scenes of Colorado towns often showed a beehive of activity — such as the view above of Golden, with horses and wagons nearly filling the street.   SHSC

Among the notables in Colorado during the 1860's was the first governor, William Gilpin — seen here in a portrait taken during his administration by an unknown photographer. The governor was a dominant figure in the affairs of Colorado until he died in the 1890's.   SHSC

Among amateur photographers, this stereographic camera was popular about 1898. The stereo card viewer (at right and below) was invented by Oliver Wendell Holmes and was used widely throughout America.

Apparatus

HE COLORADO gold rush coincided with a period of rapidly expanding popularity in America for stereographs, or stereoscopic views. From the time of Exekias, artists had attempted to represent solid forms in space by lines drawn on a flat plain, usually a canvas. One of the reasons sculpture proved so popular with artists from the Egyptians forward is that objects represented to be round were really round.

Leonardo da Vinci realized the cause of the defect in painting resulting from both eyes seeing the same thing when viewing the canvas. He wrote:

> . . . a painting, though conducted with the greatest art, and finished to the last perfection, both with regard to its contours, its lights, its shadows, and its colors, can never show a *relievo* equal to that of the natural objects, unless these be viewed at a distance and with a single eye . . .[1]

In 1838, an English scientist invented a device to overcome the problem of representing depth on a flat surface. Sir Charles Wheatstone announced that year the invention of the stereoscope. The first pictures for the stereoscope were hand-drawn pyramids, cones and other geometric shapes, which were seen as rising out from the paper like a cutout when viewed through the instrument. The stereoscope was adapted to the camera almost as soon as the photographic process had been announced. It did not gain much popularity, however, until a practical process for photographs on paper was made popular during the closing years of the 1850's. By 1859, photographs on paper (the only type of photography referred to as "photographs" at that time) had largely replaced the daguerreotype. As Oliver Wendell Holmes wrote, a few portraits were still seen on the daguerreotype plates:

> . . . But the greatest number of sun-pictures we see are the photographs which are intended to be looked at with the aid of the instrument we are next to describe, and to the stimulus of which the recent vast extension of photographic copies of Nature and Art is mainly owing. . . .

A stereoscope is an instrument which makes surfaces look solid. All pictures in which perspective and light and shade are properly managed, have more or less the effect of solidity; but by this instrument that effect is so heightened as to produce an appearance of reality which cheats the senses with its seeming truth. . . .

We can commonly tell whether an object is solid, readily enough with one eye, but still better with two eyes, and sometimes only by using both. If we look at a square piece of ivory with one eye alone, we cannot tell whether it is a scale of veneer, or the side of a cube, or the base of a pyramid, or the end of a prism. But if we now open the other eye, we shall see one or more of its sides, if it have any, and then know it to be a solid, and what kind of a solid.

We see something with the second eye which we did not see with the first; in other words, the two eyes see different pictures of the same thing, for the obvious reason that they look from points two or three inches apart. By means of these two different views of an object, the mind, as it were, *feels round* it and gets an idea of its solidity. We clasp an object with our eyes, as with our arms, or with our hands, or with our thumb and finger, and then we know it to be something more than a surface. This, of course, is an illustration of the fact, rather than an explanation of its mechanism.

Though, as we have seen, the two eyes look on two different pictures, we perceive but one picture. The two have run together and become blended in a third, which shows us everything we see in each. But, in order that they should so run together, both the eye and the brain must be in a natural state. Push one eye a little inward with the forefinger, and the image is doubled, or at least confused. Only certain parts of the two retinae work harmoniously together, and you have disturbed their natural relations. Again, take two or three glasses more than temperance permits, and you see double; the eyes are right enough, probably, but the brain is in trouble, and does not report their telegraphic messages correctly. These exceptions illustrate the every-day truth, that, when we are in right condition, our two eyes see two somewhat different pictures, which our perception combines to form one picture, representing objects in all their dimensions, and not merely as surfaces.

Now, if we can get two artificial pictures of any given object, one as we should see it with the right eye, the other as we should see it with the left eye, contrive some way of making these pictures run together as we have seen our two views of a natural object do, we shall get the sense of solidity that natural objects give us. The arrangement which effects it will be a *stereoscope* . . .

And just here comes in the photograph to meet the difficulty. A first picture of an object is taken—then the instrument is moved a couple of inches or a little more, the distance between the human eyes, and a second picture is taken. Better than this, two pictures are taken at once in a double camera.

We were just now stereographed, ourselves, at a moment's warning, as if we were fugitives from justice. A skeleton shape, of about a man's height, its head covered with a black veil, glided across the floor, faced us, lifted its veil, and took a preliminary look. When we had grown sufficently rigid in our attitude of studied ease, and got our umbrella into a position of thoughtful carelessness, and put our features with much effort into an unconstrained aspect of cheerfulness tempered with dignity, of manly firmness blended with womanly sensibility, of courtesy, as much as to imply—"You honor me, Sir," toned or sized, as one may say, with something of the self-assertion of a human soul which reflects proudly, "I am superior to all this,"—when, I say, we were all right, the spectral Mokanna dropped his long veil, and his waiting-slave put a sensitive tablet under its folds. The veil was then again lifted, and the two great glassy eyes stared at us once more for some thirty seconds. The veil then dropped again; but in the meantime, the shrouded sorcerer had stolen our double image; we were immortal. Posterity might henceforth inspect us, (if not otherwise engaged,) not as a surface only, but in all our dimensions as an undisputed *solid* man of Boston.[2]

In the accompanying stereographic photo of Leadville by Alexander Martin, we can see an ordinary street scene of the period. But put the print in an old-fashioned parlor viewer and the flat representation becomes almost real. The tall telegraph pole in the left foreground stands out from the shorter pole on the corner, which is barely visible in the flat photo. The many signs

When viewed through the stereoscope, this flat scene of Leadville during the mining boom becomes unbelievably realistic. The signs along the street stand out from each other and the horse changes from a cutout to a solid round form. This 1879 Leadville stereo card has been printed actual size at the bottom of this page so that it may be viewed through a parlor stereoscope. **SHSC**

which hang over the sidewalk form a montage when viewed without the machine, but each sign stands out distinctly from the rest when viewed through the lenses. The horse in the street is changed from a silhouette to a solid form. The illusion of actually looking at the original scene is so perfect in a well-made stereo-viewer and carefully executed stereo-photograph that it is like looking back in time and watching history through a knot hole in a board fence as a young boy might do, sneaking a look at a baseball game.

The first stereographic picture taken in Colorado was made in 1859.[3] Who took this photograph is not known; perhaps it was Sabine, or perhaps it was a traveling photographer whose name is now lost. The earliest stereo card of which I am aware is a view by Wakely of the Cherry Creek flood. This is not a true stereo-photograph, however, because both pictures on the card are identical. Probably Wakely took only a conventional camera when he shot the flood and sometime later printed the psuedo stereo-photograph to meet the ever-increasing demand for views in depth.

During the entire period of Nineteenth-Century photography in Colorado—but especially during the Seventies, Eighties and Nineties—the stereographic card was the largest-selling type of photograph. During each of the annual mountain trips made by Chamberlain and others, large numbers of stereographic negatives were made. These were later printed at the galleries and sold at prices ranging from $12.00 to $15.00 per dozen.[4] This price at least was true for 1867. By 1881, the price had fallen to around $3.00 per dozen, or 25 cents each.[5]

Many photographers had large numbers of stereo-cards for sale at their galleries. The Duhem Brothers, prominent Denver photographers during the early 1870's, advertised their collection as being over 300 views "For the Stereoscope."[6] Among the Colorado towns which they had photographed were listed: Denver, Central City, Black Hawk, Georgetown, Nevada, Granite City, Fairplay, Colorado City. It is a pity that more of these views have not survived.

Some photographers took photographs with little or no thought of their eventual value, but others were apparently extremely conscious that they were creating a valuable record of the growth of the Western frontier towns. One such photographer was T. E. Barnhouse. Barnhouse—like the Duhems—also advertised a collection of 300 stereographs, but his methods were a good deal more systematic than most of his competitors. As a contemporary newspaper editor explained it:

He has views of all the towns and camps in the San Juan from their earliest settlement; and as he has been taking pictures of the most important points every year for five years, his collection embraces a picture history of the country more eloquent than words. The views are all mounted for the stereoscope . . .[7]

The historical value of such a collection would indeed be trememdous. But the vast majority of the stereo-cards of Barnhouse have been lost.

The advantages of the stereo-photograph over other forms created such a demand for mountain scenes of this type that it soon became the main part of the output of photographers like William Chamberlain, George Kirkland, William H. Jackson, and many other Colorado photographers. When William H. Jackson traveled throughout Colorado with the Hayden surveys during the first half of the 1870's, he used a camera which produced a 5 x 8-inch collodion negative on glass.[8] He had two fronts for the camera—one with a single lens to make a single negative of that size, and the second with two lenses mounted about three inches apart, which produced two separate pictures on the single sheet of 5 x 8-inch glass. It is with this twin-lens front that he made many of the stereographic cards which were later published by the Federal government to illustrate the Hayden survey. Half of the photographs taken by Jackson during the 1873 survey were stereographic.[9]

Some idea of the percentage of stereo-photographs which some photographers made can be gained by remarking that all of the photographs by George Kirkland which are known to the writer are stereo-cards. He undoubtedly made others, and quite probably some of them have survived—but they are so outnumbered by his stereographs that they are easily overlooked. Timothy O'Sullivan, like Jackson, a famous government photographer in the West, made a large number of stereo-cards for the government while in Colorado.

Almost no field of photography is so incomprehensible to those who have not experienced it as stereographic photography. The parlor stereoscope can be purchased in antique shops for under $15.00 and because they were made in such large quantities, the cards are available for less than their original price. An inexpensive way to acquire the closest thing to a look into the past which man is likely to get is this simple and exciting stereoscope.

When printers have devised a practical way to print stereographic photographs into books, the illustrations for this volume should be redone so

Stereographic camera equipment was carried into all parts of the West. Many photographers devoted their whole time to the stereo trade.　　　　　Q-BAR

that the reader can see the photographers' work as the photographers intended it to be seen.

The question most often asked by persons interested in the history of photography is perhaps: "What happened to the negatives?" Chamberlain's, Kirkland's, Wakely's, all have disappeared. Indeed, stereographic negatives of the period are much rarer than regular negatives. The reason is probably their greater value! Paradoxically, those things with the least value are often those which have survived. The Frank Dean plates and the Garrison studio plates are two excellent examples. The Dean plates were found in the basement of Mr. Dean's original studio in Grand Junction during the demolition of that structure in 1964.* The prints had been removed for safekeeping and subsequently were lost, but the original glass negatives were left in the building when it was sold because they were believed to be of no value. The Garrison negatives were discovered in a chicken coop on the western slope of Colorado.†

Stereo-negatives, being of greater commercial value, could be sold to the large commercial publishers of views in the East. When many photographers retired from business, they probably sold their stereo-negatives. The only stereographic negatives of this period of which I am aware are half-a-dozen in the W. H. Jackson collection at the Colorado State Museum and those in Washington, D.C. Inquiries to the major stereographic view company of the period, which is still selling photographs, failed to turn up any information on Jackson's stereo-negatives. #

The rapid advance in photographic technique during the first decade of settlement of the new territory saw Colorado photographers using almost every type of photograph, from the daguerreotype through the ambrotype and the collodion negative process. By the latter half of the 1860's, some progress was being made toward shorter exposures. At the "National Gallery of Art," a photographic gallery in Central City, it was boasted: "Children taken by the new instantaneous Collodium process."[10] What was considered instantaneous in 1866, however, is not comparable to modern camera-shutter speeds. On a good day, with no clouds obscuring the sun—at about noon—the best results could be obtained. Williams and McDonald advertised at their Denver gallery:

Good pictures taken of children in one or two seconds—adults in four to six seconds . . .[11]

It is hard to imagine remaining completely immobile for four seconds while a collodion negative was being exposed. This may well account for some of the strange and rather strained expressions which portraits of the period all too often display. This difficulty was not usually encountered, however, when taking photographs outside, as so much more light was available. It made little difference when taking a picture of a house or barn how long the exposure was, assuming there were no moving objects in the scene. Long exposures caused some difficulty, however, when the subject included foliage in the foreground. On a windy day, a tree or bush would move so much during the exposure that it would record on the plate as a sweeping blur.

These difficulties did not stop a good number of people from having their ranch or farm photographed. In the days before the box camera, and before amateur photographers flourished everywhere, if someone wanted a photograph of his house, he hired a photographer to come out from town, or he waited until some photographer drove his wagon down the neighborhood lane. This was the way pots and pans, books, harnesses, Lydia Pinkham's Pills, and almost every other

* These were given to the State Historical Society of Colorado by the author.
† Subsequently acquired by the State Historical Society.

Clarence Jackson says they were left here in Denver when his father moved to Detroit (oral history interview).

Traveling darkrooms used during the "wet plate days" often were elaborate affairs covered with advertisements which looked somewhat like portable billboards. This was George Mellen's wagon from his Gunnison gallery.　　　　　　　　SHSC

article of civilization reached farms and ranches during this era—and photographs were no exception. Williams and McDonald operated such a traveling darkroom out of a specially-built carriage:

> It is neat, compact, artistic, but not gaudy. The running gear was made by Kinsey and Maxey, and while heavy enough for mountain travel, runs easy and light as a buggy. It is covered like a peddler's wagon, the photographer's room in the back part, and stepped into and the door closed, the man standing on the ground, makes as nice a dark room as any artist need want. In the fore part are compartments for stock and instruments. It is calculated for two horses, and has a buggy top for the driver, who is the artist, and his assistant. Altogether it is well done and shows a good deal of enterprise.[12]

The method of operation for traveling photographers was to set up temporary headquarters in some small town with no photographer and advertise in the local paper. Williams and McDonald were traveling near Pueblo in August, 1868, when they printed the following advertisement:

PHOTOGRAPHS.
We would inform the citizens of Pueblo
and vicinity that we are prepared to take
PHOTOGRAPHS,
AMBROTYPES,
VIEWS OF HOUSES,
VIEWS OF FARMS,
AND SCENERY OF ALL KINDS.

———

Those wishing anything in our line will please call immediately, as we will remain in Pueblo but TWO WEEKS.
WILLIAMS AND McDONALD.[13]

Photographers working in the field during the "wet plate period" needed large amounts of equipment, as this view of a U.S. Geological Survey photographer shows.   **SHSC**

Some idea of the large amount of equipment and materials needed to make photographs by the wet collodion method can be gained by reading this list of materials carried by one photographer while traveling in Colorado during 1870:

Stereoscopic camera with one or more
    pairs of lenses.
5 x 8 camera box plus lens
11 x 14 camera box plus lenses
Dark tent
2 tripods
10 lbs. collodion
36 oz. silver nitrate
2 quarts alcohol
10 lbs. iron sulfate (developer)
Package of filters
1-1/2 lbs. potassium cyanide (fixer)
3 yds. Canton flannel
1 box rottenstone (cleaner for glass plates)
3 negative boxes
6 oz. nitric acid
1 quart varnish
Developing and fixing trays
Dozen and a half bottles of various sizes
Scales and weights
Glass for negatives, 400 pieces [14]

The large size cameras in use in Colorado during the period were needed because the size of the negative determined the size of the finished print. It was the common practice to lay the negative on a sheet of sensitized printing paper and expose it to the sun. The idea of making a large photograph from a small negative had been around since the early 1850's, but these early enlargements were not widely accepted because of the extremely long printing time necessary and because the finished picture lacked considerable detail which had been present in the original negative. Both these problems were overcome, at least to a degree, by 1870. More sensitive paper was in use by that time, which reduced the time necessary to produce the large prints, and artists were hired by many galleries to restore detail lost in the enlarging process. These enlargements were usually portraits and are common today, being heavily covered in chalk, india ink and charcoal.

When these "life size" photographs were introduced into Colorado, they were considered worthy of extended notice:

SOMETHING NEW.

We heard that Messrs. Reed & McKenney had on exhibition a very fine lot of Solar Photographs; calling there, we had the pleasure of seeing three or four dozen of the finest large size photographs ever exhibited in Colorado. They have now perfected their facilities for producing those life-size photographs, which for beauty and tone far excel anything we have had in the mountains. Among others we noticed very superior pictures of B. W. Wisebart, Willard Teller, . . . Mr. Geo. Patten's children, and many others. These pictures are produced from negatives of the ordinary size. Call and examine these new pictures and you will be sure to leave your measure for one.[15]

Other photographers soon followed suit. Joseph Collier, who had had experience with enlarging while in Scotland, announced the arrival of his equipment in the columns of the *Daily Register* of Central City:

LIFE-SIZE PHOTOGRAPHS

It affords us pleasure to announce that J. Collier's apparatus for enlarging photographs to life, or any other desired size, has now been in running order for a week, and is turning out superb pictures. Of his success here we had no need of being assured, as his reputation had already been thoroughly established abroad years ago. The *British Journal of Photography*, published at London, the oldest and most reliable journal of photography in the world, in its issue of September 4th, 1868, says:

"It is in the enlargements we are most interested, for in this direction there is a great future for our art-science. . . .

"It is now nearly four years since Dr. Monckhoven delighted the photographers of London by the exhibition of specimens of enlargement effected by means of improved apparatus manufactured by himself. Since that time, new phases in the art of producing enlargements have been developed, and it is no disparagement to Dr. Monckhoven, and the early pioneers in this department of photography, to say, as in all honesty we must, that in the mammoth productions of Mr. Collier, of Inverness, we find the highest excellence that we have yet seen in any enlarged photographs that have hitherto been submitted to our notice."

. . . As the proof of the pudding is the eating, everybody is invited to call at his gallery rear of Register Block, and see samples just produced here. Any one desiring, can see the work performed.[16]

The large camera remained the standard for commercial photography, however. Charles Bohm, photographer for the firm of Perry and Bohm, used an 11 x 14-inch camera for his large prints of businesses and houses.[17] With the 11 x 14-inch negative held tightly against the printing paper, shorter printing time resulted, as well as finished prints with considerably more detail than any enlargement then possible. This method also had an advantage over the enlarging process then practiced for portraits because no expensive and delicate enlarging apparatus was necessary.

The characteristic color, tone and range of density of contact prints made in this period is imparted by the paper and method used for the printing of negatives. The negatives themselves are considered very "contrasty" by modern standards. Some of the negative areas, especially the sky, are almost opaque, while the shadows are nearly transparent. In between these two extremes is a short scale of tones comprised of varying shades of grey. Printed on modern paper of medium contrast, these negatives often produce prints of excessive contrast. When modern paper of lower constrast is used, grey prints often result. The usual expedient is to manipulate the print while it is being printed, to restrict light in certain areas and to give more light to other parts of the plate. This produces an acceptable print, but it certainly is far removed from what the original print would have looked like.

Early papers used for printing were usually albumen-coated — and printed directly by the action of sunlight passing through the glass plate and falling on the paper. No development was used, as the plate and the paper were left in the

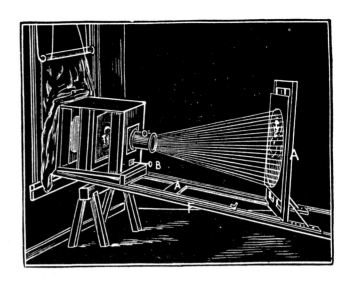

Joseph Collier used a solar camera like this one to make his mammoth prints.

sun until the image had been burned into the paper to the extent that no further chemical action was needed to bring it out. This paper was "self-blocking," which means that the darker an area becomes, the slower it reacts to the sun. A heavy shadow will get just so dark, and then the light action on it will begin to slow down, allowing the denser parts of the negative the additional time required to produce the more subtle effects on the paper. By using solar, or printing-out, paper as it is called, a wider range of tones can be achieved, without the disadvantage of the entire print turning grey.

After the paper has been exposed through the negative, it is toned or colored by submerging it in a bath of gold chloride, or other metallic solution, to produce the characteristic red/brown earth color of prints from this period. The print is made permanent by "hypo" (fixer) in the same way that modern prints are fixed. Generally, they were then dried in the air and glued to cardboard mounts with wheat paste.

A carefully-made print on solar paper, toned and mounted with care, cannot be matched—by any degree of effort—for delicacy of image and tone, while retaining such remarkable clarity and detail. The increasing interest in enlargements caused photographers to switch to developing papers similar to those used today. In these, the image is not burned into the emulsion with direct sunlight, but rather it is brought out and made visible by chemical action—like films or plates.

Following closely the demand for enlarged photographs was the interest in colored ones. The idea of coloring photographs had occured to the

Up to date in every respect, the Frank Dean gallery in Grand Junction opened its doors in 1900. Dean had been photographing western Colorado since the 1880's, when he opened his first gallery in Gunnison. This new Grand Junction studio was equipped with all the latest features of convenience to the photographer. The glass-topped shelf extending out from the second floor provided a place to expose prints in the sun, so that the photographer no longer had to climb to the roof to lay his printing frames out to make solar pictures. The diagram (below) shows the interior of such a print room and gives you some idea of how this shelf was used.   Q-BAR

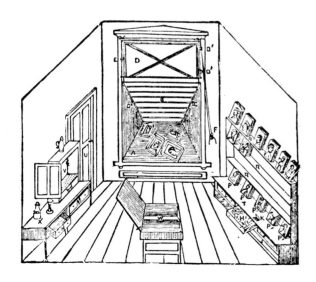

Making prints in the sun along the front of the Janes &
Sturtevant gallery near Nineteenth and Pearl streets in
Boulder.   Daily Camera Photo

earliest writers on photography. Daguerreotypes
had been hand-tinted for some time; some
partially successful attempts to take them in
natural color had even been made. But the great
interest came with the introduction of large paper
photographs. Early in 1870, the Duhem brothers,
operators of one of the leading galleries in Denver
at the time, engaged an artist from the East. She
was to prove an asset to the company, which was
soon doing a large business in oil or watercolor
photographic portraits.[18]

Before portraiture with electric light became practical,
elaborate shades, reflectors and diffusers were used to
direct light onto subjects in just the manner wanted.
Here we see a large wooden reflector sitting on the
floor. This was used to bounce light onto the left side
of the subject, while a round cloth diffuser prevented
light from falling directly onto the subject from the
skylight overhead. Photographed in the Dean Studio,
Grand Junction, about 1900.   SHSC

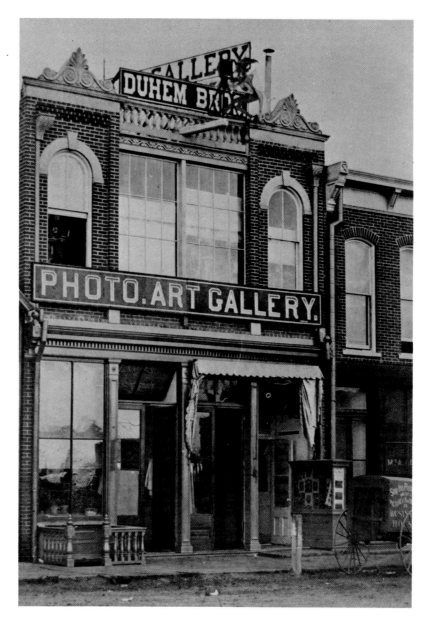

The Duhem Brothers gallery, at 448 Larimer Street, was Denver's most prestigious photographic establishment during the 1870's. Many of the leading citizens of Colorado were posed beneath their glass roof. DPL

Galleries

HE DUHEM brothers deserve special mention as they had the most elaborate gallery in Colorado at the time. The entire building was given over to the gallery:

> The block is of brick, 25 x 65 feet, two stories in height. A portion of the first floor is occupied as a sample room. The walls on the right as you enter are hung with photographs of their own make; on the left is a fine display of new chromos.* Running through the centre of the room is a counter on which are show cases, one filled with Duhems' thousand views of Colorado scenery, and another with samples in great variety of pictures taken by them. At the centre of the room is a rounding stairway by which you ascend to the second floor. This conducts you to the reception room, most elegantly furnished with Brussels carpets, silk-lined walnut tete-a-tete and chairs, and mirror.

> This new gallery is constructed with especial reference to the photographic business. The skylight faces the north, and thus gives the advantage of this light, which is smooth, soft and even on the subject. These gentlemen inform us that their's is the only gallery west of New York so arranged that a north light falls directly on the subject. All the best American, English and French photographers are adopting this principle, and are making the best pictures in the world. A large glass front, facing Larimer street, forms the side light of the operating room. The other rooms in the building, consisting of the work room, private toilet rooms for the ladies, and the apartments of the family, are all finely and handsomely arranged.

> Duhem Brothers will keep a large assortment and a full stock of frames, chromos, photographic goods, and fancy articles. They have several car-loads now on hand, which they are disposing of at low prices. *

Not all of the business of the Duhem brothers was conducted in this elegant gallery. Nor was all the business pleasant; indeed, with the tremendous expense of building a gallery, competition was fierce. Two years before they moved from their old location, one of the Duhem brothers' employees, W. Delavan, came to blows with one of their competitors named Hull. The incident involved the hanging of Sanford Dougan, accused murderer. The following day, the *Rocky Mountain News* carried this item:

> Last evening, between sundown and moonrise, as Sanford S. C. Dougan was being conveyed in an express wagon from the U.S. jail to the city calaboose, a crowd of men gathered quickly at the sound of a whistle, immediately took possession of the prisoner, without serious resistance on the part of the officers, drove him to a cottonwood tree in Cherry street, between Fourth and Fifth, and hanged him to a limb of the same until he was dead. After adjusting the rope they gave him a chance to speak, which he improved by pleading his innocence . . . He was very much unmanned, crying and sobbing like a child, calling for a Catholic Minister, and exclaiming, "O, my poor mother, don't let the news get to her, it will kill her!" &c. . . . . The corpse was allowed to hang all night, and in the bright moon light, swaying slightly to and fro it was a sad spectacle enough. We are told that certain artists were nigh fighting over it this morning for the exclusive privilege of taking photographic views of it. [2]

The story of the fighting photographers is only casually mentioned in the above account and few

* Colored lithographs.

Denver's first high school military company — photographed by Duhem in 1874, in front of their school, Wolf Hall, at Seventeenth and Champa — included several celebrities. The drummer boy was Frank Woodbury, who later became publisher of the *Denver Times;* the boy second from the right was Irving Hale. Later, General Hale accompanied the Colorado company to the Philippine Islands. The two boys on either side of Hale were the Proctor brothers, one of whom became famous as a sculptor and who designed the cowboy statue in Denver's civic center.   SHSC

In this view by the Duhem Brothers, Achert's Curiosity Shop of Denver was recorded on glass, C. 1878.   Q-BAR

Denver's finest (?) as of 1875 — by the Duhem Brothers.   DPL

The reproduction at right is from a typical advertising card of the period.   SHSC

W. H. STANDART,

WHOLESALE AND RETAIL DEALER IN

BOOTS AND SHOES,

TEJON STREET, OPPOSITE POST OFFICE,

Lynching of Duggan in Denver—Fight of Photographers for View of Remains.

other sources shed much light on the affair, but available information indicates what probably happened: On the morning after the lynching, W. Delavan arrived at the tree along Cherry Street to take stereo-views of the unfortunate Dougan. Shortly before or shortly after Delavan arrived, another photographer came on the scene with the same thing in mind. The second photographer was named A. C. Hull. [3] As the market for a stereographic-card of Dougan hanging from a tree along Cherry Street was necessarily rather limited, the two photographers quickly agreed that only one photograph should be taken. The thing upon which they were not in agreement, however, was who should get to take the picture. Delavan had the edge over his opponent in that he was deaf and could not hear the shouts of Mr. Hull. Apparently the police arrived just in time. If they could not prevent one of their prisoners being snatched away to be hung, at least they could referee the photographers' battle over the remains. We have no way of knowing for certain who won—the stereograph of the hanging, which is owned by the State of Colorado, bears the name of the Duhem brothers, but there is also extant a view by Hull.

Criminals were not always on the far side of the lens, however. In at least one instance, the criminals were behind the camera. One firm with the unlikely name of Abraham and Isaacs proved to be two of the most sought-after photographers in Colorado history. J. H. Abraham was operating a gallery on the second floor of a drugstore at the corner of Larimer Street and G (now Sixteenth) Street in June of 1868. He advertised that he specialized in pictures of babies and copying old pictures.[4] The business name was soon changed to Abraham and Isaacs with the addition of Mr. Charles Isaacs to the firm. By July 21 of 1868, the firm was being dissolved and Isaacs was to continue the business. This did not turn out to be the case for long. On July 27, the news broke that they had evacuated:

The excitement this morning on the street was the absconding of the photographers, Abraham & Isaacs, leaving all their creditors in the lurch. They "got in" to several of our citizens in various sums, $2,000 to $3,000 in the aggregate, but further, we think, into Roper than any of them, inducing him as they did to spoil the looks of his building in giving them a sky-light. They had sold their traps to the pawnbroker, Gottlieb, last night, we believe, probably being averse to working Sundays. Mr. Roper was the first to discover it, calling very early with a Monday morning "U.O.I." He was followed by a thin stream of callers, on the same errand, up to as late as 10 o'clock. These fellows took good pictures, and many excellent negatives of ladies and gentlemen of the town can be had at the "Three Balls" for a price. Doubtless the financial pressure was too much for them, however, and so they "lit out." It is the first thing of the kind that has happened in Denver within our knowledge . . . But Denver was getting dead and badly needed a sensation. From "trix" with a ring and a walking stick, and other "little games," in which Mr. Isaacs was not unskilled, as many of the boys know, he has gone on to play a trick worth all of them together. Though what he and his partner have gained by it, we are unable to see. Suppose they had run in debt to everybody—it isn't everybody that can do that. By the same token, the exercise of the same ability, being good artists and industrious and attentive to business, they could have borne the press had they been of such or of sane mind. Now what are they? "Confidence men," nothing more or less, wherever they go. Perhaps they will be brought back, though we should deem that rather unfortunate of the two. The Marshal, Deputy Marshal, and others, went after them, having heard of their leaving Maxon's for Cheyenne in private conveyance, early in the morning.[5]

Sanford Dougan — hung by a Denver mob on December 2, 1868 — is pictured in the view above. Photographers fought to obtain exclusive photographs of this gruesome scene. This is from a stereo card made by W. Delavan for the Duhem gallery. **SHSC**

The marshal and his men were unable to locate Abraham and Isaacs, and they remained "at large."

MORRISON & BROS.
CARPET STORE,
Carpets, Oil Cloths, Window Shades, &
337 Larimer Street, Denver, Col.

HENRY & METCALF'S
Livery,
Proprietors of Omnibus Line,
BOULDER, COLORADO.

The two advertising cards reproduced above are typical of the 1870's. **SHSC**

As the winter snows of 1867 melted into history, a photographic expedition was marching across Colorado. Like Fremont, 14 years earlier, the leader of this ambitious expedition—William Jackson Palmer—was determined to document his survey's route with photographs. Palmer was trying to sell Congress on the idea of building a transcontinental railroad along a southern route. His proposal was to send the line through Kansas into southern Colorado, then to Santa Fé and west to California. How Palmer got the idea of taking a photographer on the expedition is not known, but in May of 1867, he contacted John W. Browne—described as a "talented amateur from Philadelphia"—and asked him to join the party as the photographer. [6] Browne wrote Palmer that he could not spend the summer photographing the West because he had to remain in

By the mid-1870's, Denver had become a city of some pretensions, even if it was not a city of much comfort. Here we see the interior of Chain & Hardy's Parlor Book Store in Denver — from a Duhem Brothers photograph. **SHSC**

During the 1860's, the use of waterpower for mining was commonplace in Colorado. SHSC

This group of Chinese miners was photographed by the Duhem Brothers in 1875. SHSC

Miners had gathered around a forge at the time this stereo card view was made by the Duhem Brothers, C. 1869. When every piece of mining equipment had to be hauled by wagon over the prairies of Kansas and eastern Colorado, blacksmiths were in great demand for making repairs. Forges were a common sight at the mines. SHSC

The summer of 1867 saw William A. Bell — an English physician and would-be photographer — traveling the length of Colorado with a surveying party for the Kansas Pacific Railway, as Carvalho had done 14 years earlier for the Fremont expedition. This print, made by Bell, portrays the photographic outfit while it was encamped on the High Plains — probably in southern Colorado.   SHSC

Philadelphia with his sick grandmother.[7] He did, however, recommend a friend of his, an English doctor by the name of William A. Bell, as being the man for the job. Bell had learned of the proposed survey and asked Browne to see if he could get the position for him. The major problem with giving Bell the job, however, was that Bell was not a photographer.

As Dr. Bell put it:

Through the kindness of some of my friends in Philadelphia, I became attached to this expedition; but not until all the vacancies but one had been filled up. A photographer alone was wanted; and as no idle man could be allowed amongst the party, I accepted the office with, I must confess, considerable diffidence, as only a fortnight remained before starting to learn an art with which I was then quite unacquainted.[8]

I gratefully acknowledge the service rendered to me by Mr. John Browne, of Philadelphia, who, as an amateur, has acquired a high reputation amongst photographers. Mr. Browne not only initiated me into the art, but sent out after me all the necessary instruments and chemicals.[9]

Thus it happened that, taking no part in the actual surveys, I was able to move hither and thither, to travel sometimes with one party,

sometimes with another, and to take long journeys independently through regions hitherto almost unknown, but which, from their position, were of great importance to those interested in the success of the trans-continental railway.[10]

Palmer appears to have been somewhat uncertain as to the results which Bell would secure. He concluded to contract another photographer for at least part of the survey. Never content with halfway measures, Palmer engaged the most prominent American photographer of the time—excepting only Brady—Alexander Gardner. Gardner was fresh from his extensive Civil War experiences and had won a wide reputation by photographing Abraham Lincoln, first at the Brady Gallery in Washington, D.C., where he then worked, and later in his own establishment. The railroad company engaged him to travel to Kansas and take pictures along the line of the road and the neighboring regions. In addition to stereographic cards intended by Palmer and the other officers of the company as handouts to prospective investors, Gardner took numerous 11 x 14-inch plates of the most important views.[11] The reasoning behind hiring Gardner may also have been that Bell was not

Track-laying on the Kansas Pacific Railway in western Kansas was photographed in 1867 — as rails were being pushed across the seemingly endless miles of rolling prairie. This line was on its way to becoming the first railway from the east to reach Denver. This probably is about as far west as Alexander Gardner ever got with the Kansas Pacific at this time. Alexander Gardner and William A. Bell were the official photographers for the railway. Beyond this point, the images from the survey in southern Colorado and areas further west were likely the work of William Bell.   SHSC

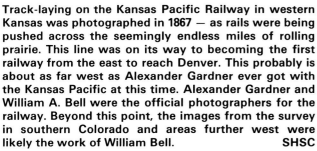

Another version of the Kansas Pacific track-laying scene was reproduced by an artist on a woodcut.

Laying the Track.

These two prints represent a watershed in the history of photography. The photograph is the earliest-known direct print used in a book about Colorado. General William Jackson Palmer — first-class promoter all the way — employed the then experimental artotype process for direct printing of photographs by printing presses. However, the process was so expensive that most of the copies of Palmer's report had no illustrations. The copies given to members of Congress — no doubt to make a good impression — were illustrated with artotypes from photographs attributed to Gardner, but quite likely made by both Gardner and Bell. The artotype process did not become commercially feasible for another 10 years, when it again made its appearance in Colorado.   SHSC

entirely trusted—at least not by W. W. Wright, the company's agent with the advance party. In July, when the expedition was still in the early stages, Palmer received a letter advising him that Wright suspected Bell of planning to use the photographs for private speculation.[12] This resulted in Gardner being appointed as official photographer and Bell being instructed that all negatives made during the survey were to be given to Gardner for printing.

With these instructions in mind, Bell set out with the survey. Advancing across Kansas, the threat of Indian attack was ever-present. At Fort Wallace, Bell met a fellow Englishman, whom he described as being of a good English family, but due to a "fatal alliance" in England, had found himself banished to Kansas, where he was serving in the United States Army. He was killed by Indians while Bell was still at the post:

The day on which he was killed he had promised to help me in printing off some copies of the photographs which I had taken on the way. I had to print off my negatives alone, and to take a photograph of him, poor fellow, as he lay; a copy of which I sent to Washington, that the authorities should see for themselves how their soldiers were treated on the plains.[13]

. . . Sergeant Wylyams lay dead beside his horse; and as the fearful picture first met my gaze, I was horror-stricken. Horse and rider were stripped bare of trapping and clothes, while around them the trampled, blood-stained ground showed the desperation of the struggle . . .

Traveling on into southern Colorado, Bell scoured the area, taking views of the major features as he went. Passing farther south, the party often camped early to give the animals a chance to graze. At one camp, Dr. Bell wrote:

As soon as tents were pitched, I retraced my steps down the ravine, with photographic "outfit" strapped on a mule, accompanied by Mr. J. Bell, whose kindness in assisting me on so many occasions I shall ever remember with gratitude. Our object was to penetrate, if possible, into the Great Cañon and take some views of it. We were, however, prevented by the escape of our mule, who broke away while we were engaged in taking a view in one of the valleys, and ran back to camp as fast as he could.

Next day we brought back the defaulter, and pushed forward towards the cañons; but the huge rocks and fissures which blocked up the sides, and the trees and brushwood which choked the passage, made our advance so difficult that we were obliged to relinquish the idea of taking any views of the gorgeous scenery, the sight of which amply repaid us for our trouble.[14]

This view of the survey camp of the Kansas Pacific Railway has been reproduced from an artotype, which was photographed somewhere in southern Colorado during 1867. This view has been attributed to Alexander Gardner, but it is more likely that William A. Bell shot it.   SHSC

Not one to be easily daunted, Bell found the cañons of southern Colorado, and more particularly New Mexico, perfect subjects for his camera. The sight of the body of his friend laying on the desolate prairie of Kansas had not left him, however, and the danger of Indian attack could not easily be overestimated:

I was photographing with a companion one afternoon in the cañon, about half a mile in the rear of the surveyors, when suddenly a succession of shots ahead made us start up from our work. The gloomy grandeur of such a place was not good for the nerves; and we feared terribly an Indian attack, where the advantages of position were so much against us. Leaving the camera, black tent, and the rest to take care of themselves, we hastened towards the front. A horse, minus his rider, dashed rapidly past, which did not increase our confidence. On arriving, however, at the scene of action, we were not a little relieved on finding that a fine flock of turkeys had so tempted the foremost of our party, that, forgetful of the alarm they would cause, they had seized their rifles and fired at them. The explosion caused by even a single shot in such a chasm sounded like the report of a dozen cannon, so great was the reverberation, and so many the echoes which followed it.15

As the party traveled toward Santa Fé, Bell became interested in the inhabitants, as well as the topography of the area being surveyed. At

Santa Fé, he found much to interest him and he lingered to make a series of photographs of the place:

I found the *fonda*, or hotel, very comfortable: the bedrooms were large, usually containing each three beds. Mine opened upon the court-yard, and as light was admitted by a trap-door at the top, which also acted as a ventilator and could be put up or down at pleasure, I converted my chamber with ease into a dark room, and used the court-yard as my photographic studio. Thither, in the morning, I brought the Navajos, and with a good deal of difficulty and persuasion obtained a capital group . . . I then let them mount their horses, and took another view of them in travelling rig.

The photographic studio was kept going all the time, and whenever I could decoy a Pueblo Indian wandering about the street, or a picturesque little black-eyed señoritta, or any other study into my net, they did not escape without leaving an impression behind them. The fair sex were rather hard to manage, as they had an idea that they were turned upside down in the camera, and strongly objected to such a liberty being taken with them. Often, after spending much time and trouble in collecting and forming a group, some knowing one would start this idea, and all would run for their lives, and hide.16

It appears that Dr. Bell had the field to himself by this time. Whether Gardner, who had seen action with the Army of the Potomac during the

Civil War, had been frightened by the Indian threat, or for some other reason, he appears not to have gone farther west than Kansas. His name still appeared as the official photographer of the survey, but no evidence has come to light which suggests that he actually took many of the pictures which bear his name.[17]

In October of 1867, Gardner was still in Kansas. He had made about 400 negatives during his stay. Bell, traveling with the advance party in the West, had sent back—probably via Gardner—only 100 negatives. General Palmer received word from headquarters that "the pictures taken by Dr. Bell are not of much account."[18] It seems that Bell had not quite mastered the wet collodion process in the two weeks he had studied it in Philadelphia before joining the surveying party. The fact that Bell had asked for no salary as photographer and had agreed to pay his own expenses[19] may account for the tolerance of his shortcomings—he wasn't much, but he was cheap. In fairness to the English doctor, however, some of his pictures are masterpieces of composition. His principal problem seems to have been that his pictures were uniformly low in contrast, with everything tending to blend together.

Whatever his contemporaries may have thought about Dr. Bell's photographic undertakings, he forms an interesting sidelight to the history of photography in Colorado. He was probably the first amateur photographer of note.

A Denver photographic establishment of note during the 1870's is the firm of Perry and Bohm. Charles Bohm had arrived in Denver as a boy in 1866. Mary Bohm, daughter of the photographer, wrote:

> . . . they returned to the East for a short time, but the call of the West took my father again to Denver in 1870, and with him, as partner, went Mr. Chas. Perry and a complete photographic outfit.
>
> They established a gallery on Fifteenth street, just east of Larimer. During the summer months they explored the canyons and parks of Colorado, taking views and photographs of the towns and camps, and even the top of Pike's Peak, which was indeed an undertaking when one recollects that this was before the day of dry plates and the photographer had to be a chemist as well as "push the button."[20]

The local press described the new business in the curious journalistic style which had become the stock in trade of the newspapers of the period:

A NEW ART ESTABLISHMENT

The photographic rooms of Messrs. Perry & Bohm are now open to the public. These gentlemen have been busy for several weeks arranging their model establishment, and are at present prepared in every particular to meet the demands of their many friends and the public generally who are anxious to secure first-class pictures of every description. The rooms are located on F street, immediately above Ingols' jewelry store, the entrance being at the end of the building nearest Larimer street. In every particular, the gallery is arranged with an eye to convenience and elegance, and patrons will find not only the auxilliaries of a model establishment of this character, but also gentlemen well versed in their profession, and capable of producing as fine work as can be obtained in New York, San Francisco, or any other centre noted for their first-class works of art. This is a desideratum that has long been felt in Denver, and our citizens may well congratulate themselves that the means are now within reach, here at home, to meet every want of this character. No reason exists why first-class pictures cannot be produced here, such as are made in the most prominent art centres of the country, and we are sure, from the specimens of work we have seen, that Messrs. Perry & Bohm will take a leading position in their line hereabouts. They are ready to furnish photographs of every description, which are acknowledged, from their excellent and delicate finish, superior in every respect as perfect likenesses. Mr. Bohm possesses rare artistic atainments, and devotes much of his attention to this last mentioned class of work. The photographs

The Charles Bohm gallery can be seen in this print, produced during the 1880's. The "shooting space" was located on the roof, in the glass enclosure. Prints were made in the racks at the left — along the wall of the lean-to shed.   SHSC

made by this house are noteworthy for their artistic excellence, fine tone, and general superiority to anything heretofore produced in the territory.

There is another branch of business to which Messrs. Perry and Bohm devote their attention, and that is lithographing and copper-plate work in all its branches. Mr. Bohm has had long experience in this line, and is a superior workman. . . .

Those desiring artistic photographs or work of the latter class detailed above, will conserve their best interests by calling at the establishment of which we are writing. The proprietors are both young men of acknowledged ability, and are justly entitled to a large share of public patronage. Their work speaks for itself, which is as high a recommendation as could be paid, but aside from

this they are enterprising, public spirited, and bound to succeed. [21]

They were indeed "bound to succeed"—and the Bohm gallery prospered for quite some time. As was reported in 1875: "They seem to have all the most desireable customers . . ."[22] Mr. and Mrs. Bohm were at the center of the amateur theater circle in Denver at the time. The reception room of the gallery was the location of many social gatherings. As their daughter remembered:

As I look back from a grown-up standpoint it seems to me that the young people of Denver had very good times indeed, at any rate, that particular group of which my mother and father

formed a part. There were not many large halls or rooms in Denver in those days, so that the reception room of my father's photograph gallery at 284 (then) Fifteenth street, came to be used as a gathering place after business hours. Here were held the rehearsals of the private theatricals, the Snowy Range Minstrels, the fancy dress balls, and masquerades at which the gay young participants had more sport than at the event itself. We had living rooms adjoining the gallery, so that I, though only a small child, was present from necessity at all these frolics. So often did I hear the plays repeated that, with the precocity of childhood, I soon learned the speeches by heart. . . .

Looking back over the gulf of years, it seems to me there was never a time in those days when "private theatricals," as they were then termed, were not the aim and end of existence. There were always rehearsals at the gallery of an evening and many farces and plays, and minstrel shows, not to speak of tableaux and entertainment for the different churches were perfected in these rooms. The grouping and costuming of tableaux was always the work of my artistic father . . . My father always played the "juvenile," and usually Miss Jessie Witter (Mrs. Ed. Rollins) was his opposite, Mrs. Horton the star and my mother and I were both critics and promptors at all the rehearsals . . .

A group of these gentlemen, friends of my father, gathered one Christmas night at the gallery and with much ceremony presented him with a huge hand-painted porcelain punch-bowl as a token of their regard. On the New Year day following, my mother and a number of ladies received calls in the good old New Year way, with the punch-bowl to crown the feast, and at every successive gathering of the crowd the punch-bowl

was always brought out. My father valued it to the time of his death as his most precious belonging, and today it forms the chief ornament of my dining room . . .[23]

The brilliant social events were soon clouded with financial problems. The engraving and lithographing part of the business did not do well. It had been assumed that an enterprise of this type would produce a brisk business, as there was no competition. But the expected business did not materialize and the firm was in deep financial trouble by 1873.[24] Charles Perry quit the firm and Charles Bohm carried on the photographic end of the business. He continued to be one of the leading portraitists in Denver during the 1870's.

Many descriptions of galleries of this period have survived, but it is rare that anything was written about the actual procedure of having a portrait taken. In the following description of a setting at the Bohm gallery in 1883, the writer of the following had never been to a gallery before and left this delightfully humorous account:

Most people would be unable to buck up courage to face the photographer's gallery during such weather as prevailed yesterday afternoon, but I am not proud of my good looks—which accounts for my invasion of Charley Bohm's gallery. I don't think the picture does me justice. However, that is what the majority of people say, and then, I believe that I just remarked that I was not proud of my looks. I had an awful time trying to keep my face straight while Charley was leveling the gun at me . . . He threatened to use the "instantaneous process" on me—the dry plate—which is generally employed in taking the

Upon the death of Charles Bohm in 1885, his wife, Mary, took over his photographic gallery.   SHSC

He said I was the worst case he had for some time, and if there was to be any exception in the matter of price, he would be compelled to make it the other way. That is to say, he wanted to charge me extra.

Inasmuch as this was my first introduction to a photograph gallery, I made myself as obnoxious as an inquisitive person could. Charley submitted to the intrusion very gracefully for awhile, piloting me all through the dark recesses, mysteries and secrets of the business. Among other things that surprised me, was the fact that artists—good artists I meam—rather preferred a dark day for sittings. The best and clearest negatives are obtained when the sun is cloudy. This information rudely dispelled a supposition I had always labored under: that a cloudy day was decidedly not the day upon which to sit for a picture, unless the subject didn't care whether the result was good or indifferent. I was escorted to the little dark room where the artist rushes into after he takes the plate from the instrument. There on one side was the box of plates prepared by acid, alcohol and pumice-stone used for the negative experiments. Beneath was a nitrate of silver bath, into which the plate is plunged after the sitting, to be developed . . . It was a dingy little nook, full of strong odors and bottles of chemicals . . . Mr. Bohm stood the test bravely until I ventured an inquiry as to the profits of his business. This audacity got me fired out, but as I was passing through the storeroom to the office I lingered long enough to see 14,000 negatives boxed up, the boxes being shelved in rows like sample coffins in an undertaker's shop . . .

I pity the photographer. His path is anything but a rose bed. While I was in the office arranging for the postponement of my bill, indefinitely, I had ample occasion to sympathize with him.[25]

The Bohm gallery continued to flourish until the death of Charles Bohm in 1885, when it was taken over for a short time by his wife, Mary.

negatives of bawling babies, but I wouldn't stand it. I couldn't stand such a reflection on my dignity . . .

I had quite an awful and awkward time of it in endeavoring to give my legs (excuse me if I seem vulgar) a fair show. They give me a great deal of trouble now and then; get tangled into snarles and knots and all that, and make life a nervous and pitying misery to those of my friends who happen to be around during the agony. You cannot observe it in the picture, but in all confidence and sincerity I would state that they had to be straightened out by a friction application and then anchored to the floor . . . (by) an invisible mooring that was placed behind me. I did like most people do—made a fight for a reduction of rates—but Charley wouldn't stand it.

84

At about the same time that Perry and Bohm were getting started in their business venture in Denver, Joseph M. Collier was opening his new gallery in Central City. In August, 1871, his doors were opened to the public. He had been a blacksmith in his native Scotland and had taken up photography when an injury had forced him to give up his former profession for some time. He seemed to be reasonably prosperous in Central City and to have been quite prolific.

Collier was not very popular with his competitors, however. In January, 1872, he announced in the press that he had just received an express shipment from London containing: "the quickest-acting photographer's lens known to science."[26] With this lens, which he assured his customers was the only one of its kind to be found west of Chicago, he was prepared to take pictures of babies and other subjects which would not remain still long enough for the usual exposure time.[27] Collier's primary competition in Central City at this time was the firm of Reed and McKenney. After Collier's announcement, they replied that he was "humbugging the public"[28] with the story of his miracle lens. Collier responded by challenging them to participate in an impartial investigation. After a short and technical exhange of slanders and optical data in the newspaper, the argument gradually diminished, leaving behind not only a very confused public, but probably a good deal of animosity between the two leading photographic firms in Central City.

Collier used a donkey cart to haul his camera and equipment through the Colorado Rockies. His cart was seen in widely scattered areas as he gathered negatives which would later be printed in his gallery in Central City.[29] In 1873, he presented a set of his stereographic views to Julia Grant, the First Lady, while she and the President were stopping at Central City on their Western tour.[30]

Never content with doing things the way everyone else did them, Collier was always an innovator. He had brought with him from his former home in Scotland the latest European ideas in photography. One of his most novel introductions was the forerunner of the modern 35-millimeter stereo-slide. As usual, the local press gave him good coverage:

STEREOSCOPIC TRANSPARENCIES

Mr. Joseph Collier, the eminent photographer of Rocky Mountain scenery, has been engaged through the winter in making and perfecting appliances for doing a kind of work never before attempted in Colorado, and, so far as we know,

Joseph Collier is portrayed here with his traveling camera equipment.   DPL

not done elsewhere in the United States. (sic.) These new pictures are called transparencies. After the negative is taken it is transferred to plate glass as a positive, and the plate, after finishing and toning, is backed by another plate of ground glass. The glass for this purpose has to be very perfect, and Mr. Collier uses British plate, the ground glass being finished in Venice. The first and only stereoscopic picture so far issued is No. 118 of his series, "The Garden of the Gods." To hold this picture up to the window light, merely, makes a very much finer view than to look at an ordinary good stereoscopic view through a stereoscope; and to look at it through a stereoscope, makes the finest picture in the world. The perspective is wonderful. It is not difficult to imagine that you are looking at the scene itself. Indeed, it makes all the stereoscopic views seem cheap and crude. The price of this style of view is necessarily considerably higher than the ordinary style, as each one has to be carefully finished and toned, and the materials are much more expensive. We do not know the cost, but one is worth a dozen of the old kind, to one who can appreciate absolute perfection.

Portable frame to hold photographic backdrops.

> . . . Applied to our Rocky Mountain scenery, the effect is magnificent. We congratulate Mr. Collier upon his great success, and urge him to prepare for an unprecedented demand by both citizens and tourists. [31]

The stereo-transparencies doubtless had great publicity value, but it is not likely that they enjoyed a wide distribution. Some copies were probably sold to wealthy tourists and the landed citizens of the Colorado area, but the cost was quite likely out of the range of the average "seven-to-seven" blue-collar worker. None of Collier's Colorado transparencies are known to have survived.

Collier was quick to get in on another innovation of the 1870's: the sciopticon. This device was a modification of the older "magic lantern," which had been around for quite some time. In the magic lantern a kerosene lamp was housed in a light-tight box with a lens attached in front of the only opening. With a photograph on glass placed behind the lens, images could be projected upon a screen much like the modern slide projector. This type of projection had been first used with pictures of Colorado in 1859, when a lecture on the gold fields of the Pikes Peak Region had been illustrated by hand-colored lantern slides. [32] The small amount of light produced by a kerosene lamp, however, limited the size and brilliance of the projected image. The magic lantern was less of a novelty in 1870 than it had been 10 years earlier. The revival of the device came with various attempts to improve the source of light. In the sciopticon, the simple kerosene lamp was replaced by a lamp with three parallel wicks set edgeways to the lens. This lamp burnt petroleum [33] or paraffin. [34] With these improvements, a picture 10 feet in diameter could be projected on the screen. This set the stage for a series of illustrated lectures on everything from the Civil War to mountaineering in Colorado.

Collier was quick to get on the bandwagon. His experience with the transparent stereographs had taught him a good deal about the practical side of making quality photographs on glass. The photographs were often toned by immersing them in a chemical stain which had the effect of complementing the scene depicted. A snow scene could be given a slight blue color to suggest cold, amber was often used to represent the hot sunlight of summer, and so on. By the end of October, 1874, Collier was preparing slides for a lecture on Colorado, which was to be given by two professional lecturers. [35]

The impact of these new, improved slide shows was great. The public interest which was aroused is reminiscent of the curved-screen movie fad which swept the country some years ago. Each new magic lantern show was a major social event. One benefit performance which took place in Guard Hall, Denver, in 1874, was described the next day by the *Rocky Mountain News:*

COLORADO'S COUNTERFEIT.

The dissolving views illustrating the scenery of the "Switzerland of America," as the uninventive correspondents and guide books call Colorado, exhibited at Guard Hall last evening for the benefit of the Ladies Relief Society, were pronounced by the large audience who viewed them to more than hold the mirror up to nature. As exact reproductions of the scenes they purported to illustrate, they could hardly have been excelled, while as a work of art, each and every view ranked high. Not only were the buildings of local interest in our city of Denver portrayed with a fidelity to which the hearty applause of the audience continually testified, but the grand scenery of the neighboring mountains was depicted with even greater exactness. Besides views in Denver, the programme embraced all the prominent points in the Clear Creek cañon, including representations of Golden, Black Hawk, Central (City), Georgetown, Idaho Springs and contiguous hamlets . . . [36]

In spite of the efforts made by Collier to remain up-to-date, he could not make a go of it in Central City. By January of 1877, he had outlasted all other photographers in the city, [37] but even without competition, he was not inclined to stay. The following year he sold his gallery and moved to Denver.

Stereoscopic Views of Colorado Scenery.

LEADVILLE.

The "boss" mining camp of the world, both as to wealth and population, having within two years acquired a population of over 28,000, and possessing the greatest and richest mines in the world. The bullion product for this, its second year, is estimated at $20,000,000. Altitude, 10,000 ft.

Photographed by CHAS. WEITFLE, Central City, Colo.

Headquarters for Colorado Views.   *Over 300 different Views for sale.*

This advertisement appeared on the back of some of Charles Weitfle's view cards.

In 1878, a new name appeared on the photography scene in Colorado: Charles Weitfle, a veteran of 24 years in the photographic business by the time he arrived in the Centennial State. Like Timothy O'Sullivan, Weitfle had acquired practical field experience in photography during the Civil War, and had earned an international reputation before he moved to Colorado. When he arrived in Colorado, at 42 years of age, he was at the height of his artistic and practical capabilities and his work during the next five years shows him to be second to none. He operated principally out of Central City and Denver, but was also connected in some degree with several other galleries in the central mountain area.

Weitfle's views of Rocky Mountain scenery were widely known and distributed. He won first prize for the best collection of photographs exhibited at the Colorado Mining and Industrial Exposition at Denver in 1878. He got into the view business by accident and not by design, however. When he first came to Colorado, he planned to engage in the portrait business, but one look at the Rockies changed his mind, and he immediately embarked on a whirlwind career in Colorado.[38] For five years he roamed up and down the Front Range, and far into the heart of the Rockies—taking views of almost all the major mining camps and tourist resorts. His views were uniformly good and enjoyed great popularity.

In 1880 or 1881, he moved his headquarters to Denver and began to acquire the negatives of other photographs to sell under his hallmark. He acquired a collection of negatives by the Central City artist, Joseph Collier, when he purchased Collier's studio in 1878.* Within the first few years of the new decade, Weitfle had acquired glass plates by William G. Chamberlain, as well as the collection of Mrs. Thurlow of Manitou Springs, and several others. With his combine of several branch studios in various key cities, and negatives from the best photographic houses in the state from north to south, Weitfle appeared to be on the verge of cornering the view market. His studios began to turn out stereographic cards and cabinet size (5 x 9-inch) prints, literally by the thousands.

Weitfle's star set as quickly as it had risen, however. On Halloween night of 1883, a kerosene lamp in the chemical rooms of the Denver Weitfle gallery exploded, throwing flaming kerosene and hot glass in all directions. By the time the fire was extinguished, nothing remained of Weitfle's 30 years work in photography. In this fire, one of the finest collections of Colorado negatives ever amassed was lost through the carelessness of whoever neglected to put out the lamp before leaving the studio. The $3,000-worth of insurance on the collection did not begin to cover the loss, even at 1883 prices. Weitfle closed his galleries and disappeared disheartened into obscurity.[39]

* The number of Collier negatives acquired by Weitfle is uncertain.

Typical of the many small galleries in rural Colorado was James Thurlow's "Cottage Photograph Rooms" at Manitou Springs. In the barn at left, Thurlow's traveling photography carriage is partially visible — in this 1874 photograph.　　　　　　　　　　SHSC

The Nast photographic gallery was located on Sixteenth Street in Denver, at the turn of the century. Notice the billboard-style advertisement on the side of the building proclaiming Nast as "the great baby photographer."　　　　　　　　　　SHSC

Photographic darkrooms were rarely photographed prior to World War I. In this unusual print, O. E. Aultman, a Trinidad photographer, is seen in his developing room, about 1908. Photographed by an unknown photographer, he evidently burned magnesium powder to illuminate the darkroom.   SHSC

This rare interior photograph shows a typical portrait studio of the 1890's. The camera, mounted on a trolley, was equipped with a vignette attachment to soften and fade the bottom of the image for head and shoulder portraits. At left, a kerosene burnisher can be seen sitting on a table. Prints were run through the hot burnisher to impart a smooth, glossy finish.   SHSC

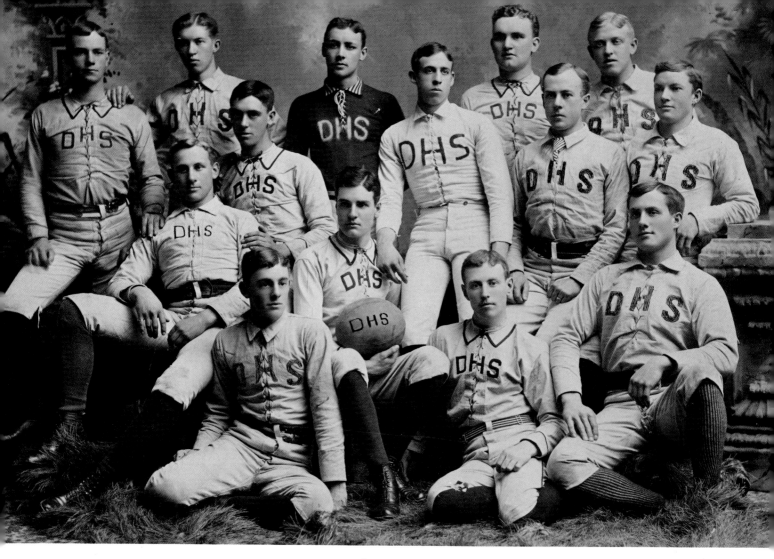

Denver High School's football team posed in the Rothberger studio in Denver, about 1889. For those players who lacked the school's monogram on their sweaters, the photographer obligingly supplied the missing letters with a retouching pen later.   SHSC

Opposite, below: Photographic galleries were always located on the top floors of buildings. This was necessary because portraits were almost universally made with natural light which fell through a skylight. It was also handy when making prints, as direct sunlight was needed for this process, also. This studio is typical of many galleries during the '80's and '90's; stores were on the first floor, perhaps the photographer's family lived on the second floor, and the studio and printing rooms were on the top floor.   SHSC

Many of the photographs which were made in Colorado during the Nineteenth Century were the product of small and unobtrusive galleries, such as this one, which was recorded for posterity in the middle 1890's. This is from a stereo card made by the Koch Studio, located in Golden.   Q-BAR

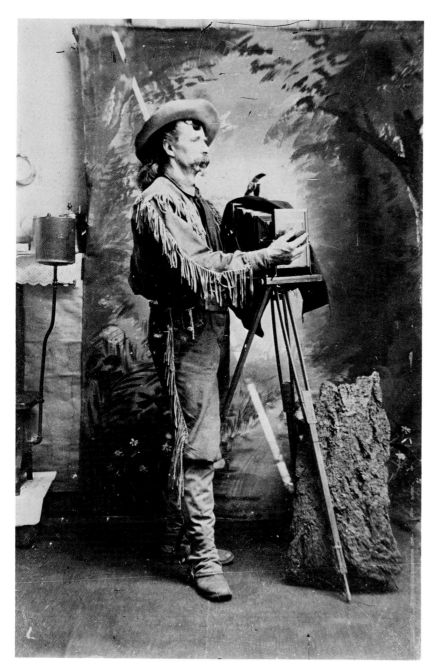

Boulder photographer, J. B. Sturtevant, was portrayed in his traveling costume. Photographers often were as colorful as their subjects. This is a Boulder Daily Camera photograph

Opposite, above: This detail from a picture of La Veta, photographed in 1883, shows the tent of an unknown photographer, pitched in a vacant lot. Many photographers used tents similar to this one in their travels in search of views. Q-BAR

Opposite, left (below): The early photographers following the frontier had no studios and had to rely on makeshift shooting stages. Some of the more affluent photographers had tents with skylights built in. This jolly group was having "afternoon tea" beneath the canvas roof of one such tent. SHSC

Opposite, right (below): Many photographers went from mining camp to mining camp throughout the Rockies. Many used tent studios like this one of Charles Goodman in Bonanza, C. 1887. These tents were specially made as studios, and were equipped with a skylight and an area for developing. Q-BAR

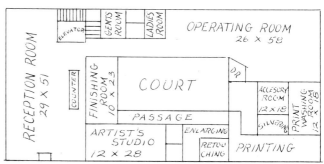

The illustration at left is from a business card printed for J. Bevier Sturtevant of Boulder City, 1886. The sketch above shows a typical floor plan of a photographic gallery during the 1880's. SHSC

Opposite, above: One enterprising photographer traveled with a tent which had a skylight. He is believed to be Frank Dean, pioneer photographer of Gunnison and Grand Junction. A detail view of this studio was shot by William H. Jackson, C. 1883.   SHSC

Opposite, below: E. F. Bunn, a Fort Collins photographer, traveled through northern Colorado in this sleek rig, making prints of farms, orchards and the scenery of the area. Many photographers used wagons similar to this one during the days when anyone wishing a photograph of a house or farm had to rely on a traveling artist to wander down the country road.   DPL

Here, a rugged western slope cowboy posed in front of a backdrop in a tent studio and was photographed by either George Mellen or Frank Dean, C. 1885. Gary Christopher collection.

When this print was recorded, Lewis Clark Coggshall, Georgetown photographer, was at work photographing subjects near the Georgetown Loop — about the turn of the century.   SHSC

Many photographers combined business with pleasure while on camping trips in the Rockies. Here, O. E. Aultman had set up a camp in the mountains west of Trinidad. The sale of scenic view cards was a large part of the photographic industry until the halftone process made mass-produced postal cards possible. SHSC

Opposite, above: Some photographers would do anything for a picture. Lawrence P. Bars & Company took this view of an enterprising photographer knee-deep in Grand Lake, attempting to get just the right angle, C. 1890. SHSC

Opposite, below (left): George Beam, photographer for the Denver & Rio Grande Railroad, spent most of his professional career turning out negatives along the railroad system — from one end of the line to the other. Using 8 x 10-inch glass plates, he created a record of the road valuable not only from an historic point of view, but one of unusual beauty as well. The original caption on the back of this photograph — written in Beam's own hand — reads, "G. L. B. awearied, at Marble." The photograph was taken about 1910. SHSC

Opposite, below (right): O. E. Aultman — the Trinidad banker who turned photographer when he foreclosed on a studio which had been unable to repay a loan to his bank in 1889 — is shown on the following page. He has his portable photographic outfit, ready to set out in search of something to photograph. SHSC

The Hayden Expedition of 1870 posed for this homey lunch scene. William Henry Jackson is the handsome young man on the right, standing just above the deer carcass — which probably served as the principal ingredient of the day's noon meal.　　SHSC

Scenery of the Union Pacific Railroad,

PHOTOGRAPHED BY

JACKSON BROS., OMAHA, NEB.

William Henry Jackson

VI

ITHOUT question, the most famous Colorado photographer was William Henry Jackson. He achieved worldwide acclaim for his photographs of the western United States. Of all those who photographed the West, Jackson's name stands alone. Next to Mathew Brady and Alexander Gardner, William H. Jackson probably is the most famous American photographer. When he was discovered by F. V. Hayden, head of a Federal survey of the territories, he had made a series of photographs along the line of the Union Pacific Railway as part of a promotion campaign for that line. Hayden was impressed with Jackson's work and offered him the position as official photographer with his survey.

Jackson wrote copiously about his travels and photographic experiences in Colorado. As his account cannot be improved upon for giving a feeling of the man and his task as a pioneer photographer during the 1870's, we will relate his story in his own words:

. . . Then, the so-called "wet plate" was in general use, involving a complex process of many operations, and required practice and experience to attain the necessary manipulative skill. It was so messy chemically, and encumbered with so much apparatus that there is little wonder that photography was rarely the hobby of amateurs and that the making of pictures by this means was almost wholly the work of professionals . . .

I had accumulated but little experience in landscape work before undertaking survey photography; such as it was, having been acquired in making negatives along the Union Pacific Railway during the construction years of 1868 and 1869. Three years of rather strenuous work, however, with the Survey in the northern territories had rounded out my experience so that when I came to Colorado I was about at my best, not only in the particular kind of photography required, but also in the usages of camp life and of travel in uncharted regions.

Up to this time, I had worked along with the main body of the Survey, under the direction of its chief but was now provided with a separate outfit, to be officially known as the Photographic Division and given *carte blanche* within designated areas as to character and extent of the photographic work to be done. In the organization of this Division, two packers and a cook, besides myself, were to be permanent features. I never had a professional assistant, but as there were generally two or more extra members assigned to the party each season— botanists, entomologists or other collectors with occasionally a young man with no other prescribed duties than to be useful—I had all the help needed. On our first expedition I had with me Coulter, the botanist; Lieut. Carpenter (on leave of absence), entomologist; and a young son of Senator Cole of California. The next year Coulter and two young men from Washington made up our quota to seven, while for 1875 Barber, special correspondent for the *New York Herald*, was the only additional member.

The "wet plate process" was, briefly, making on the spot the sensitive plate for each exposure. This required a portable "dark-room" (box or tent) to work in, and nearly all the material and appliances ordinarily used by the sedentary photographer in his "gallery"—all of which had to be condensed within our very limited carrying capacity. The preliminary planning to provide well-balanced supplies was a matter of some care, as, once afield, there was slight possibility of making good any deficiency.

My first outfitting was for three series of negatives, 11 x 14, 5 x 8 and stereoscopic. The glass alone—some 400 pieces, was no inconsiderable

53116—Cliff Palace, Mesa Verde,

At the turn of the century, William H. Jackson closed his photographic gallery in Denver and joined a group of businessmen in Detroit in a new business venture. The company had acquired the rights to a newly-perfected process for printing photographs in color. Jackson was asked to join the firm because of his large collection of glass-plate negatives, which he had made during 30 years of photographing the American West — and indeed many other regions of the world. The color views produced by Jackson and the Detroit Photographic Company were among the best ever produced — up to that time. Although not quite as realistic as modern color photographs, to an audience which had never seen colored photographs, these renderings of Jackson's views — which originally had been shot in black-and-white — seemed miraculous. Above is one of Jackson's views of the Cliff Palace in Mesa Verde National Park. SHSC

William Henry Jackson was first an artist and later a photographer. His field sketches, made during the Civil War, were vivid documents for his family at home. At left is Jackson's self portrait in oil, which he had painted for his family during the mid-1860's. His early art training was to be a great asset later in life, when he went into the color printing business. SHSC

The myth of the noble red man must have received considerable impetus from prints such as this one. This noble-looking youth is Pedro, a Ute brave and the view was published in 1900 by the Detroit Photographic Company.   SHSC

Falls of the Rio San Miguel, 200 ft, Sep. 20th 1875

In the quiet moments around the campfire, Jackson filled his diaries with sketches and drawings, as he had done while serving in the Union army during the Civil War.   SHSC

item, while the collodions, silver nitrates, iron sulphates and a score or two of other chemicals and articles, made up in bulk what they lacked in weight. My dark tent was made of white canvas lined with orange calico and supported over a folding tripod, being just large enough to crawl into on my knees. At other times I used a folding box, set up on a short tripod, that opened like a trunk lid with an attached hood into which I inserted the upper half of my body.

A working outfit of cameras and enough material for a day's work, made a light, convenient pack. With good photographic subjects along the trail from one camp to another, the photo mule would be dropped out while the view was made, and then he jog-trotted along to overtake the train again. Sometimes there were so many of these diversions, frequently some distance from the trail, that we did not reach camp until long after the others, occasionally, not until far into the night. As the loading and unloading on these side trips devolved almost entirely upon me, I eventually became an expert packer.

More frequently, however, a lay-over camp was made where good grazing, as well as good scenery, were near at hand and sidetrips made therefrom. In either case the regular procedure after locating a point of view was to bring up the pack mule as near as possible and quickly unload. While I was setting up the camera and making the final focal adjustments, the assistant arranged the dark tent, being careful to make it light-tight all around its contact with the ground, and place inside the bath-holder and the bottles of collodion, developer and fixing solution, with a cup of water from the rubber water-bags that are always attached to the pack for use when a natural source of supply is not at hand. With everything ready, I took one of the plates inside the tent and proceeded first, to flow it with collodion, which, when "set" was immersed in the silver bath until the proper chemical reaction had taken place, when it was placed in the plate-holder ready for exposure—an operation that usually took five minutes. In some instances the camera was placed so far from any possible location for the dark-tent that there was a long interval between the coating and the development of the plate. Wet blotting paper against the back of the plate with a wet towel and the focusing cloth around the holder would keep the plate sufficiently moist for development for half an hour at least. With the exposure made and back to the tent, the plate was flooded with the developer by a dexterous sweep, the image appearing almost immediately. It was then well rinsed and "fixed" with the cyanide solution equally quick in action, and finally was taken outside for more thorough washing. After drying spontaneously, or by artificial heat, the plate was put in a grooved box and when back in camp was varnished and packed securely for further transportation.

When hard pressed for time, I have made a negative in fifteen minutes, from the time the first rope was thrown from the pack to the final repacking. Ordinarily, however, half an hour was little enough time to do the work well. Thirty-two good negatives is the largest number I ever made in one day and this was possible only in a region like that including the Garden of the Gods and Monument Park.

We broke camp early for the '73 expedition— the 24th of May. We were the first of the four divisions to leave the rendezvous at Miers Fisher's ranch on the Clear Creek bottoms. Going first to Estes Park we skirted the range southward, bucking our way frequently through deep snow in the timber, trying to reach good view points. We succeeded finally in getting Arapahoe and neighboring peaks from back of Ward, and the James

Peak region from near Central City, but it involved a lot of hard work for men and animals.

... After working the region from Hoosier Pass to Buffalo Peaks, we made a short cut over the range to Twin Lakes and from there up to the foot of LaPlata Mountain, on Lake Creek, where we stopped for three days to make a panorama from the summit of the mountain. When we were descending this peak I had a mishap that bothered me a good bit for a while. There were three of us, each packing some portion of the apparatus, mine being mainly the bath-holder with its content of silver bath. In making my way over the rough, broken rock-fields my footing gave way and I fell heavily on my back, cracking the holder so badly that the solution was entirely lost. Repeated efforts to make permanent repairs proving fruitless I finally discarded it and used a flat tray, which while inconvenient to handle in my small tent, was as serviceable as the old dipping bath.

Crossing the range over to the headwaters of the Gunnison we gradually made our way into the heart of the Elk Mountain region where for nearly a week I had a busy time depicting its grand as well as picturesque scenery. In leaving this place I had another mishap. Our camp on Rock Creek [now the Crystal River] was at the bottom of a deep gulch, or canyon, the climb out being very steep. While the train was worrying its way up the mountain, the mule carrying my boxes of 11 x 14 glass and negatives, slipped its pack and both boxes went tumbling down the hill, one of them breaking open and spilling the plates all over the rocks. An inventory of the damage showed that the loss was almost entirely among the plates made from LaPlata and Mount Lincoln. The season was getting late and storm clouds were threatening through the mountains, but in face of these handicaps I made good all losses. . . .

We did not get away from Denver on the '74 expedition until July 21st, two months later than the year before, though we had a longer route mapped out before us.[1]

Having worked over most of the territory assigned to us, we finally reached the Rio Grande on our way into the heart of the "San Juan" via Cunningham Pass. On the 27th of August we camped early in the day at Jennison's (Chemiso) ranch, as it was too late to make the Pass that day, and also to do some photographing in the neighborhood. Another and equally potent inducement to stop was the opportunity to get a good square meal served by the rather attractive young hostess of the ranch, as we were almost out of "grub" and no more to be had until we reached Howardsville.

While we were unpacking, a burro pack train came along and went into camp near-by. As they passed us there was much hilarity over the very comical appearance of one of the party, who was astride a very small burro, with another one of the party following behind with a club with which he

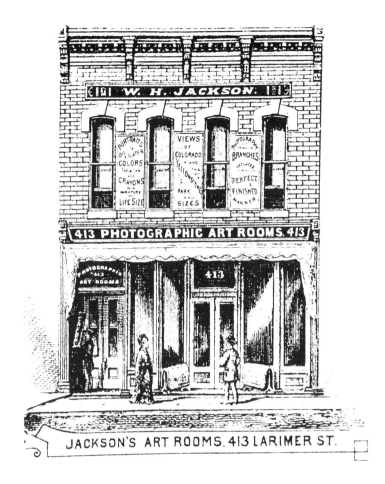

JACKSON'S ART ROOMS, 413 LARIMER ST.

was belaboring the little jack to keep him up with the train. On our return to camp from our photographing later in the day, this same man had come over to visit us. A mutual recognition followed our meeting as I remembered him as a fellow townsman in Omaha when I was in business there a few years previously. With all of us grouped around a rousing big fire after supper, we talked long into the night, Tom Cooper explaining that he was one of a small party of miners working some placers over on the LaPlata, that he had been out for supplies and was now on his return to their camp. As he appeared well acquainted with this part of the country, we "pumped" him for all the information he could impart. As he was naturally loquacious, he had a great deal to say, and understanding in a general way the object of our expedition, urged us by all means to come over to the LaPlata and he would undertake to show us something worth while.

It was generally known that many old ruins were scattered all over the southwest, from the Rio Grande to the Colorado, but Cooper maintained that around the Mesa Verde, only a short distance from their camp, were cliff dwellings and other ruins more remarkable than any yet discovered. All this interested us so much that before we "turned in" that night, we had decided to follow him over to his camp as soon as we could outfit for the trip.

By the time most of the Indians had either been killed or shunted off to reservations, the late Victorians developed a fascination for them. Here William H. Jackson had issued a colored version of an earlier print of the Ute chief, Buckskin Charlie. Reproduced from a colored original published in 1899.   SHSC

The famous "hanging bridge" in the Royal Gorge was a mecca for tourists in the Rocky Mountains. Passenger trains regularly stopped on the bridge to allow sightseers a chance to get out and gaze up at the mighty canyon walls. This print was reproduced in 1899, from a black-and-white original — photographed by William H. Jackson during one of his many excursions into the region.

SHSC.

Advertisement on the back of a William H. Jackson print.

Cooper had not travelled over the country where the more important of these ruins were to be found, but had his information largely from John Moss and his associates. Moss, he explained, was high "muck a muck" or "Hi-yas-ti-yee" of the LaPlata region, who, through his personal influence with the Indians had secured immunity from trouble, not only for his own operations, but for others also travelling through the country.

A few days later, after dividing our party in Baker's Park [site of Silverton] and travelling light —just Mr. Ingersoll[2] and myself with the two packers—we were on our way to the LaPlata. Soon after leaving Animas Park [on the Rio de las Animas], we overtook and passed Cooper's outfit, and a few miles farther on were very much surprised by the appearance of Moss himself coming up from behind on a jog trot with the evident purpose of overtaking us. Riding along together until we reached the camp, cordial relations were established very soon, and with a good deal of preliminary information, he promised us his co-operation, and possibly his company, in our further operations.

Moss, at this time appeared to be about 35, of slender, wiry figure, rather good looking, with long dark hair falling over his shoulders, and as careless in his dress as any prospector or miner. Quiet and reserved in speech and manner generally, he warmed up to good natured cordiality on closer acquaintance, and as we found out later, was a very agreeable camp companion. Jogging along together over the trail, he described in a general way what we might find, the natural features of the country and the difficulties to be met with. He also had a good deal to say about a recent treaty with the Southern Utes, by which new boundary lines had been established excluding them from the

mountain regions, very much to their dissatisfaction, not only on account of the loss of their hunting grounds, but also because of the failure of the government so far to make some promised awards. As one of the consequences they were frequently ordering all white men off their reservation, and while there was little hostility, there was a good deal of uncertainty and apprehension. Moss explained that when he first came into this country, he had made a treaty of his own with the principal chiefs, and by the payment of a liberal annuity in sheep and some other things, had secured their good will and freedom from molestation in his mining operations.

. . . We had three pack mules, "Mexico" carrying the photographic outfit—a little rat of a mule but a good climber, and could jog along at a lively pace without unduly shaking up the bottles and plates. "Muggins" and "Kitty" carried the "grub" and blankets, and as both were reduced to bare necessities, their packs were light and they could be pushed along as fast as we cared to ride. Steve and Bob, with their packs, kept close to the trail most of the time, while the rest of us were roaming all over, investigating every indication of possible ruins that came to our notice; and when photographing was decided upon, "Mexico" would be dropped out, unpacked, tent set up, and the views made while the others jogged along until we overtook them again.

Our first discovery of a Cliff House that came up to our expectations was made late in the evening of the first day out from Merrit's. We had finished our evening meal of bacon, fresh baked bread and coffee and were standing around the sage brush fire enjoying its genial warmth, with the contented and good natured mood that usually follows a good supper after a day of hard work, and were in a humor to be merry. Looking up at the walls of the canyon that towered above us some 800 or 1,000 feet we commenced bantering Steve, who was

* Ernest Ingersoll, correspondent for the *New York Tribune.*

This print shows Jackson himself (at far right) with the members of the photographic division of the 1874 Hayden survey, ready for their first expedition into Colorado.   SHSC

a big heavy fellow, about the possibility of having to help carry the boxes up to the top to photograph some ruins up there—with no thought that any were in sight. He asked Moss to point out the particular ruin we had in view; the Captain indicated the highest part of the wall at random. "Yes," said Steve, "I can see it" and sure enough, on closer observation, there was something that looked like a house sandwiched between the strata of the sandstones very near the top. Forgetting the fatigue of the days work, all hands started out at once to investigate. The first part of the ascent was easy enough, but the upper portion was a perpendicular wall of some 200 feet, and half way up, the cave-like shelf, on which was the little house. Before we had reached the foot of this last cliff, only Ingersoll and I remained, the others having seen all they cared for, realizing they would have to do it all over in the morning. It was growing dark, but I wanted to see all there was of

The years that Jackson traveled with the surveys in the West saw him trying every type of portable darkroom from a tent almost big enough to walk in, to a platform on a tripod. The view at right shows the small tent he used during the 1874 season. Just big enough to crawl into, the orange calico lining let in enough light to see fairly well, but not enough to fog the plates.   SHSC

After a difficult climb from the canyon floor early on the morning of September 9, 1874, Jackson uncapped the lens of his camera and captured Moss and Ingersoll, and the first cliff ruin they had discovered in the Mesa Verde area.   SHSC

Before photographic reproduction of photographs by the printing press was possible, all illustrations were engraved by artists on wood or metal. Jackson's artistic ability served him well when illustrating his official reports of the surveys. In the rendering above — of his first photograph in Mancos Canyon — Jackson had eliminated Ernest Ingersoll, but left Moss in, probably to show scale. In the lower left corner, Jackson had included his initials.   SHSC

108

This view is a pirated print of "Susan," sister of Chief Ouray, whose picture was widely circulated after she helped the captive white women following the Meeker Massacre in 1879. The collodion negative in the Jackson collection appears to be the original, but the oldest print known was produced by Chamberlain. SHSC

Opposite: William Henry Jackson is shown here at the beginning of his Western career in Omaha, Nebraska, during 1868. Two years later, he began his work with the Hayden survey, which started his climb to prominence in the American West. SHSC

William H. Jackson's portable darkroom tent was set up among the rocks — at left in this unusual view — as his two companions posed among the ruins along the Rio San Juan in southwestern Colorado. Q-BAR

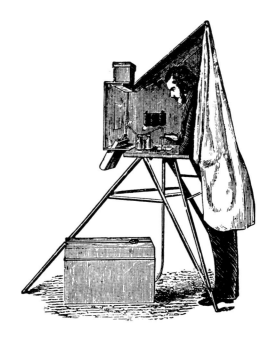

This is a diagramatic sketch of the type of darkroom tent used by Jackson when he made his negatives of the Mesa Verde cliff ruins.

The ancient ruins in the Mesa Verde area of southwestern Colorado held a special fascination for William H. Jackson, and he was always proud of his part in bringing them to the attention of the world with his photographs. Later, when even larger and more impressive ruins were discovered not far from where he had made his original discoveries, he returned to the area and made additional views — one of which is reproduced here as he originally produced it in 1892.   SHSC

it, in order to plan my work for the next day, and Ingersoll remained with me. We were "stumped" for a while in making that last hundred feet, but with the aid of an old dead tree and the remains of some ancient foot-holds, we finally reached the bench or platform on which was perched, like a swallows nest, the "Two-Story House" of our first photograph. From this height we had a glorious view over the surrounding canyon walls, while far below our camp fire glimmered in the deepening shadows like a far away little red star.[2]

. . . It was getting quite dark, so we delayed no longer than to assure ourselves that it was all we hoped for, and to prospect a way up when we should return the next morning with the photographic outfit.

Bright and early, as soon as breakfast was dispatched, we commenced the ascent. "Mexico," our little pack-mule, with the apparatus upon his back, by sharp tacks and lively scrambling over the rocks, was able to reach the foot of the precipice of which I have spoken above. From this we hauled the boxes containing the camera and chemicals by the long ropes taken from the pack saddle. One man was shoved up ahead over the worst place, with the rope, and tying it to a tree, the others easily ascended.[3]

And now I want Ernest Ingersoll to take up the story. When we returned to Denver he sent the full account of our preliminary discoveries to his newspaper, and the *New York Tribune* thus was the first to publish, November 3, 1874, a description of the ruins which subsequent explorations established as the most remarkable in this country:

"... There, 700 measured feet above the valley, perched on a little ledge only just large enough to hold it, was a two-story house made of finely cut sandstone, each block about 14 by 6 inches, accurately fitted and set in mortar now harder than the stone itself. The floor was the ledge upon which it rested, and the roof the overhanging rock. There were three rooms upon the ground floor, each one 6 by 9 feet, with partition walls of faced stone. Between the stories was originally a wood floor, traces of which still remained, as did also the cedar sticks set in the wall over the windows and door ... Each of the stories was six feet in height, and all the rooms, upstairs and down, were nicely plastered and painted what now looks a dull brick-red color, with a white band along the floor like a base-board. There was a low doorway from

William H. Jackson (left) became an expert at packing his photographic equipment on mules during the Hayden survey expeditions. SHSC

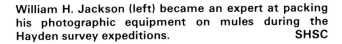

Members of the photographic section of the Hayden survey posed outside their tent with the developing apparatus and chemicals used with the wet collodion negatives. Photographed by William H. Jackson. SHSC

Utes at the Los Pinos Indian Agency were photographed by Jackson in 1874.   SHSC

One of our objectives in going south was to be at the Los Pinos Indian Agency at the time of one of the annuity distributions, for the purpose of obtaining photographs of the Indians. We came upon them first, in some 60 or 70 tepees, on the Cochetopa at the junction of the Los Piños. Making our purpose known to the Agent he assured us of his co-operation and in due time arranged an interview with Chief Ouray who was domiciled in an adobe house within the Agency square. A little later we found him at home reclining on a rude couch covered with Navajo blankets of which there were a great many covering other couches. The furnishing otherwise was simply a chair and a stool with a few colored prints decorating the walls in addition to many articles of beaded buckskin wearing apparel. The interview was quite a long one, Ouray asking many questions about our work and travels and why we wanted to photograph his Indians. Inasmuch as we came from Washington he took it for granted that we knew something about the recent curtailment of the reservation. At the end he promised to say a good word for us to the other chiefs and to sit for his own portrait. Bearing in mind the adage to "strike while the iron is hot" we extemporized an open air studio on the porch of the Agent's residence and began operations by making individual sittings of the Agent's family; then came Ouray arrayed in his bravest attire of beaded

the ledge into the lower story, and another above, showing that the upper chamber was entered from without. The windows were large, square apertures, with no indication of any glazing or shutters. They commanded a view of the whole valley for many miles. Near the house several convenient little niches in the rock were built into better shape, as though they had been used as cupboards or caches; and behind it a semi-circular wall inclosing the angle of the house and cliff formed a water-reservoir holding two and a half hogsheads. . . . 4

Jackson continues:

Passing over many incidents of our experiences, which if detailed would fill a volume, I will relate two or three only which remain most clearly impressed on my memory.

We traveled "light" so far as the photographic outfit was concerned, using only a 5 x 8 camera, and in place of the tent of the previous year had a folding box that was more handy for working small plates. This served every purpose until, one cold morning, our pack mule, "Johnnie," in a bucking spree, turned a somersault squarely on top of it, and the only thing that was not smashed was the cloth hood. A carpenter in Silverton made good the damage, however.

Chipeta, wife of Chief Ouray, was photographed in 1874 at the Los Pinos agency by W. H. Jackson.   SHSC

buckskin accompanied by his young and comely wife, Chipeta, equally resplendent in buckskin and beads. Heavy rains cut off any further portrait work for that day.

Next morning we went down among the tepees. Began operations by having a preliminary pow-wow with some of the head men. After passing the pipe around, with a whiff or two from each one in the circle, and an interval of cogitation, a lively discussion followed, mostly in their own tongue, in which it soon became apparent that the "Medicine Men" had worked up an antagonism to our project, leading to a general expression on the part of those present that it was "no bueno"—Shavano, Guerro and some others protesting against the making of any pictures. Notwithstanding this opposition I set up my camera and dark box in front of Piah's tepee, ready for business, as he had earlier in the day promised to stand for his picture and to get others to do the same. With his assistance we got together a few groups and were going finely until a downpour of rain stopped any further work.

Then came Issue Day. We anticipated great results from the crowds that would be on hand for their rations—flour, sugar and many other things, with "beef on the hoof." We began by photographing groupings of tepees and ponies and then with

With the help of the Indian agent's wife, Jackson made this picture of Pi-ah's papoose without the father's consent. When the fact was discovered, Jackson lost the support which he had had from the chief and was nearly chased off the reservation. This stereo card was made in 1874. SHSC

Jackson had unusually good luck in getting these Ute warriors to pose at the Los Pinos agency in 1874. SHSC

the connivance of the Agent's wife made a negative of Piah's papoose on its cradle board. We tried to get his squaw to pose, but Piah got wind of it and ordered her away from the building. He was in quite a different humor from the day before and his good nature was now turned to hostility. Planting my camera on the Agency porch to take in the whole assemblage on the issuing ground and preparing to make an exposure, Piah, with half a dozen others rode up in front of me, protesting vehemently, pulling at the tripod legs and occasionally throwing a blanket over both camera and myself, all the time declaring that "Indian no sabe picture—make'm heap sick—all die—ponie die—papoose die." His idea seemed to be that there was no harm in making single pictures of the men, but I must not include the squaws, papooses or ponies. Defeated in this quarter, for a mounted delegation followed me closely, I went into the cook house intending to make a picture out of the doorway, but when the camera was set, one of the Indians tried to ride his horse through the door on to me, and failing in that, remained before it with a blanket over his arm, effectually blocking the view.

There seemed to be so much antagonism that we gave up any further attempts, particularly as heavy

One of Jackson's claims to fame during his career was his pioneering use of large-format cameras to make mammoth prints. As early as 1875, he had used a 20 x 24-inch camera on the Hayden survey. Carrying the equipment required the use of two mules, one for the camera and tripod, and the other one for the glass plates. NEWHALL

clouds threatened the usual afternoon storm, but even after I had packed up, Piah demanded that I destroy the plates already made, at the same time trying to snatch the plate box from my hands. A little argument convinced him this was going too far and he left us, but in all this controversy neither the Agent or Ouray was in evidence anywhere—probably very busy elsewhere.

The rest of the day we looked on at the distribution. The issue of beef was novel and thrilling. Mounted and armed Indians were drawn up in line and as the cattle were liberated, one by one, from the corral, allowing the bovine a fair start, each little group pursued its assigned steer as if hunting buffalo, popping away with rifle and pistol until it was brought down. By the time that nearly 20 such groups were scattered over the field, it made a lively scene, reminiscent of a wilder life on the plains. It would have been a fine subject for a "movie."[5]

One of the most ambitious photographic experiments undertaken on the American frontier during the 1870's was the use of a mammoth 20 x 24-inch camera during Jackson's 1875 expedition. Jackson was the first to attempt to manipulate such huge

sheets of glass while in the field.[6] The problems encountered while using these huge plates were numerous. Jackson describes the use of the mammoth camera:

This was something unheard of so far in the annals of mountain photography under similar conditions—a useless expenditure of energy and material, viewed in the light of modern methods of enlargement; but 50 years ago there were no such methods.

It was something of a problem to carry a camera of that size over the trails we had to contend with, which because of its bulk was made a top pack on the aparejo, another pack mule being required for the glass and other adjuncts for operating. For dark-work room I had a tent, built on the same lines as the one I used in '73, but on a proportionately larger scale, and for the silver sensitizing bath, a wooden tray. We took this outfit over some of the hardest trails in the San Juan; up Lake Fork, to the San Miguel and finally over Mosquito and Argentine passes on our way back to Denver by way of Georgetown.

For every plate made there was some unique

114

experience well worth relating, but the story of how we photographed Uncompagre Mountain is typical of all.

From our camp above Lake City we began the ascent a little below Henson Creek. The trail was very steep and the bulky camera perched on the top of an aparejo was an awkward load on a 45 degree grade. When well up the mountain where small trees obstructed the trail "Old Mag." lost her balance, and rolling backwards was saved from greater disaster by lodging between some trees. With difficulty, in a ticklish situation, the camera was released from the pack and carried to a practicable loading place, and then the mule, with more difficulty, was put on her feet without tumbling still further down the grade. Getting well up towards timberline we made a temporary camp from which I prospected for the best point of view and Bill went out with his gun for game. Returning later, I found that Bill had brought in a mountain sheep but had gone in search of our animals, which had pulled up their picket pins and taken the back track. He did not return until next morning, the stock having gone all the way to the camp above Lake City.

The point selected for a close-up view was about three hours from where we camped and well above timberline. By the time I had the tent pitched and the camera in place, clouds obscured the sun and high winds were sweeping over the bare plateaus. I made only one exposure which turned out poorly—too much wind for the long timing required. Giving up the attempt for that day we cached the whole outfit under the rocks and went down about 1,500 feet to where a fire could be made for an all night camp. It was raining nearly all this time but the morning came in clear and we were soon back to where the apparatus had been left. (This was the 4th of July, by the way.) We had time to secure one fairly good negative only when the winds and the clouds became more aggressive than before, bringing occasional light flurries of snow that hastened our return to the home camp.[7]

Jackson never intended to remain permanently attached to the U.S. Geological Survey. He felt that the government was getting quite a bargain with the limited salary he received. He had been completely unknown in 1869, when Hayden had hired him, but his views of Yellowstone, Yosemite and Mesa Verde had made him widely known in Europe and America. He made a scale model of the ruins in Mancos Cañon, Mesa Verde, which was exhibited at the World's Fair at Philadelphia in 1876. In 1879, Congress failed to provide money for a photographer with the next survey, so Jackson left Washington and headed for Colorado. He found a building under construction at 413 Larimer Street in Denver, and agreed to occupy the upper floor if the plans would be remodeled to his specifications. From this studio he made trips

An interesting example of early trick photography — Jackson made this print when exposures were far too slow to capture a pancake in mid-air. He took the picture of the cook with a skillet poised and added the pancake later by dabing the negative with black paint to create the floating flapjack. Reproduced from a stereo view card, C. 1874.　　　　　SHSC

all over Colorado and the entire country. From Grand Junction to the eastern plains, almost no town escaped his camera.

Jackson had been toying with the idea of opening a gallery in Denver at least since 1874. At that time, William Chamberlain was trying to sell his business in Denver. Jackson met Chamberlain while camping during that summer. As he noted in his diary:

Intended to have gone back into camp early but I got up into Chamberlains and got so interested in talking over the pros & cons in regard to buying his place that I did not get away before 11 or 12 or near noon. C. wishes to sell very much indeed & if I was only free & had just a little more ready money I should not hesitate a moment to take the place, for it's the best in the region.[8]

Jackson's principal object in coming to Colorado was to work with the Western railroads as he had done in 1868 and 1869, before being associated with the Hayden surveys. He did a good deal of work for the Denver and Rio Grande Railway, as

When the home of William H. Jackson and his family — on Twenty-third Street in Denver — was photographed in 1882, everyone seemed to turn out for the event. The neighbors were stationed in front of their house, and Jackson's son and daughter, Clarence and Emilie, were posted in front of their mother — and even the maid was included, positioned off to one side, of course. SHSC

This was the drawing room of William H. Jackson's Denver home was photographed about 1890. SHSC

Jackson traveled throughout the West in private railroad cars during the years after he left the U.S. Geological Survey. Here, he posed (right) with traveling companions in the car he used on his trip to Mexico during 1883. SHSC

well as other Western lines, traveling in more comfort during his subsequent trips than he had during his days with the Hayden survey. He usually had a special car provided to him by the railroad. This car was fitted up with a darkroom, living quarters and usually a black porter.[9] On occasion, his family was able to spend the summer with him, traveling around the Rockies in the private railway car. His mother spent one summer with the family. She was quite old by then, but spent most of her time on the observation platform with her grandchildren, getting covered by soot and ash from the steam locomotive.

Jackson's specialty during this period was his

18 x 22-inch glass plates. It was much easier to carry these when traveling by rail than by pack animal and he made a good many of these giant plates all over Colorado. He received $10.00 for each 18 x 22 picture.[10] This may not seem like much money by modern standards, but in 1892 it was considerable. Several hundred of these large glass plates have survived to the present day.

Jackson remained in business in Colorado until the turn of the century, when he moved to Detroit to begin reproducing colored photolithographs of his 40,000 negatives. The Western negatives were later returned to Colorado and have been preserved by the State.

W. H. Jackson

029 HECLA CASTLE, NEAR CALUMET.

DETROIT PH

Opposite: No, this is not the proper way to ride on a locomotive — especially through a tunnel! The men in this view obviously were posing for their picture at the Denver & Rio Grande's scenic Toltec Tunnel, along the Colorado - New Mexico border. The locomotive was but 2 years old when W. H. Jackson placed his 11 x 14-inch glass-plate camera on the edge of a sheer cliff to record this scene. When he produced this view in 1880, the "San Juan Extension" of the D&RG was brand new; and, as was often the case, Jackson was on hand to photograph the first year's operation.   SHSC

The Rio Grande system had an extremely steep seven-mile-long branch to Calumet — which was built in 1881. William H. Jackson was called upon to photograph this narrow-gauge line, and naturally aimed his lens at a rock formation called Hecla Castle, near the end of the branch. Locomotive Number 401 was brand new when photographed here — with the train's conductor, "Towser" (the dog) and the locomotive engineer, seated on her pilot beam. This print was made from one of Jackson's superb 11 x 14-inch glass-plate negatives.   SHSC

A scene at the National Mining Exposition in Denver was photographed by William H. Jackson in 1882. This delegation of Utes came to visit the show and Jackson could not resist photographing them.   SHSC

The majestic Windsor Hotel was the most opulent hostelry in Colorado when it was built in 1879. These two rooms were typical of the posh furnishings. These interior views no doubt were used for advertising purposes after Jackson shot them, C. 1881.   SHSC

Mining machinery in Stray Horse Gulch, near Leadville, was photographed during the 1880's by William H. Jackson. SHSC

The "News" office at Grand Junction was at Number 6, B Street, in 1882, when William H. Jackson recorded this view. SHSC

When William H. Jackson visited the Grand Junction area in 1882, the settlement's first school looked like this. SHSC

William Dingle's drugstore in the Tabor Building at the corner of Sixteenth and Larimer streets — in lower downtown Denver — was photographed by William H. Jackson about 1885.

SHSC

This photograph of Sixteenth Street, as viewed from Curtis during the 1860's, shows the
Tabor Opera House, as a cable car and trailer rattled past.   SHSC

Crewmen and passengers were pushing this cable car and trailer — probably to regain the cable. This was at the corner of Sixteenth and Curtis streets, in the heart of Denver's main business district, C. 1893. The cars have signs reading, "16th St. & North Denver" and "Zoological Garden, Berkeley & Sloan Lakes." Cable cars continued to operate in Denver until 1900, when the last route was electrified. This scene is an enlargement from one of Jackson's 8 x 10-inch prints, showing a detailed portion of it.

SHSC

As W. H. Jackson shot this view, horse cars were pulling away from the Denver City Railway Company's building in lower downtown Denver. Jackson exposed this scene from the tower of Denver Union Depot during 1893. SHSC

During the late 1880's, the corner of Fifteenth and Lawrence streets, in Denver, was in the center of the business district. In this print, William H. Jackson captured a cable car as it paused on its journey up and down the cable line. SHSC

Sherman Street in Denver during the 1880's was the avenue of wealthy capitalists and speculators. Here, a carriage with liveried coachman and matched team were awaiting their owner at the curb step. A W. H. Jackson photograph. SHSC

Opposite: During the 1890's, the People's Bank of Denver was a major banking institution. At the time, several cable car lines ran to all parts of the city. This combination grip car and trailer was running on Sixteenth Street. The destination sign on the end of the grip car (the smaller of the two) reads "Elitch's Gardens." Photographed by W. H. Jackson. SHSC

127

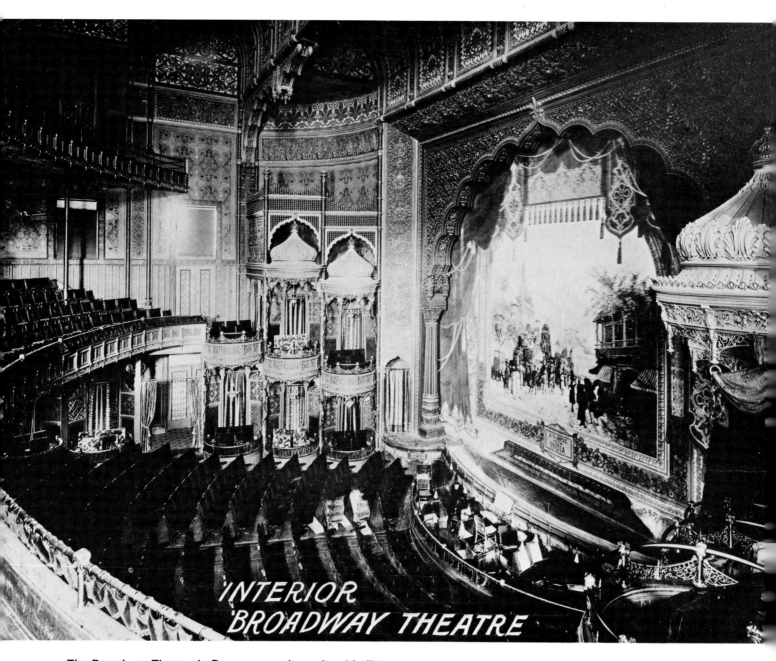

INTERIOR
BROADWAY THEATRE

The Broadway Theatre in Denver was planned and built as the rival of the Tabor Grand Opera House. The interior was as lavish and modern as the Tabor had been when it was completed. In this view of the interior — made about 1895 — William H. Jackson captured the opulent Victorian appointments of the designers. **SHSC**

Opposite: The Mining Exchange Building in Denver was the symbol of the wealth and economic power generated by the mineral industry of Colorado. In this Jackson view, the building is seen as it appeared during construction — as an Eleventh Avenue electric streetcar rattled past. **SHSC**

3827. MINING EXCHANGE   THE PHOTOCHROM CO. DETROIT

In 1884, William H. Jackson photographed a Denver & Rio Grande Railway locomotive on one of the big wooden trestles that once marked the route of the famous narrow-gauge line over Marshall Pass. Steam locomotives were often posed atop spidery trestles by early-day photographers. Q-BAR

On March 29, 1884 — with winter snow still on the ground — William Henry Jackson made a series of views of the recently-completed Georgetown Loop on the Colorado Central Railroad. This print probably was made at that time, and shows Jackson's special photographic train in the foreground, and three other trains posed strategically at other points along the loop. The three pages following this view show the same picture enlarged two different sizes to illustrate the wealth of detail Jackson's large-format camera recorded. SHSC

1854. THE LOOP IN THE U.P. RY NEAR GEORGETOWN. W.H.J.&C.

Opposite, above: Probably the most famous railroad engineering feat in the early history of mountain railroading, the Georgetown Loop on the Colorado Central Railway drew tourists from all parts of the country. It was even recorded on moving picture film shortly after the turn of the century by the American Multiscope & Biograph Company. This print, one of probably millions taken of the loop, was made about 1884 by W. H. Jackson. SHSC

William H. Jackson often placed his photographic train in scenes he shot along the narrow-gauge lines of western Colorado. In the view above, his train had stopped enroute to Durango, along the Silverton Branch of the Denver & Rio Grande, a short distance above Rockwood, in 1886. At this point, the railroad was (and still is) high above the turbulent water of the Rio de las Animas. Q-BAR

COLORADO MIDLAND EXCURSION TRAIN
11 MILE CANON
W.H. JACKSON & Co PHOT. DENVER.

Colorado Midland locomotive Number 17 was photographed by William H. Jackson above Ute Pass — in Woodland Park — in 1887. The track had just recently been laid and the railroad's equipment was nearly brand new. Jackson aimed his large 11 x 14-inch camera at Pikes Peak, dramatizing its majestic dimensions beside the diminutive special train.　　　SHSC

Overleaf: An excursion-train ride on the Colorado Midland was not soon forgotten. Eleven-Mile Canyon — west of Colorado Springs — provided sight-seers with a perfect excuse to get out into the fresh mountain air, pick wildflowers, and — of course — take pictures. William H. Jackson captured the scene printed on the preceding two pages on a large-format 18 x 22-inch glass-plate camera in 1888.　　　SHSC

138

During the 1880's a cattle drive on the open range was photographed by William H. Jackson.   SHSC

Overleaf: Railroad tunnels were a must to photograph back in the "good old days." Here, we see Tunnel 10 in Eleven-Mile Canyon, along the mainline of the Colorado Midland. In 1888, W. H. Jackson made a tour over this line with a specially-equipped caboose and locomotive, and this was one of his "photo stops." His family caught their breath as he recorded this view on an 18 x 22-inch glass plate.   SHSC

This log cabin on Quartz Creek was photographed in 1880 by William H. Jackson.　SHSC

"Josie" Meeker by 1880 had become famous from her part in the Meeker Massacre in which her father and nearly all male members of the staff of the White River Ute Reservation were killed by the Utes. Jackson made this portrait to sell like post cards to the curious who crowded the lecture halls across the country to hear Ms. Meeker tell of her harrowing experiences and captivity among the Indians.　Q-BAR

Other rigs of the pioneer freighter David Wood were being loaded with cargo when William H. Jackson shot this stereographic view of Telluride in 1893.   SHSC

O 225 P . MANITOU CANON FROM THE TEMPLE

Some photographs required considerable effort to secure. In these two scenes we see that W. H. Jackson, or an assistant, had climbed to the top of a canyon wall to capture an unusual view of the gorge through a hole in the rock formation called the "Temple of Isis." These views were photographed in Manitou Canyon, near the Cave of the Winds and the Garden of the Gods.   SHSC

William Henry Jackson

See page opposite: William Henry Jackson, at the twilight of his long career, posed with one of the early types of cameras he used as a youth. Jackson lived to see his work recognized and acclaimed as the milestone it had become.   SHSC

On one of his summer trips throughout the Rockies during the 1890's, Jackson was joined by his mother. She spent many hours on the platform of their private car looking at the mountains and being covered by cinders and soot from the engine.   SHSC

GLACIER POINT. YOSEMITE.

William H. Jackson's work took him many places outside the Centennial State. Here is his famous view of Glacier Point in Yosemite National Park, California. From far and wide — all across Colorado and the vast reaches of the American West — Jackson's cameras had been put to use recording an era as no other man was able to do.   SHSC

Album of the 1870's

The railway was a new institution to Colorado in 1870 when the *Walter Cheeseman*, a trim 4-4-0 "American Standard" steam locomotive, was photographed along the route of the first line to serve Denver, Governor John Evan's Denver Pacific. SHSC

Curecanti, an important Ute chief and the man for whom the settlement and landmark in the Black Canyon were named, is shown here with his two wives — from a *carte de visite* produced by G. A. Goehner in 1877. Q-BAR

Very early in the history of photography, the art-science was used on solemn occasions to provide a record of what occurred. Indian conferences often were concluded with a group portrait such as this one. Here, we see a stellar cast assembled on both sides. In addition to Chief Ouray and his wife, Chipeta (seated on the floor), Otto Mears can be seen at the extreme right. J. B. Thompson, second from the left in the center row, enscribed on the picture that it was made about 1874. He presented the original to the State Historical Society in 1921. SHSC

In 1873, when T. J. Hine made this photograph, the Ute Indians had not fully accepted the camera. This seemingly deserted village was only evacuated because of the photographer's presence. SHSC

A group of Utes pose in front of Ben Gurnsey's studio in Colorado Springs, C. 1875. From a stereo card made for an advertising campaign of the Denver & Rio Grande Railway.

SHSC

This is Douglass, Ute chief of the White River Agency. He was instrumental in the Meeker Massacre. He paid for his "crime" by being confined in Fort Leavenworth, Kansas, until he became insane. His wife, Susan, helped the Meeker women when they were held captive by the Indians. Photographed by W. G. Chamberlain. SHSC

Captain Jack and his squaw, photographed in 1879 by Jacob Whitter of Freeport, Illinois. Whitter was one of many Eastern photographers who came to Colorado to shoot and purchase negatives of Rocky Mountain scenes. This portrait of the famous Ute couple was obviously made in a studio, either one borrowed by Whitter, or it is a print from a negative which he did not actually make himself. Q-BAR

Mining machinery was becoming more sophisticated during the 1870's. The scene at right shows a horse-powered mining hoist which operated near Nevada City on Bald Mountain, C. 1872. Reproduced from a stereo card by the Duhem brothers. SHSC

Professional hunters who supplied meat to construction camps and settlements were beginning to disappear by the end of the 1870's. Here, Joseph Collier has posed one of these hunters with his prize, about 1878.   SHSC

A hunter posed with his trophy and faithful hunting companion, C. 1875, in this stereo card by B. H. Gurnsey.   -BAR

William Byers (standing right), founder of the *Rocky Mountain News,* and a group of friends pose in Bartholomew Velarde's gallery after a successful buffalo hunt during March of 1873.   DPL

The myth of prospectors "striking it rich" brought thousands of people to Colorado during the gold rush, and continued to be the romantic staple of storytellers and picture-makers for 100 years. In this obviously posed scene, two miners near Manitou Springs make the all-important discovery which will lead them to wealth. This stereo card was produced for the tourist trade during the 1870's by James Thurlow of Manitou Springs.   SHSC

155

The commerce of the mountains was carried-on by means of wagon trains from the beginning of settlement in the territory until long after the turn of the century. Any place the railroads did not go was the territory of the wagon. Here, a wagon train was heading up Ute Pass with goods destined for customers now long-forgotten. Photographed by Gurnsey about 1878.
SHSC

WAR DEPARTMENT, CORPS OF ENGINEERS, U. S. A.

Geographical

EXPLORATIONS and SURVEYS WEST of the 100th MERIDIAN.

No. 84   T. H. O·Sullivan. Photo.

Roman Catholic Church, Plaza of Guadaloupe, Guadaloupe Co., Colorado. Built not many years since of adobes. Dimensions, length 120 feet; width 60 feet; height 25 feet. Grave yard in the fore-ground surrounded by an adobe wall about 6 feet in height.

The photographer Timothy O'Sullivan made several brief visits to Colorado. These two 1874 prints show life at Fort Garland, one of the state's leading military establishments at the time. The first view shows an officer and his family outside their quarters, while the second one shows soldiers taking their ease at one of the entrances to the post. SHSC

Francisco Plaza, in La Veta, was photographed shortly after the celebration marking the admittance of Colorado into the Union in 1876. Both the Republican and Democratic parties wished to hoist the Union flag during the celebraton, so two flag poles were raised for the purpose, allowing each to have the honor. SHSC

Fort Garland in 1874 was photographed by Timothy O'Sullivan.

159

Engine 92 of the Denver & Rio Grande Railway was posed atop Veta Pass shortly after the narrow-gauge line was built in 1876.　　　　　Q-BAR

An Atchison, Topeka & Santa Fe Railway work crew is shown here building the original "hanging bridge" in the Royal Gorge. This was during 1878-79 while the gorge was still called the Grand Canyon of the Arkansas. The right-of-way through the gorge would soon be lost to the Denver & Rio Grande Railway during the so-called "Royal Gorge War." The photographer of this view (above) is unknown.   Q-BAR

In 1879, the Denver & Rio Grande Railway and the Santa Fe System faced each other in a showdown over possession of a right-of-way through the Royal Gorge. This was the only practical route west through southern Colorado into Utah. As a result of the ensuing court litigation, the Rio Grande won the right-of-way through the gorge, but lost the right to build south of Colorado through New Mexico to reach the line's original goal, El Paso, Texas, and old Mexico. During the court battles, considerable show of force was made — as illustrated in these posed pictures by Boston & Ziegler — showing gunmen hired by the railroads.   Q-BAR

Opposite: One of the first men to prospect for gold in southwest Colorado was Charles Baker. Here we see his log cabin overlooking Bakers Park — the site of the famous San Juan mining town of Silverton. His cabin was photographed during the 1870's by an unknown photographer.   Q-BAR

BLACK HAWK

Blackhawk, C. 1878 — with a Colorado Central Railway train bound for Central City in the background — was photographed by Charles Weitfle and sold by him as a stereo card. The train is crossing what was known as the Blackhawk Trestle, above the town's streets in renowned Gregory Gulch. Because the grade was too steep up the gulch, the Colorado Central had to resort to a double-ended switchback in order to reach Central City. This consisted of three sections: The train was on the middle section — its engine pointed toward the lower end of the line. The track in the foreground was part of the lower section — as well as a portion of the mainline up from the junction at Forks Creek. The upper section of the switchback can be discerned running along the hillside in the background.   Q-BAR

The 1870's saw great strides made in scientific equipment for mining. The steam drill quickly replaced the sledge hammer and hand drill used during the early years of the gold rush. Here three steam drills are shown at work in the San Juan Mountains of southwest Colorado in 1879 — from a stereo card by Luke & Wheeler. The San Juans were rich in gold and silver, and saw much mining activity.   Q-BAR

In this Alex Martin view of Gilman, we see the mining town clinging to the slope of Battle Mountain. Drifts of the Eagle mine — which became the largest mine of the area — now crisscross the interior of the mountain. In fact, many of the hillsides in this area have been honeycombed with tunnels, driven in the search of

gold. The Eagle mine continues to produce zinc, lead, silver, gold and copper — and is served by the Rio Grande system by way of sidings laid in the depths of the Eagle Canyon, over 500 feet below. Years ago, little cablecars moved supplies from track level to the town.

SHSC

1 Herbert J. Parker. 5 Harry G. Schoenfeld. 9 Thos. B. McCormic.

2 Aaron S. Shallcross. 6 Dr. R. G. Buckingham. 10 Dr. H. K. Steele.

3 Dr. John Elsner. 7 Dr. C. M. Parker. 11 William N. Town

4 Dr. W. H. Williams. 8 Dr. J. M. Norman 12 C. W. Kuhl

Sept. 1893.

As the 1870's drew to a close, Denver had become a city of gas lights, horse-drawn streetcars and substantial buildings. This reproduction from a Chamberlain stereo card shows a section of Fifteenth Street late in the decade.
Q-BAR

Opposite, above: Many of Denver's most prominent doctors posed outside the McCormic & Shallcross drugstore during September of 1873. The proprietors, Shallcross and McCormic, are seated on the iron rail on either side of the steps.
SHSC

Opposite, below: The "Solid Muldoon" was excavated on Muldoon Hill, between Pueblo and Beulah, in 1878. Exhibited all over the United States as a "petrified man," the figure was proved to be a hoax, planted at the behest of George Hull, a "con artist" from New York. The material used was pulverized stone, bone, plaster and clay, which had been fired in a kiln. This photograph was part of a promotional scheme to induce people to pay to see the "man" on exhibit.
Q-BAR

Fairplay in 1878 had a timid blacksmith who retired to the interior of his shop, where he can be seen peering out at Dana B. Chase, who made the stereo card from which this print was produced.   Q-BAR

Sixty-five tons of silver bullion and ten tons of silver ore await loading in this view of Platte Station in South Park. Photographed by Ben Gurnsey in 1879.   Q-BAR

In 1878, Cherry Creek went on a rampage through Denver as it had done 14 years earlier, in 1864. In this stereo card view by Chamberlain we see the Blake Street bridge abutments shortly after the bridge began its downward journey toward Nebraska. SHSC

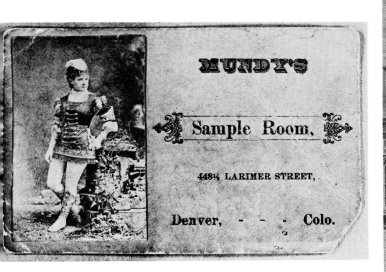

MUNDY'S

Sample Room,

448½ LARIMER STREET,

Denver, - - - Colo.

It pays to advertise — and here we see how a local Denver "wine room" placed "lurid" pictures on their business cards of 1879 to stimulate patronage. SHSC

Denver's Larimer Street horsecar of 1878 pauses on the turntable for a turn up Fifteenth Street — from a W. G. Chamberlain photograph. Q-BAR

This photograph of William L. Hallett's home in Estes Park featured four generations of his family. He came to Colorado in 1878 as a young engineer on a vacation. He remained, to become one of the region's largest cattlemen, running some 35,000 head of cattle. He also was a part of the famous Wyoming Rustler's War.   Q-BAR

A summer idyl in the late 1870's — complete with black servants and a sun shade in a tree — was sold as a stereo card by Chamberlain.

A monument to black enterprise during the decade of the 1870's, Barney Ford's *Inter-Ocean Hotel* was one of Denver's leading hostelries. Reproduced from a Chamberlain stereo card. Q-BAR

During the mid-1870's, the New York Store of Central City was photographed by by J. Freedman & Company of Denver.   SHSC

The great Leadville boom of the 1870's created a town almost overnight. Many of the first people to stake their claims soon found themselves in conflict with the new town. In this view of Harrison Avenue — photographed during July of 1879 — one of the early settler's cabins can be seen sitting squarely in the middle of the

street! Leadville, at an elevation of 10,152 feet, is magnificently situated high in the upper valley of the Arkansas River. Bearing one of the greatest names ever to exist in the world of mining, large quantities of silver, gold, lead, zinc, manganese and molybdenum have been mined locally.

SHSC

Some of David Wood's freighters in Canon City during 1879, with typical six and eight-mule teams. Because of their great stamina, mules often were used to haul wagons over the rough — and ususally steep and narrow — mountain roads of Colorado. This view is from a stereo card by E. G. Morrison.   Q-BAR

The tent in this view was serving as a field station of Western Union Telegraph along the narrow-gauge line of the Denver, South Park & Pacific Railroad in 1875. Little actual construction was done on this line until the following year. This print was sold by Mrs. M. A. Mathews at her curiosity shop in Denver. Q-BAR

Top right: Construction was underway on buildings of the Territorial State prison at Canon City when this view was made early in the 1870's   Q-BAR

Right: By the mid-1870's, mining operations in Colorado had moved away from the individual miner toward "big business." In this view of Chases Gulch — near Central City — which was made by Chamberlain during that period, at least three smelters can be seen. Q-BAR

175

In this scene of Golden in the early 1870's you are looking north; in the foreground is Twelfth Street. Most of these brick buildings are still standing.　　Q-BAR

One of the most innovative uses of photography in Colorado during the early 1870's is this card and printed message. It was sent as a mailing price to churches in England and in the eastern United States as an appeal for funds to complete the building. The photographer is unknown.　　SHSC

Grace (Episcopal) Church,

COLORADO SPRINGS, COL.

To cost when completed, - - $7,500
Present subscription, - - - 4,000
Amount yet required, - - 3,500

New Horizons

VII

URING the years since photography had been first introduced into Colorado, much change had taken place in both the light-sensitive camera material and the finished product. At no time was the change more apparent than during the 1880's and the early 1890's. It seemed as though the farther the art-science of photography advanced, the faster it changed, until it reached a temporary leveling-off place with the invention of rolled film, about 1890. One of the innovations which was introduced into Colorado during the early 1880's was the printing of photographs on printing presses.

William G. Chamberlain, at the twilight of his long career, became interested in the newly-perfected method of illustrating books and other documents with photographs printed on ordinary paper with ink. In February, 1881, Chamberlain announced in the *Rocky Mountain News* that he had sold his photographic business to F. D. Storm. He stated at that time that he would remain at his old gallery:

> . . . giving my whole attention to the artotype, which is a photomechanical process, particularly adapted to commercial work, such as book illustrations, maps, drawings, copies of oil paintings, portraiture, views, machinery, etc.
>
> As no chemicals are used, the artotypes do not fade or turn yellow any more than a steel engraving, and are superior to ordinary photographs whenever permanency of the print is desired.
>
> The public are invited to call at the gallery and see specimens of artotype work and to give me their patronage.[1]

The halftone process which today reproduces photographs in almost every newspaper and most books—including this one—was only a crude idea in 1881. All of the pictures reproduced in papers in Colorado up to that time were the work of artist-engravers working either on a block of wood or a piece of metal, cutting the image into the material which would later be inked and used in printing. The artotype process was a refinement of a process which had been announced in Germany little more that 10 years earlier.[2] This process had been used with limited success in 1869 by William Jackson Palmer to illustrate his survey report with photographs by Bell and Gardner.

The essential feature of this process is the fact that gelatin, which has been hardened by the action of light, will not absorb printer's ink. An ordinary glass negative was placed over a piece of glass coated with a special light-sensitive gelatin, which was then exposed to light, developed and fixed in the usual manner. When printer's ink was applied to the resulting glass positive, it did not stick to the hardened parts, but did adhere to the rest of the plate. When this inked plate was pressed against a sheet of paper, a beautifully graduated halftone print resulted. The number of prints which could be obtained by this process was numbered in the thousands, but the fact that the image was usually reversed from right to left was somewhat of a disadvantage. It is not known how long Chamberlain was involved in the artotype business. One artotype print from the early 1880's, which is owned by the State Historical Society of Colorado, shows Castle Rock at Golden. It was obviously taken from one of Chamberlain's negatives and is presumably a product of his company. This print was published by the "Artotype Company of 359 Larimer Street, Denver."* This was

---

* This appears on the lower right-hand corner of the print.

LEADVILLE.

A rare example of a Colorado "Artotype" reproduction — featuring the mining camp of Leadville — as published by the Artotype Company of Denver.   SHSC

Results from an Artotype and paper photograph from the same negative are shown in this view. This scene is Castle Rock at Golden, Colorado. Photographed by Chamberlin, C. 1879.   SHSC

CASTLE ROCK, Golden,——1000 ft. above City

Artotype Co, 859 Larimer St,

Denver's chief of police, John Farley (center), inspects the department's collection of "mug shots" in this photograph, taken during 1900. At that time, the collection — which had been inaugurated in 1885 — already comprised 2,000 portraits.   SHSC

the address of the firm of Charles C. Wright. Whether Chamberlain had entered into a joint business venture with Wright or simply sold some negatives to him is not known.

Prints produced by the artotype process by Chamberlain, his rivals or successors, are not common. The Colorado Artotype Company made a brief appearance in 1886 under the direction of H. M. Williams, but the firm had disappeared from the directories by the following year and no prints are known. It is likely that Chamberlain had in mind printing the thousands of negatives which he had taken in Colorado between his arrival in 1861 and his retirement 20 years later. In this idea he anticipated the picture postcard which was soon to make its appearance.

As photography became more common during the first half of the 1880's, it began to be used in many new ways. The so-called "dry plate" was slowly gaining acceptance during this period. It came "ready-made" from the factory in a lightproof box and had only to be exposed and developed. The shorter exposures possible with these plates opened up new fields to photographers. One of the most unlikely uses for photography which was instituted during this period was the police "mug shot."

In May, 1885, the Denver Police Department began the systematic collection of photographs of criminals. These were hung on the wall of the police station in a case with a glass front. In the lower part of the case were displayed knives and other plunder of the department.[3] The business in criminal photography was so good that by August of the following year a new case had to be acquired to house the collection. This case had a dropleaf door which covered the photographs when not being viewed. The photographs included not only the more formal portraits, but also several lynchings, hangings and a few losers of shootouts. A reporter for the *Tribune Republican* of Denver happened in at the police station one quiet

Among the novel innovations of the 1880's were "mug shots." In this example, the prisoner refused to hold still long enough for the photographer to expose his plate, and therefore he was tied to the door to keep him immobile. He promptly closed his eyes! Photographed in 1880-1881 by the the sheriff of Arapahoe County.   SHSC

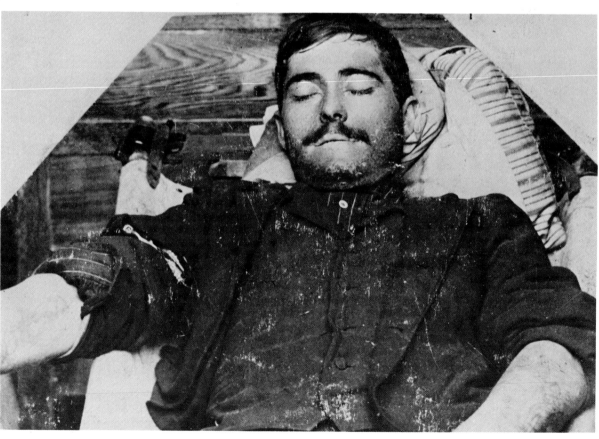

Monday, where he had an interview with a detective about the "rogue's gallery":

"Do you have much trouble in obtaining photographs of criminals?" asked the reporter of Detective James Connor who was present.

"Yes, considerable, sometimes," answered the detective. "You see there are a great many men who are ashamed to have their photographs appear in the Rogue's Gallery, and the most of them are sharp enough to know that we don't have their pictures taken for our private albums. They are onto the scheme, and some of them hate it like the mischief."

"What classes dislike it most?"

"First-class criminals, certainly. You see, there are grades in crime as well as in anything else. When we get hold of an educated bank robber, who has used skill and knowledge in the way of forcing combinations and that sort of thing, you don't suppose he wants to leave his picture with us, do you? No, indeed, he doesn't, and he will avoid it in every way that he possibly can. But he can't usually make his point, and is generally obliged to come along and do as he is told. In such cases you will usually find the heads hung down, and a sullen look of acquiescence on the face, but that doesn't matter much; it's the features of the 'birds' we're after, that they may be readily identified should they ever be at large again.

FORCE IS NOT USED.

"No, we never use force with prisoners in the matter of having their pictures taken. You can't do it. What you accomplish with them has got to be done by coaxing. You can't drive a prisoner with any degree of success anyway, and particularly when you want his picture. You've got to humor him, and be as friendly as you can. In short, if an officer wants to command the respect and obedience of a criminal, he has got to inspire the latter with trust and confidence. So we talk as pleasantly with them as we can about this matter, and, as a general rule, meet with no serious trouble. There are instances, however, where criminals 'kick' about going to the gallery, and where they wink, make faces, and swear all the time they are being photographed. I have known it

Here we see Sadie Leichens, pioneer Denver policewoman who was photographed by the police photographer during 1889. SHSC

to take a photographer an hour to make a picture of a criminal, but I have much oftener seen it done in less than five minutes. When we get hold of a man who has at one time occupied a position of trust and prominence, you can imagine that he is mighty chary of sitting for a portrait for the Rogues' Gallery. Such men are not generally brazen, when it comes to this stage of the game, although they may be brave enough, if it comes to a question of their lives. They are possessed of sufficient delicacy to want to keep out of the 'Gallery.' You see, it isn't a part of a criminal's scheme to be found out. . . .

"We have one man whose photograph we were unable to get until we took him over to the County Jail and bound him to a cell door. There we at last had him in our power, but even then he shut his eyes, and we were unable to make him open them when he was photographed. He was a hard one to manage, sure enough.

Opposite, below: A macabre page from the record book of the Denver chief of detectives, the original caption reads, "Tattood on right arm picture of woman standing on tip toe on a star, on left arm was an inscription: 'To the memory of my mother' also a picture of a woman. This man was shot & killed while committing a burglury at Florence Colo. morning of Sept. 29, 1890. Afterwards identified as one of the assailants & murderer of Ed McKnight." SHSC

TAKING AND BEING TAKEN.

Taking pictures of wild game had intrigued Colorado photographers since Solomon Carvalho first made deguerreotypes in the state. The difficulties of long exposures, however, were not easily overcome. Here we see a wood cut of an attempt by one photographer to get his pictures by first shooting the animals with a gun and then proping them up for their picture. In this case, he appears to have been premature. SHSC

"Yes, the lower classes of criminals are proud of having their photographs taken and would be delighted to have their pictures in the *Police Gazette,* but such pictures are seldom used there, because they are not sufficiently high-toned. That is such criminals are not usually daring enough to commit deeds of such a desperate nature as to secure them a place in the *Gazette.* It's the photographs of the big fellows they want there, and I assure you, sir, very few such fellows are ambitious to shine there. But with the lower classes of criminals it is quite different. . . .

"They step very briskly when the word photographs is mentioned, and frequently 'primp' at the mirror if allowed to do so, before sitting. I took a fellow to the gallery the other day who insisted on being shaved before having his photograph taken, but I didn't see fit to humor him that much. He was as proud of his photograph as any dandy would have been, and begged to have one to keep personally.

WOMEN AND PHOTOGRAPHS.

"No, it has never been necessary to photograph any woman whom the Denver police has ever arrested. We can always find a photograph in a woman's room. Being photographed, you know, is as common as eating is with the fair sex, and the habit saves us a good deal of trouble, where women who are criminals are concerned. Sometimes the photographs are a little old, but they do very well."[4]

As the collection became even larger, the practice of keeping the photographs more or less on display had to be abandoned. In the first part of 1889, a cabinet was purchased from a firm which specialized in such things. It stood on the floor and measured eight feet high by four feet wide. It had a capacity of 2,000 photographs.[5]

There seems to have been no limit to the criminals available for photography.

Deer Drinking.
(DEER, N° 33)

COPYRIGHT, 1894, BY A.G. WALLIHAN.

Wildlife photograph of mule deer by A. G. Wallihan, 1894   **SHSC**

Another one of the many things which were being photographed for the first time with the newly popular dry plate during the late 1880's was big game. From the earliest photographers onward, attempts had been made to capture animals in their natural habitat. In 1853, Carvalho had made daguerreotypes of buffalo on the eastern plains, but these were only of herds grazing quietly in the far distance. The long exposures necessary precluded photographing anything which was not perfectly still—or at least so far away that movement was minimized.

Because of the increasing speeds of emulsion available to the would-be photographers of wild game in the late 1880's, several people entered the field at this time. The earliest photographer of big game in Colorado may well have been Frederick H. Chapin. Chapin was a writer and mountaineer, the author of several books on Colorado mountaineering. He spent several summers in Colorado measuring snowfields. During his first year of experimenting with wildlife photography, he wrote:

. . . For the work on snow a camera was requisite, and this was a sufficient burden, without lugging a rifle; but I was always on the alert to capture big game with the former instrument, and once on the terminal moraine of Hallett Glacier I photographed a grizzly. On Ypsilon Peak we met with five cinnamon bears in one day. One of them approached very near to me as I carried my camera over the boulders, but he was moving at a lively gait on ledges above my position, and would not pose for me.

Later, however, farther away from the ranches, I met with rarer game, and found opportunity to study it carefully. This was big-horn or Rocky Mountain sheep, a beautiful creature that has disappeared from the foot-hills and valleys and is to be found only on the wild mountain tops. Even by early travellers this animal is described as very shy and difficult of approach. . . .

183

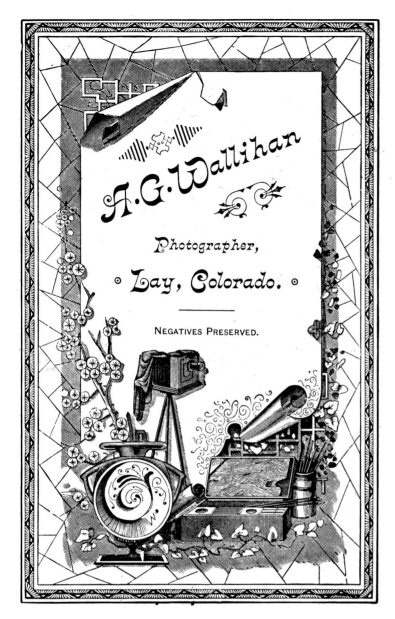

Advertisement on reverse side of view card.

In July, 1887, I had a chance meeting with big horn. . . . I was making the ascent of the gradual slopes of Table Mountain, over the top of which lies the only direct pass between Estes Park and Middle Park; for the wooded slope on this mountain marks the only break in the solid rock-wall which extends from Long's Peak to Willow Cañon. Our route was along the brink of a mighty gorge, 2,000 feet deep. Icy lakes lay in the bottom of the cañon, from which the eye followed up the ravine, over rushing cascades, dazzling snow, and ancient moraines, to a large ice-field which hangs from the mountain-top like a true glacier. From over the ice-field the tapering cone of Mount Hallet looks down upon it. From the opposite side of the gorge a vertical wall rises to a height of 1,200 feet . . .

While threading our way among the boulders, we were keeping very quiet, and were on the look-out for ptarmigan, when we came upon the big-horn quietly browsing upon the scant tufts of grass only a few hundred feet distant on our right. Our leader told us to duck, and said in an undertone to me, "Follow me with your camera." I did so. Dropping our packs we all advanced, almost crawling along, and soon saw the big-horn again, though they had not observed us. The wind was blowing a gale in our faces, so they had no scent of us. Luckily my instrument was focussed. I pointed the lens at the animals and exposed one plate, although they were not as near to us as when we first saw them. They now discovered us, and after a glance in our direction, trotted off over the slope to the brow of the hill. It was remarkable how easily they moved over rocks and boulders among which we could hardly find a way. Imagine our surprise when they turned and walked a little way toward us again. I asked my friends to return to the packs for more plates, and while they were gone I focussed more carefully on the still distant animals, as they stared at me, their curiosity overcoming their fear. My companions now brought up the relay of fresh plates, and returned behind some ledges farther off. At this moment, as I remained there alone by the camera, the ram stood up on his hind legs, and struck out with his fore feet as if inviting combat; then the three stood looking at me. We were in one of the wildest spots on the mountains; a seemingly endless field of ledge and boulder all around, snow mountains and rocky peaks only in the panorama; all signs of valley or glen, tree or river far below. I had a moment to reflect on what I was beholding, and carefully adjusting the glass again on these rare creatures, closely watched them.

Our leader crawled up to my side, and as the quarry showed signs of alarm I attempted to take another picture, but I was now so excited that I took a slide out of one plate-holder before putting the cap on, and that ruined piece of glass now lies among the rocks to amuse the conies [pikas] and ptarmigan; while the slide which I had placed on the camera was whirled far away by the strong wind. Even so experienced a hunter as my companion lost his head as the big-horn were trotting away, and exclaimed: "Take them quick!" . . . Then as they stopped once more and looked at us, he called himself bad names, saying: "I might have known they would stop again, and that there was no need of haste." But lo! what did those sheep do but turn around and walk deliberately toward us, until they were within about a hundred feet. We were fairly trembling with excitement, and I first took off the cap without pulling the slide. When I made this blunder, they were all facing us, standing on granite pedestals a little elevated above the general level, and in line with the broad snow-field on the cliffs back of them, which showed them in relief with startling clearness. . . . The next moment I succeeded in capturing them . . . and then the animals decided to trot off, and we saw them no more.

Portrait of an Elk.

Photographed from life by A. G. Wallihan.

Classic wildlife photograph of a Rocky Mountain elk (wapiti) by A. G. Wallihan, 1895.   SHSC

Hunters talk of the excitement which a novice experiences when he shoots at his first buck, but I could have shot those three big-horn without being one-half as nervous as when trying to photograph them.

Of the five plates which I used in trying to capture the big-horn on glass, three proved worthless, besides the light-struck one already referred to, and it was indeed exceptional good fortune that I was enabled to secure even one picture of these very shy animals. When one reflects that hunters are obliged to use every precaution when approaching their haunts, and sometimes are obliged to lie concealed for hours, or to crawl on the edge of dizzy precipices in order to obtain a distant shot, he will appreciate the

value of what we saw and took away with us.

The photograph of the big-horn naturally occupies the place of honor among a great many pictures which I took in the Rockies, most of which were secured from very high elevations. The reader will perhaps pardon a little boasting when he realizes that such luck has probably never befallen a mountaineering photographer before.[6]

The man who is often given credit for being the first to take pictures of wild game, and certainly the most famous of Colorado wildlife photographers, is Allan G. Wallihan. He started work later than Chapin, but did considerably more picture taking and became so conspicuous that he has long been regarded as Colorado's pioneer nature photographer. He worked with his wife, out of their home in Lay, Colorado.

In 1894, Wallihan's photographs were published in book form, with an introduction by a member of the United States Civil Service Commission, Theodore Roosevelt. Roosevelt, an ardent sportsman, had been impressed by the photographs of game and had been induced to contribute an introduction to the book, part of which is printed below:

> It has never been my good fortune to see as interesting a collection of game pictures as those that have been taken by Mr. and Mrs. Wallihan . . .[7]

When the second book of Wallihan photographs was being prepared in 1901, President Theodore Roosevelt again wrote the introduction:

> It is a pleasure to write an introduction to Mr. Wallihan's really noteworthy book, for his photographs of wild game possess such peculiar value that all lovers, whether of hunting or of natural history, should be glad to see them preserved in permanent form. The art and practice of photographing wild animals in their native haunts has made great progress in recent years. It is itself a branch of sport, and hunting with the camera has many points of superiority when compared to hunting with the rifle. But, even under favorable conditions, very few men have the skill, the patience, the woodcraft and plainscraft which enabled Mr. Wallihan to accomplish so much; and, moreover, the conditions as regards most of our big game animals are continually changing for the worse. The difficulties of getting really good and characteristic photographs are such as to be practically insuperable where game is very scarce and very shy, and throughout most of the United States, game is steadily growing scarcer and shyer. Photographs in a game preserve, no matter how large this preserve, are, of course, not quite the same thing.
> Mr. Wallihan's hunting was in northwestern Colorado and western Wyoming—regions where I have often followed the game he describes . . .
> Mr. Wallihan is not only a good photographer, but a lover of nature and of the wildlife of the wilderness. His pictures and his descriptions are good in themselves as records of a fascinating form of life which is passing away. . . .
> Theodore Roosevelt
> Dated: Sagamore Hill, Oyster Bay, New York, May 31, 1901[8]

Wallihan got started in photography almost by accident. He was postmaster of Lay, Colorado, in 1888 and had enough spare time to do considerable hunting. As he recalled many years later:

The blacktail or "mule" deer of the western United States in this region—northwestern Colorado—summer in the high mountains and, in October and November of each year, slowly return to the lowlands to the westward to avoid the deep snows of the high mountains in winter time, returning again in April and May to the high mountains, where feed and cover are better for them. Prior to 1900, there were thousands upon thousands of them here and in this migration they followed well-beaten trails or paths across country. They traveled day and night, and on one of the largest of these trails near our home my wife was seated on the ground with rifle on her lap for a band to come along, hoping to get a buck for our winter's meat. I was on a hill nearby, on another trail, to give her a chance to get her buck if she could without in any way interfering with her chance. We had lunches in our pockets and about noontime she ate her lunch and sat watching some ants carrying away the crumbs that were dropped. Hearing a slight noise, she looked up and found herself surrounded with a band of about 100 deer of all sizes and ages. They were so close that she held out her hand to them to come nearer. After gazing her fill at the pretty creatures so close, she thought of her rifle and, when she began to raise it, they all ran off. When they were about 100 yards away, she fired at one who, like Lot's wife, "looked back," and killed it.

When I came down to her to dress the deer, she said, "If I had a camera then, I could have gotten a wonderful picture of them so close. I am going to get a camera and we will get some pictures of them." From that time on, for more than a year, she dreamed of a camera and photographing the deer and possibly other game. The following summer there came two young men—missionaries—on their summer vacation through the mountain country, and one of them had a camera. She soon bargained with him for it, paying partly, I remember, in buckskin gloves of her own make, from buckskin I tanned.

Then she set me to learning the loading of the camera with dry plates—which had been in use but a short time, the focusing, and exposing, and then I had to learn the chemical part of mixing developers, fixing baths, washing and drying the plates and then the printing of "blue print" proofs from them and finally printing out on regular photographic papers and mounting the finished prints on cards. This was a necessity as we were in the wilderness far from any photographer, and the handy "roll film" of later years was as yet unknown. I had been many years on the frontier and had become a very good shot and hunter, and I found that what I considered was a very close distance for a rifle shot was too far for a "camera shot" so I had to exercise all my skill to get closer and closer to them until I learned that a deer cannot tell you from a stump or rock. He will see the slightest motion, or hear the smallest noise very

In the Snow.
(COUGAR, Nº 3)

COPYRIGHT 1895 BY A.G. WALLIHAN.

Wildlife photograph of a treed cougar (mountain lion) by the A. G. Wallihans, 1895. SHSC

quickly, and if the wind happens to blow to him from you he stampeded with all his might when he gets scent of you. Many a time I have had them pass within 10 to 20 feet without knowing I was more than a rock by the wayside.

The first camera was a very crude one. The bed was screwed to the tripod and then a screw released the bellows, and it was pulled out by hand to the focussing point, and moved back and forth until the proper focus was obtained, and the screw tightened to hold it in place. It was very clumsy and slow. Fortunately, it was small and not so heavy, and was soon discarded. It was 4-1/4 x 6-1/2. The next one was 5 x 8 and was much better, with an 18-inch extension of bellows, which gave the use of the rear half of Gundlach 5 x 8 lens, which made the images larger and is a very sharp, clear lens. With this, much of the work was done. Finally an 8 x 10 Rochester Optical Company camera was obtained and was used for most

of the last year's work. This was much heavier, especially with the heavy glass plates.

In October, 1888, I began my attempts to get close enough to the shy deer to get photographs of them. The large trail which passed about two miles from my home, runs crosswise of the ridges and valleys where I would select a point behind a sage bush and set the camera on its tripod, and with lens focused on some spot on the trail which was thought would make a good view, await the coming of the deer. As they scattered over about one-half mile of a strip, it was uncertain whether they would come on the trail selected or go on one just out of reach on one side or the other. A band would come along on my trail to within 100 yards, then they would straggle across to another trail and I could not move over to get them. Perhaps another band would come in five minutes or it might be two or three hours before there would be another possible chance. Then the wind might shift and they would

187

get my scent and another opportunity would vanish. Then would come a band right up to the point of focus, and as I had no shutter to begin with, I had to make a time exposure by taking the cap from the lens and replacing it as quickly as possible. Then the slide would be put into the plateholder and the plate on the reverse side made ready for another exposure.

Then at night would come the task of developing the plates exposed during the day, in a room made dark by shutting out all light at windows and cracks around doors or other places and developing them by the light of a ruby lamp, and our hearts would beat with nearly as much excitement as we watched the image develop on the film on the plate, as we experienced in taking it in the field. Perhaps it would be a good negative, or at first, it was likely that some of the subjects moved, or it was under or over-exposed. The main fault at first was that the deer were too far from the camera, so it was gradually moved up closer and closer to the spot on the trail where they were wanted.

By studying the lens-makers' and camera-makers' catalogue, it was learned that the longer focus the lens was, the larger the image on the plate, and a camera was necessary that had a greater opening length, so a better lens and camera were obtained in 1889, and better results were had and at later dates other lenses and cameras were secured and two Bausch & Lomb fast shutters were fitted to the better lenses, and faster exposures could be made and snap shots when the light was right. Plates and films were not so ultra fast as they now are, so it was necessary to judge the light pretty closely. The two closest and best exposures ever made were both lost—one by light getting to the plate, and the other by the shutter being set wrong and an over-exposure made. In this latter one, the camera was set up on the front side of a small cedar tree and I stood behind the camera so that watch could be made of the trail in the distance. A large band of 50 to 75 came up within 60 yards on the trail I was on and then straggled off to another trail on my left. In a short time, a smaller band came slowly up to the same point and stood around, seemingly enjoying their first taste of the cedar trees since the springtime migration in the other direction. A still larger band

came up on the trail to my right with much bleating of fawns. Presently they scented me and stampeded with much snorting. The band in front looked over their way, but paid no further attention, and finally came right up front and a buck and doe walked up within 10 feet and stood and peered at the object in front of them, and as I gently released the shutter, I congratulated myself on what a wonderful picture it would be. The deer, after looking at the camera a couple of minutes, passed on by me and the rest followed, paying no attention to the camera and myself as they went by. When they were all gone, I straightened up, and on fixing the camera for the next exposure, I found I had set the shutter wrong.

. . . My photographs were all taken from live wild game, as wild as game can be, not in any preserves and further I or my wife were with the cameras and made the exposures at all times. There were no set cameras for the game to touch off the shutters by breaking a thread, nor were they baited with delicacies at any time, but they were taken by sheer skill and persistence, under all kinds of hardship, freezing cold in winter, and the hottest suns of summer days. Hard riding on a sure-footed pony after the hounds after cougars, through cedars, over hills and mountains . . . fording rushing mountain streams and rivers, one time being swept off a ford into swimming water, the horse I was riding never having been in swimming water, he knew nothing of swimming and sank until the water was up around my waist, when his hind feet touched bottom and he came up to the top, only to sink a second time and bounce up again, and that time he began to swim and took me out. I was on him bareback and with only a rope around his neck, so I could not guide him. Another horse fell with me and lit on top of me, which crippled me for a week or more, and this was a long ways in the mountain wilderness of Wyoming. After mountain sheep in Wyoming the work was especially hard, as they rove on the high ranges in almost inaccessible places, making the work doubly hard.[9]

The pictures that Wallihan took are striking, even by modern standards. It is unlikely that anyone ever again will be so fortunate as to have so much wildlife at his back door, and to record it so beautifully.

Women

VIII

F THE 11 photographers who are known to have been in Colorado in 1860, two were women.[1] This does not conform to the stereotype most people have of the "Wild West" or the position of women in business at the time, but women were a part of the photography business in Colorado even in 1860. The distiction of being the first woman photographer cannot be assigned with any degree of certainty, but the earliest reference to a female photographer came in June of 1860, in the *Rocky Mountain Herald:*

> Ambrotypes—We call attention to the advertisement of Miss Mickel, in this morning's paper. We have examined some of her pictures, and pronounce them good. She is located on Blake street, over Cook and Company's store.[2]

Whether or not Miss Mickel was the first woman to take photographs in Colorado, she was doing business in Denver less than one year after the first gallery had been opened by George Wakely. She advertised her business as the "Ladies Ambrotype Gallery"—specializing in portraits of children. Whether she was an itinerant photographer by design, or business was insuffcient to sustain her, she disappeared from the scene after 1860, and was not heard from again.

Less than three months after the opening of the Ladies Ambrotype Gallery in Denver, the town of Golden had a woman photographer. The *Western Mountaineer* of that community noted under the date of September 13, 1860:

> Ambrotypes—Miss D. Ferris has fitted up rooms over West, Blunt and Company's store where her friends can "secure the shadow ere the substance fades."

Miss Ferris did not last any longer than her counterpart in Denver. Apparently the idea of a woman doing anything constructive in the business world was so revolutionary in 1860 that the solid middle class probably did not patronize such "shocking" establishments. There was quite likely less of this attitude in the West than elsewhere, but even the Western women were surely operating under this additional encumbrance, with which the men had never to contend.

The names of 36 women photographers in Colorado are known between 1860 and 1900.[3] Beyond the names, the location of their galleries, and the dates they were active, little is known about the vast majority. What would induce a woman to become a photographer? For some it was the need to express themselves through some media—in England, Julia Margaret Cameron was rapidly becoming the greatest portaitest of her age. For many, it was a chance to escape dependence and make an independent living. It would be almost 75 years, however, before a woman would be recognized as outstanding in the field of photography in Colorado. Not until Laura Gilpin achieved national acclaim during the 1930's, did women photographers in Colorado receive the recognition they deserved.

The life history of one woman photographer can be briefly outlined as perhaps typical: Lucinda Cumverse married Mike Dougherty, the popular comedian of the Langrishe Company of Players. The marriage was at the home of the father of the bride in Denver, on October 22, 1861. The friends of the groom toasted the couple with exuberant good wishes:

> May your career, Mike, in the connubial cast be as successful as it is and has been in the "art dramatic."[4]

The couple did not enjoy many years of happiness, however, as Mike was apparently fond of drinking to excess.[5] He died in Central City in July

With the advent of wet plates, it became easier to make photographs away from the gallery darkroom. Women in numbers began to show an interest in photography during the decade of the 1890's — as this view shows. **SHSC**

of 1865.[6] For three years Lucinda remained a widow. It is not known how she lived during these years; perhaps she lived with her father in Denver. In October, 1868, she married Robert A. Clark at a ceremony at Black Hawk.[7] Robert was the city marshal of that town. Less than one year after their marriage, another tragedy occurred. Two brothers named Cramer had passed through Central City on July 10, 1869. During the time they were in town, one of the pair assaulted a man, causing painful injuries. One of the pair was under arrest for a short time, but soon escaped. Constable Peter Herbert of Central City asked Marshal Clark to help him overtake the fleeing men. The local press reported:

They pursued until they reached a cabin a short distance beyond Dora's Ranch, which is four miles from here, where they found their wagons standing in the road and their stock feeding. As they approached, the men who were inside shut the door. Herbert and Clark dismounted and tied their horses to one of the wagons. Herbert went up and rapped. The door was opened, and Herbert stepped far enough forward to prevent its being closed. He found there only the one whom he had in custody, and inquired where the other assailant was. He answered with an oath that it was none of his business. Herbert went upstairs to a loft or garret and found the assailant there. He asked him what he wanted. Herbert told him he must go back, as he had the original warrant for his arrest . . . He answered that he would be down in a moment, and Herbert descended. In the meantime, the other began to abuse Clark, and refuse to be arrested and attacked Clark with a club. Clark told him it was useless to resist as he was an officer and must do his duty. Cramer then said he did not want any shooting. Clark and Herbert answered that there would be none. Just then the one who remained upstairs commenced shooting through the cracks, and the first ball passed through Clark's head, killing him instantly. Herbert returned fire, but the second shot from the house struck Herbert in the right forearm, the bullet passing through the flesh and lodging in the upper arm, from which it has since been cut, but breaking no bones. The one outside started to run away, but the one inside cried out, "O, Sam, I am killed, don't leave me!" Herbert, unable longer to maintain the fight, stooped down and spoke to Clark, but he did not answer or move, and believing him dead, he mounted Clark's horse and came to town as rapidly as possible. . . . Sheriff Grimes and posse went out and found Clark dead and brought his body in. The two brothers fled, the one who did the shooting taking the horse left by Herbert. At last account, neither of them had been caught. Mr. Clark was one of Gilpin county's best citizens, and the best City Marshal Colorado ever had. He was a man of correct habits, honest, industrious, and universally esteemed, and but for his untimely end he would have been a prominent candidate before the Rep. Convention for Sheriff at the coming convention.[8]

Lucinda was once more alone. It is not known how or when she learned the photographic trade, but in November of the following year, this notice appeared in the *Daily Register* of Central City:

Mrs. R. A. Clark has opened photographic rooms at Black Hawk, and solicits the patronage of her friends, believing that she can execute the various styles of pictures usually done in photographic rooms to their entire satisfaction.[9]

Throughout the winter months, Lucinda Clark worked at making the gallery a success. The demand for photographs was not great in Black Hawk and it was hard for men to make a success of the photographic business in the town. For a woman it must have been impossible. In July of 1871, eight months after it opened, Mrs. Clark's gallery was offered for sale "with all its appurtenances, at a low figure."[10] What happened to the photographer is not known; perhaps she married again, perhaps she returned east to whatever town she had come from originally. Since she sold her equipment with the gallery, it is unlikely that she was willing to try her hand at photography again.

Not all women photographers were stationary. In 1876, two ladies, Mrs. Harkullas and Miss Arm-

Mrs. G.N. Barrett, Del Norte photographer, made this print of a church fair in that city during 1876. The original caption reads, "old woman in the shoe." SHSC

NEW TO-DAY.

NEW PHOTOGRAPH ROOMS.

Mrs. R. A. CLARK

Announces to the citizens of Black Hawk and vicinity that she has opened a Photograph gallery, and is prepared to execute pictures in the best style of the art.   n10

strong were traveling around south-central Colorado, photographing as they went. They set up a temporary gallery in Las Animas and advertised in the local paper that they would remain at that location for about three weeks.[11] As business was rather slow in the photography line as a rule, the ladies also mentioned in their advertisement that they would give a "magic art entertainment" on Thursday evening. This, no doubt, helped to augment their income, as entertainment was probably more sought after than photographs. Mrs. Harkullas' name appears in the state business directory for that year as being located at Trinidad, where she remained for some time. After 1881, she disappeared from the record.

The difficulties faced by women photographers traveling around the state during the period before

One of the few prints known from a woman photographer in Colorado during the Nineteenth Century, this view of the first law office in Creede, Colorado, was made by Mrs. H. D. Newton from Salida. SHSC

railroad travel became common between most cities is illustrated by a trip made in 1874 by Mrs. G. H. Masters, a Fort Collins photographer. Mrs. Masters was from Denver, but decided to relocate in Fort Collins when she heard that the telegraph line was to be extended to that place. She went to Fort Collins to settle some matters in connection with a brick building she was having built there.

Jennie Aultman made her living as a retoucher and receptionist before she married Trinidad photographer O. E. Aultman. After her marriage, her photographic activities were largely limited to helping out at the studio occasionally and taking snap-shots of her family. Here, her husband has photographed her in the garden of the Aultman home in Trinidad as she was photographing her son, Glenn. SHSC

This building was to be used as a photographic gallery and a telegraph office, as she was expert in both fields. After completing her business in Fort Collins, Mrs. Masters prepared for the trip to Denver. As reported in the *Rocky Mountain News*:

In company with a gentleman of this place, the lady started on Friday for Greeley, on her way to Denver. Their conveyance was a single horse and buggy, the horse being tinctured with a runaway disposition; a smashup occurred before they were out of town. Mrs. Masters was thrown from the carriage, receiving severe bruises, but no dangerous wounds. The driver was dumped in a pile of lumber and considerably scratched, while the buggy went to pot with a broken shaft and other damages. The horse was corralled between some buildings in a lumber yard. The sad fruits of this accident were two buckets of eggs that were

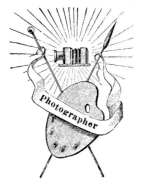

MRS. G. N. BARRETT,

Photographer

Corner Sixth and Columbia Avenue.

DEL NORTE, COL.

smashed in a jiffy. Strange to say, the same party, after recovering for a time, undertook a second expedition with the broken and bruised members of the same outfit, and when five or six miles on their way, the freak was repeated with far more serious results. The lady was severely injured, and the gentleman received several cuts about the head and a catalogue of bruises that will last him for many days. Mrs. Masters is now undergoing careful medical treatment at the Greeley house, with convalescent symptoms, and the horse is in the hands of a skillful veterinary surgeon. [12]

Whether or not Mrs. Masters fully recovered from her carriage accident is not known, but she did not remain in business at Fort Collins after 1874. Nothing more is known about her. She is like so many of the other women: one newspaper article, one advertisement, or one mention in a city directory and they disappear without a trace.

With so little information, it is impossible to know what impact the women photographers had. Judging from the handful of their prints which have survived, some of them were second to none in their profession.

Mrs. H.D. Newton, Salida photographer, traveled to Crestone at the turn of the century to record this view of the main (and only) street.   Q-BAR

The Amazon Guards — women's auxiliary of the Grand Valley Guards, Grand Junction — which were organized to protect the valley from Indian attack.　　SHSC

Mrs. Clara Brown, leader in Colorado's black society during the 1870's and 80's, was known for her helping hand to all those she met. She lived for a time in several mining communities before settling in Denver. She died In 1885, in her mid-80's.　　SHSC

Max Platz
Studio

88 NORTH CLARK ST.
CHICAGO.

Dr. Florence Sabin, outstanding woman in the field of
medical research, was selected as Colorado's woman
of the century for her contribution to health care in the
state. Her statue was placed in the rotunda of the U.S.
Capitol, Washington, D.C., by the grateful State of
Colorado.   SHSC

Mother Pancietis Bonfils is shown here in the Lorentine
veil worn when she was an administrator at Loretto
Heights College in Denver. Photographed about 1885 by
an unknown photographer.   SHSC

197

Sincerely Mrs John Elitch Jr

Jones & Lehman,   1615 Arapahoe St., Denver.

The Lady of the Gardens, Mary Elitch Long, directed the growth and expansion of Elitch Zoological Gardens in Denver for many years following her husband's death. It was at a select private *soiree* in her theater in the gardens that motion pictures were first projected in Colorado.   SHSC

Hook Photo.

Bound for Pikes Peak.   429

646. LEADVILLE, FROM CAPITOL HILL.

200

In an attempt to show how gas was simple to use, safe and clean for heating, the Denver Union Gas Works commissioned H. H. Buckwalter to make a series of photographs of domestic scenes, made more comfortable by the use of gas. In this view, a child and her companion were whiling away the hours in a home heated by a new gas space heater.   SHSC

Opposite, above: A proper little girl, riding side saddle on her pet burro in Leadville, was recorded by William H. Jackson about 1883. At this time, the Catholic Church was under construction and its tall steeple had not yet been erected. Reproduced from a cabinet-size print.   Q-BAR

Opposite, below: A quiet stroll — somewhere in the Rockies — where mother and baby posed during the 1880's for some long-forgotten photographer.   SHSC

Opposite: During the 1880's and 1890's, almost everyone was photographed at least three times in their lives: once when they were christened, once when they were married and once — if they lived long enough — during their silver wedding anniversary. Here a bride was posing for her wedding portrait at the Bellsmith studio in Denver, about 1894.   SHSC

Among the most famous and individualistic women in Colorado's history is Margaret Brown, *nee* Tobin, the one-and-only Molly Brown. Shown here at right, the ''unsinkable'' Molly Brown made her mark early on Colorado and remained virtually a landmark for many years. (She obtained her title as the unsinkable Molly Brown after surviving the sinking of the ocean liner, *Titanic.*) Photographed at the turn of the century with a companion who is unknown.   SHSC

A Victorian family group in Denver was photographed
by Mrs. Thomas Hood in 1888.   SHSC

In the view above, Irene Jerome Hood
— probably the most outstanding
woman photographer of the Nineteenth Century — is shown with her
"Kodak." On the page opposite, we
see an interesting self portrait. Both
views were taken about 1890.   SHSC

Opposite, above: Young upper-class Victorian girls in the 1880's posed before their home for the camera of Irene Jerome Hood. SHSC

Opposite, below: "The Girls," photographed in the late 1880's by Irene Jerome Hood. SHSC

In the days before wash-and-wear fabrics, keeping children's clothing in proper order must have been a difficult job. One suspects, however, that this outfit was more of a problem for the maid than for the mother. From a print by Mrs. Thomas Hood, about 1890. SHSC

When the first "Kodak" arrived on the scene, the idea of a fixed focus, fixed aperture camera with only one shutter speed was unproven. The lenses used had such fall-off at the corners that the prints were masked round to eliminate the bad corners. Here is an early "Kodak" print, made by an amateur, Mrs. Thomas Hood. SHSC

Opposite, top: During the early 1880's, women of fashion aspired to the "Langtry Look" — wearing their hair and even being photographed prone like the famous beauty, Lily Langtry. SHSC

Opposite, below: This photograph of a burro pack train hauling ore from the "Bachelor" mine near Creede was taken on July 24, 1895, by a photographer from Salida, Mrs. H. D. Newton. SHSC

Maggie Cooney, woman photographer, is shown here at her stove — as photographed by another woman photographer, Irene Jerome Hood, in the early 1890's. SHSC

By the 1890's, women were becoming more emancipated. Here, two "modern women" of the era tucked up their skirts to wade into Grand Lake — in this photograph by L. P. Bass. SHSC

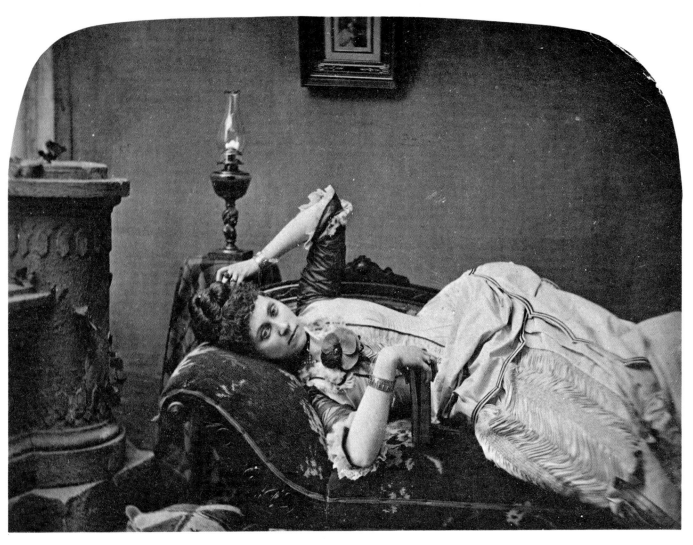

209

"Polly Pry" — Mrs. Lionel Ross Anthony — Colorado's celebrated journalist and socialite, is shown on this page in a stately pose — and in a more "relaxed" posture on the page opposite, riding in a sling over the rim of a canyon during the construction of Cheesman Dam. She was an indefatigable champion not only of women, but of all down-trodden people.   SHSC

Portraits of famous — and infamous — persons were mass produced
to sell like postcards. This print of the second Mrs. Horace Tabor —
better known as "Baby Doe" — was widely circulated by the Rine-
hardt studios in Denver shortly after she gained notoriety because of
the divorce and remarriage of H. A. W. Tabor, one of the great "silver
kings" of Leadville.   SHSC

A shocking example of Victorian "pornography," this photograph
belonged to Baby Doe Tabor.   Q-BAR

The three Becker sisters are shown here on the Rio Grande Ranch in the San Luis Valley, where they were born. With the shortage of labor during this period, some women became ranch-hands of necessity. O. T. Davis made this photograph in 1894.   SHSC

Overleaf, above: As national magazines carried on weighty discussions pro and con on women "baseballists," the *Boston Bloomers* team toured the country, playing exhibitions as they went. The knee-length costumes of the players brought many "lascivious men" to the games, according to opponents of women playing this "manly" game.   SHSC

Overleaf, below: A group of young women in the latest ski fashions took to the slopes at Breckenridge, 1889.   SHSC

On page 217: Mrs. O. A. Aultman is portrayed here as she was photographed in the Trinidad studio of her husband and his brother, O. E. Aultman, about 1890-'95. The glass plate used to make this portrait measures 18 x 21 inches. Mammoth portraits like this one were never common because of the cost of the plates and the printing paper, coupled with the handling problems, drove the cost beyond the means of most photographic patrons.   SHSC

216

The Reverend Nona Brooks, founder and pastor of the Divine Science Church in Denver, was a pioneer in the ministry for women in the state. Her religious and charitable work at the turn of the century earned her a prominent place in the community.   SHSC

By the 1890's, women had learned they could begin to free themselves from the narrow limits they had known previously. Here, two women try their hand at shooting waterfowl in this "Kodak" print made about 1900.   SHSC

By the beginning of the Twentieth Century, the years of Indian wars were beginning to be forgotten, and friendships were developing among the more enlightened Westerners and Indians. Here, an unidentified white woman posed with a group of her acquaintances — probably from the Ute tribe. Photographed for H. H. Tammen, about 1900. SHSC

Opposite: Ola Aftinson Garrison began her photographic career as a retoucher and colorist shortly after the turn of the century. She worked for Frank Dean in his gallery in Grand Junction before going to De Beque in 1910 to establish her own gallery. After the collapse of the oil boom at that place a few years later, she moved to Rifle where she worked for Fred Garrison at his gallery. Later, Ola married Mr. Garrison — and she often claimed afterward that he married her to avoid paying her a salary! SHSC

In the view above, art class was in session when this photograph was taken in Wolfe Hall at Thirteenth and Clarkson, Denver, in 1889. The photographer is unknown.   SHSC

The Columbine Woman's Band flourished in Grand Junction during the 1890's. Here, a member of that group posed before the camera of Grand Junction photographer Frank Dean.

Dr. Susan Anderson, Fraser physician for nearly half a century, was forced to leave Denver because of prejudice against her sex.   SHSC

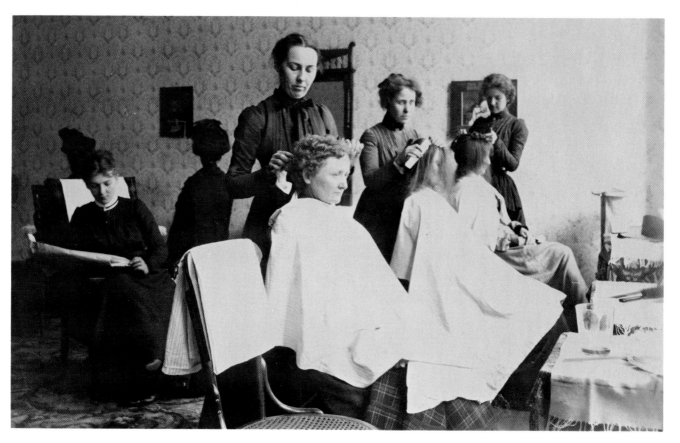

Another of Buckwalter's experiments with fast plates indoors was this view of a turn of the century beauty salon in Denver.   SHSC

In the early 1890's, Aspen was a city overrun by burros. As they became lame or overworked, they were turned loose to graze and recuperate on their own. Many of the local children would entice these animals with carrots or clover and semi-domesticate them for playmates and transportation. Photographed in 1889 by the traveling photographer, James M. Davis, from New York. SHSC

Overleaf, above: In the days when it was still fashionable to lampoon blacks, amateur dramatic companies often included a blackface routine for comic relief. Here, the Nevadaville Dramatic Society is seen in a pose from one of their productions for the 1893 season. Photographed by V. M. Kepler, Central City's woman photographer. Q-BAR

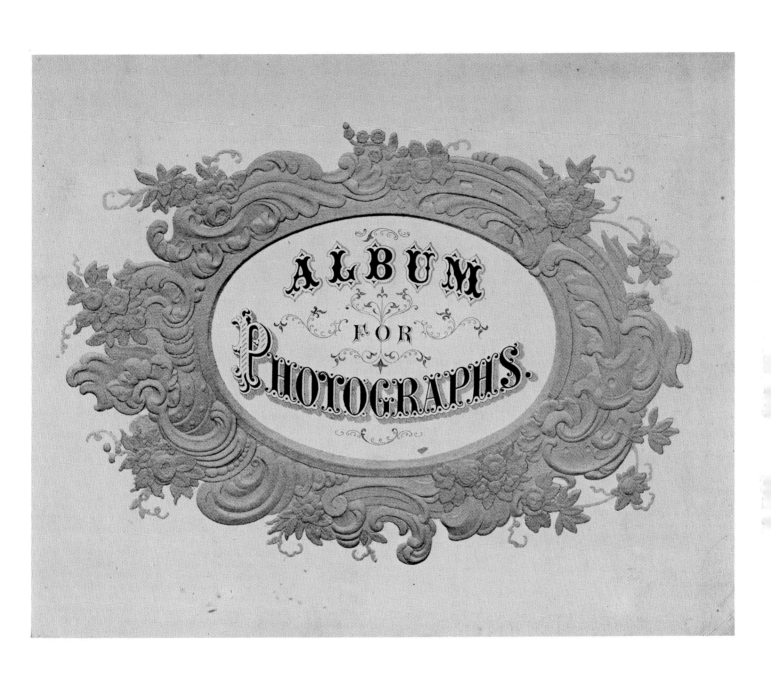

Album of the 1880's

The summer of 1880 saw the inauguration of passenger service on the narrow-gauge Denver, Utah & Pacific. Here, the first DU&P was about to pull out of Longmont — probably enroute to Denver (on what now is Burlington Northern trackage). The barefoot boys were typical of those youngsters of the period who "hawked" their wares to railroad passengers.   Q-BAR

What appears to be an Atchison, Topeka & Santa Fe mixed train is shown here as it paused at the Trinidad depot, about 1880. A Trinidad Transfer Company omnibus had just pulled up to the depot platform. From here, the AT&SF climbs famous Raton Pass — past "Uncle Dick" Wootton's ranch and toll gate. Wooton had built a toll road over the pass in 1865, on the mountain Branch of the Santa Fe Trail. He sold his rights to the AT&SF in 1878.   Q-BAR

An 1881 view of the yacht, *"Dauntless,"* on lower Twin Lake — by Ben Gurnsey.   Q-BAR

By 1881, Alma was beginning to draw attention to itself in mining circles. Promising deposits were discovered, and soon major mining operations were underway. This stereo card was photographed along the Arkansas River by T. C. Miller during his short stay in Colorado from 1881 to 1886.   Q-BAR

Opposite: In the days when photographic plates would not record detail in certain shades of light, photographers often resorted to supplying missing detail by hand on the glass. In this view produced during the 1880's, the Brisbois studio of Leadville had added considerably to this mammoth ice mound.   SHSC

BRISBOIS PHOT. Leadville.

231

Tintypes were popular as cheap photographs for 20 years following the Civil War. Generally, these images were reversed from right to left. Their popularity was a result of their relatively low cost, and this was in spite of the fact that they contained few grey tones. Almost no views were taken on this type of print and only portraits are common. These two prints are typical of the quality and style of tintypes of the 1880's. Q-BAR

Opposite, above: The renowned La Veta Hotel in Gunnison, the most prestigious building ever built in that city, is portrayed as it looked in the early 1880's. When the narrow-gauge railroad arrived from the east slope, the La Veta was provided with "next-door service" — and passengers could literally step from the coaches onto the porch of the hotel! Photographed by Mellen on an 11 x 14-inch glass plate.   SHSC

Gunnison was jealous of its commercial pre-eminence on the western slope during the early years of the 1880's. Here, George Mellen, a photographer from that city, lampooned the newly staked-out town of "Grand Junction" by showing this view of the "new town," as of September, 1881.   SHSC

By the early 1880's, interiors of buildings were becoming more popular subjects to photograph. This stereo view by Luke & Wheeler shows a store in Leadville. Cards like this were often sold as souvenirs by Colorado merchants.   Q-BAR

Overleaf: Lake City, the mining camp which became the county seat of Hinsdale County, is shown in this view as it appeared in 1882 — during its palmier days. The photographer is unknown.   SHSC

By the 1880's photographs of sports and political personalities were being distributed nationally. This print of the noted pugilist, Charles Norton, was distributed through the *Police Gazette* and hung in bars across Colorado during the mid-1880's.　　　SHSC

Jack Dempsey, famed Colorado pugilist, was nationally known during the 1880's. Shown here in a print circulated by the *National Police Gazette,* Dempsey was later eclipsed by another Colorado boxer of the same name.　　　SHSC

Brisbois *Leadville,*

Although not as spectacular as the view business, the portrait trade was the staple of most photographers in Colorado during the Nineteenth Century. Intent on capturing more than just simple head-and-shoulders shots, many photographers turned out charming and interesting portraits for their clients. Here, two long-forgotten Victorian ladies were posing in the Brisbois studio in Leadville during the 1880's.   SHSC

A studio view of an award-winning skater was taken in the Brisbois studio, Leadville, during the 1880's. The ice and the snowy backdrop are studio props. SHSC

237

Opposite top: Denver's National Mining and Industrial Exposition hall was built as a showplace for the mining and industrial wealth of the state. Built on a Victorian rambling style, it is shown here in its prime, in the 1880's.   Q-BAR

Opposite, below: The "Monarch Pass, Gunnison & Dolores Railroad" offices in Arboursville, Colorado, represented one of those projected lines which never got beyond the paper stage — only far enough to have an office. Photographed on a bright, sunny day, C. 1880, by an unknown photographer.   Q-BAR

During the 1883 National Mining and Industrial Exposition, a large number of photographic art contest entries were hung on the balcony overlooking the mineral exhibits.   SHSC

"Rocky Mountain canaries" and their masters lined up for their group portrait in Alma during 1883. Burros were used as pack animals throughout the West for many years, and at times, even photographers made use of these hardy beasts for field trips. Photographed by T. C. Miller.   Q-BAR

National Mining and Industrial Exposition Denver - Colo:- MARTIN. PHOTO

Opposite: The smokestack of a stationary steam engine can be seen in front of this saw mill near the Palmetto mine in the Lake City area. Photographed about 1882 by an unknown photographer on an 11 x 14-inch glass plate. SHSC

Before Colorado's narrow-gauge railways had finished laying their network of tracks across the state, goods and equipment had to be laboriously freighted from the rail lines to the towns and settlements far from the track. Here, Dave Wood's freighting outfit was crossing the Uncompahgre River, near Montrose, on the road to Telluride. Q-BAR

In this view — photographed on the eastern slope of Marshall Pass — we see a Denver &
Rio Grande locomotive on one of the wooden trestles during the construction days in
1882. Otto Mears' toll road can be seen in the foreground, the main route between
Salida, Gunnison and Lake City prior to the coming of the railroad.   Q-BAR

On the turntable at Monarch Colo — Aug 1" 1884   Goodman PHOTO

Chas. Goodman photographed the gallows turntable of the D&RG on the Monarch Branch, west of Salida, in 1884.   Q-BAR

The mining town of Silver Cliff on laundry day, C. 1882 — from a stereo card by Frank Kuykendall. At this time, Silver Cliff was a silver boom town and was one of the largest settlements in Colorado.   Q-BAR

Opposite, top: This view is M. W. Mealey's 1882 photograph of Pueblo's famous hanging tree — a cottonwood that stood in the middle of South Union Street until 1883. Notice the horsecar tracks have been built to avoid the tree. Q-BAR

Opposite, below: A boxing match at Harry Rogers' camp, near Beaver City, C. 1883. Rogers' camp would have been on the "other side of the tracks" if Beaver City had had tracks. Drinking, gambling and fighting seemed to be typical of social life in many of the mining camps. Q-BAR

George A. Crofutt was the man who wrote more guide books about the West than any other person; from 1869 until 1892 he had published more than 1,500,000 copies. He was born in Danbury, Conneticut, on August 13, 1827. Where and when he died remains a mystery. For Coloradans, his most famous guide book was *Crofutt's Grip Sack Guide of Colorado,* first published in 1881. SHSC

Bob Ford, who won fame by shooting the infamous train robber, Jesse James, was in turn shot for his trouble in the saloon at right, in Creede, Colorado. Always eager for a newsy photograph, the man who recorded this view, Charles Goodman, arrived in time to produce this picture of the body being removed in a wagon. Q-BAR

245

HARTMAN'S RANCH.

No. 180. FIRST POST OFFICE IN THE GUNNISON VALLEY. 1876.   FIRST CABIN BUILT 1870.

Mill workers and their families assembled for photographer T. C. Miller, outside the Nester Mill in Alma, about 1883.   Q-BAR

Opposite, above: This rather primitive "skiing event" was photographed by G. Miller of Gunnison City, in Gunnison County, during March of 1883.   SHSC

Opposite, below: Already an historic structure in 1883, when this picture was made, the Hartman Ranch was said to be the first settlement in the Gunnison Valley. George Mellen, who produced this view, noted on the glass-plate negative that it was the first post office in the area, being established in 1876.   SHSC

Overleaf: J. S. Randall's *Georgetown Courier* was photographed by Alex Martin, C. 1884-1888.   SHSC

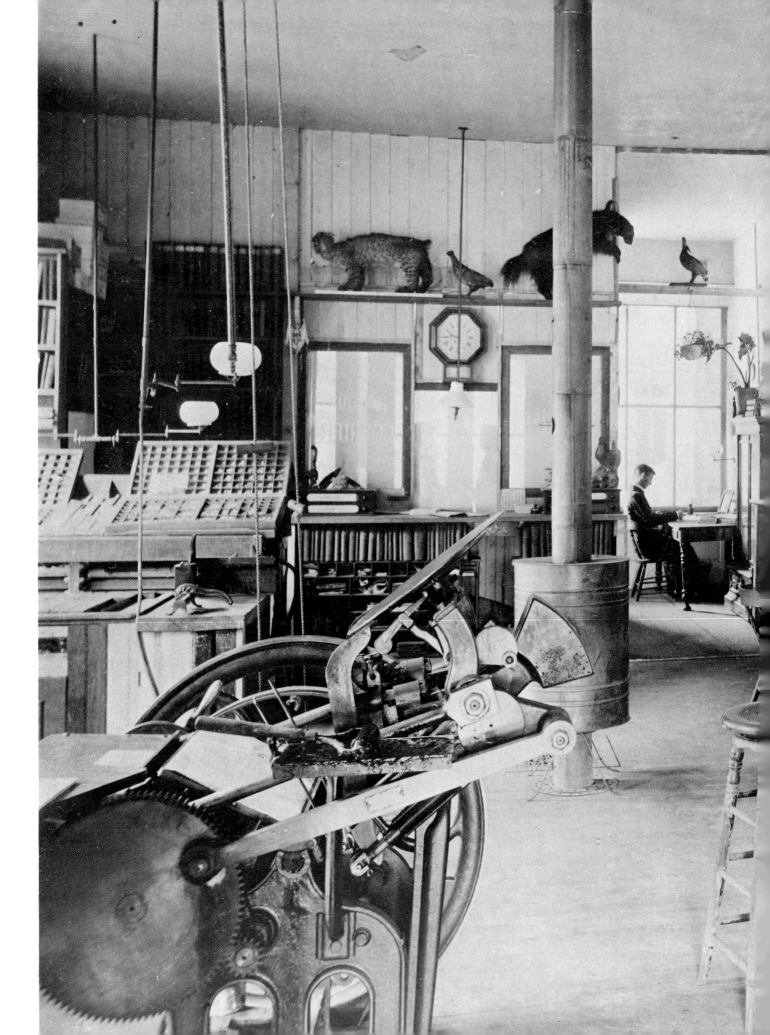

The view above is of a Silverton-bound stagecoach pausing in Ouray during 1884. By this time, stereo cards such as this one (enlarged more than two times) were widely distributed in the East. A notation on the back of this card by Kuykendall & Whitney noted that "Persons wishing duplicates of this picture can obtain it at any time by addressing us and giving us the No. of Negative."

Q-BAR

250

In this view, an unidentified Boulder family posed outside their home during the middle 1880's. Photographed by an itinerant photographer.　　　Q-BAR

E. N. Clements, Leadville photographer, took this view of a mountain family at their log cabin and post office about 1885. The little sign on the cabin reads "Post Office."　　　Q-BAR

H. S. Brodie, jeweler, optician and watchmaker, posed in front of his new store on Larimer Street in Denver, while having this photograph taken by Joseph Collier in 1885. SHSC

In the view below, left, a group of Ute Indians were visiting Denver in 1885 and had their picture taken in Alex Martin's studio. Q-BAR

Opposite, above: This scene, by an unidentified photographer, provides us with a general view of the main street of Blackhawk, C. 1885. The steel trestle near the center of the view carried the Colorado Central narrow-gauge railroad over Gregory Gulch and the street below. Q-BAR

Opposite, below: With the Meeker Massacre fresh in their minds, National Guard units were organized by many western slope towns during the early 1880's. This is the Grand Valley Guards, photographed in 1884 at Grand Junction. SHSC

ROSE & CO., Photographers.

DENVER, COLO.

EVERETT HOOK AND LADDER TEAM, GOLDEN, COLO.

WON FIRST PRIZE AT STATE TOURNAMENT, BOULDER, 1885.

500 Feet, Hook and Ladder, 25 3-5.   Dry Test, 600 Feet, 31 4-5.   800 Feet Speed Race, 32.   600 Feet Speed Race, 23 1-5.

254

Hot Baths 5 Cents — Wanita Hot Springs near Gunnison at its prime in the late 1880's was photographed by the young Gunnison photographer, Frank Dean. Q-BAR

Horace Tabor's toilet and bathtub were considered the last word in plumbing when this scene was photographed. SHSC

Opposite, below: The pride of Red Cliff in 1887 was the town's brass band, shown here in full uniform. The photographer is unknown. SHSC

Charles Goodman photographed the last run of the Ouray to Montrose stagecoach at Montrose in August of 1887.   Q-BAR

Francis & Gritten photographed this interior view of a "flophouse," in Baltimore, Colorado, C. 1886.

The view above shows the interior of the shaft house of the Caribou mine — as photographed by J. Collier in 1886. The Caribou silver mining camp — about six miles above Nederland — was established in 1869 and was quite a profitable operation for many years.   SHSC

Small galleries sprang up in almost every town across Colorado during the early days of settlement. Portraits could be had at prices ranging from less than $1.00 for tintypes in lower-class galleries to over $20.00 each for "Imperial Size" prints.   SHSC

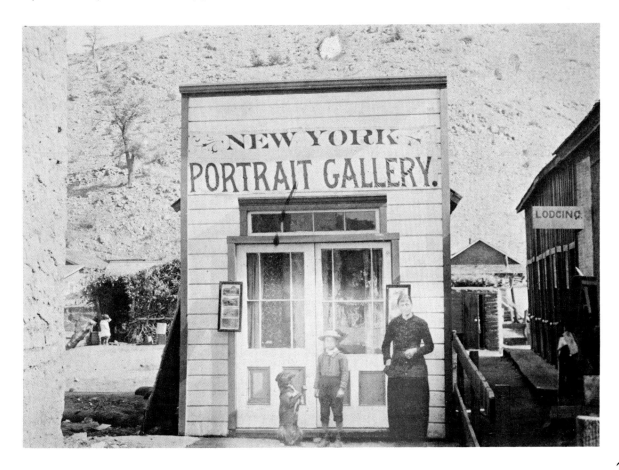

"Fancy Groceries and Provisions" — Birks Cornforth grocery store in Denver was photographed in 1886, the same year that Russell Brothers, view photographers, held their grand opening. SHSC

Birks Cornforth posed in one of his store windows along with his Thanksgiving display — and was most properly photographed by Russell Brothers — in 1886. SHSC

The Tabor Grand Opera House was photographed during a celebration of the Grand Army of the Republic C. 1887. The photo is by Alex Martin.   Q-BAR

Alex Martin photographed one of Denver's horsedrawn streetcars, C. 1885. Apparently this car ran from Union Station out to Colfax Avenue to serve the eastern part of Denver.   Q-BAR

JOHN P. LOWER

10 Blocks Colorado Red Sandstone (100 Tons in all) enroute to Kansas City, Mo., May 29th, 1887, from the Quarries of

THE FORT COLLINS RED STONE CO.

Bellevue, Larimer Co., Colorado.   Address, Box 2730 P. O., Denver.

Boring First Artesian Well, Montrose, Colorado. July. 1886

Throughout the arid western slope of Colorado, water is essential for settlement. This was an early attempt to sink an artesian well at Montrose, Colorado. Photographed in July, 1886, by Charles Goodman. **Q-BAR**

Opposite, above: This view of a Fort Collins Red Stone Company shipment is an example of advertising photography near the turn of the century. **Q-BAR**

Opposite, below: Montrose in 1888 could boast of numerous brick buildings, gas street lights and a "California Laundry," presided over by Yee Wa Lee, who — one suspects — was a member of Colorado's substantial Chinese minority, mostly recruited to build the railroads across the Rockies. **SHSC**

A county fair exhibit of the Reeves & McFann store in Montrose, 1888, was photographed by Charles Goodman.

Opposite, above: Civil War veterans assembled in many towns and cities every Decoration (Memorial) Day for many years to honor the Union's war dead. Here, Charles Goodman recorded a typical Decoration Day parade of long ago — on one of the main streets of Montrose in 1888.

Opposite, below: Company A, 22nd Regiment, of the U.S. Army was photographed at Fort Lewis (near Durango) by A. B. Salsbury in 1885.

Decoration Day, Montrose, Colo. 1888.

C. P. McCary's blacksmith shop in Grand Junction, about 1887. Probably photographed by T. E. Barnhouse.

The first trolley car in Grand Junction, C. 1888, showing "Charley," the motive power, the only horse to fill this distinguished position. He pulled the car until the line was electrified. Frank Catalina, the driver, was a member of Grand Junction's Black community.   SHSC

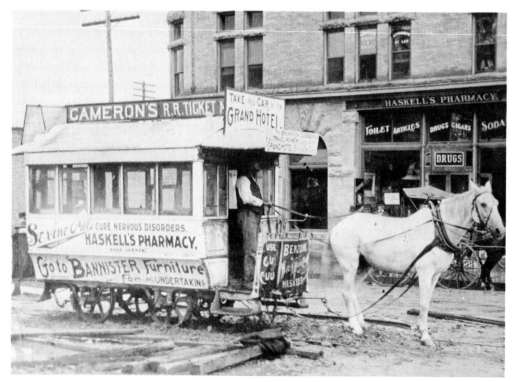

A group of miners were photographed at Montgomery, about 1886. James W. Nutt from Alma was the photographer.
Q-BAR

The perils of mountain travel included everything from bandits to snowslides. Here, an enterprising road crew on the Ouray to Silverton toll road had tunneled under a massive slide, much too big to remove. Charles Goodman, Montrose photographer, captured this unusual scene on July 6, 1888.

SHSC

4th of July in Telluride. Colo. 1887.

The Fourth of July, 1887, in Telluride was complete with a brass band and a hose cart for the race between competing fire departments.　SHSC

Tin cans already were being used in abundance when Alex Martin made this stereo view of miners along the Eagle River in 1888. The strategically placed shovel, ax and picks were to emphasize the stereographic quality of the image when viewed through a stereoscope. This print (at left) was made from a badly cracked glass-plate negative.　SHSC

Overleaf: This picture of the main street in Buena Vista was taken by C. W. Erdlen in 1887. Founded in 1879, at the confluence of Cottonwood Creek and the Arkansas River, Buena Vista has long been a trading center and shipping point for products of local ranches, farms and mines.　Q-BAR

267

The last days of Andrew Green were spent in jail in Denver awaiting his execution. This photograph was made shortly before Green was led from his cell to become the last person publicly executed in Denver, July 27, 1886.   SHSC

The lynching of George R. Witherall at Canon City on December 4, 1888, was recorded for posterity. This lynching occurred after Witherall had murdered Charles R. McCain of Pueblo. He was arrested in Denver, October 30, 1888, returned to Canon City and lynched.   SHSC

270

This view shows the hanging of Jose Otiz on July 16, 1889. Scenes like these of the crowds eagerly awaiting the spectacle led to the end of public executions in Colorado. SHSC

The Main Street business buildings of Como looked like this when George Stephans photographed them in 1885. At that time, Como was an important point on the Denver, South Park & Pacific Railroad. Q-BAR

A perfect day for "Iced Congress" and seltzer or a ginger ale, or, if not up to that, perhaps some "St. Jacobs Oil" would be in order. The drugstore in the

Tedmon House at Fort Collins had almost everything
one wanted. This print was made by the traveling
Denver photographer, David Lamon, about 1887. Q-BAR

2 - Joe Davis
3 - Ben Robinson
4 - Geo. Robinson
5 - Jim Nash
6 - "Kanaki" Joe Felton
7 - Ike Marshall
8 - Jim Belmer
9 - Frank Leslie
10 - John Dunham

11 - Alfred Dunham
12 - Harve Wallace
13 - Sam Todd
15 - Sant Bowen.
16 - Nels Peterson
17 - Bob Nash
19 - Will Belmer
20 - Judd Pierce

21- "Te He" Bill Crozier
22- Jim Mears
23 Billy Randall.
24- Ruf Bloise
25- Al Herndon.
26- Andy Jensen.

This view, entitled "Dinner Scene of Plateau Cow Boys," was photographed in 1887 by J. W. Carpenter of Telluride. SHSC

Garfield looked like this in February of 1888. This community is on the D&RG's branch to Monarch, west of Salida. Photographed by C. H. Clark. SHSC

Aspen, the great silver-mining metropolis of the Roaring Fork region, as it appeared late in the 1880's. This town was once served by two rail lines. SHSC

Even in the 1880's, cameras were taken on fishing trips. This print of a fishing expedition into the Rockies was made by H. M. Taylor, a rather accomplished amateur who used 5 x 9-inch glass plates. No record remains as to what group this was or why the two men in the center are holding pieces of a deer. **SHSC**

The hamlet of Dallas, Colorado, looked like this in 1886. Dallas was situated a short distance from Ridgway in the heart of the spectacular San Juan Mountains. Charles Goodman of Montrose photographed this panorama, which graphically illustrated the broad sweep of the high mountain peaks. **Q-BAR**

Lemonade, Cigars, Milk Shake, Bath, Shave — the Windsor Bath House in Creede was virtually a "shopping center" in 1889. Recorded on glass by E. E. Pascoe.   SHSC

Uncle Dick Wooton's stage stop and ranch near Raton Pass appeared like this, C. 1889. Photographed by Henry Brown, a Santa Fe camera artist.   Q-BAR

Opposite, above: In 1889, Central City had what one could almost call a "metropolitan flavor," with gas lamps, concrete sidewalks and fine brick buildings. Goldman's saloon sold imported fruits, as well as wines and liquors.   SHSC

Opposite, below: Not pasteurized, but fresh daily — Beeman's Dairy wagon brought dairy products to the townspeople of Harmon. This photograph is by an unknown photographer, C. 1889.   SHSC

279

INTERIOR, ROBERTSON & DOLL CARRIAGE CO.'S REPOSITORY.

This interior view was made of the Robertson & Doll Carriage Company's repository (showroom) in Denver, during 1889.
SHSC

Opposite: The Tabor Grand Opera House in Denver was lavish in every detail. Here, an unknown photographer has captured the interior of the barbershop as it appeared in 1889.
SHSC

INTERIOR CITY TICKET OFFICE, DENVER AND RIO GRANDE R. R. COMPANY.

The city ticket office of the Denver & Rio Grande Railroad was photographed in Denver during 1889 by an unknown photographer. SHSC

Opposite: The Colorado Central had this attractive little depot and concession building at the Forks of Clear Creek during the 1880's and '90's. The early morning passenger train had just come down the Central City Branch, on its way to Denver. Photographed by Charles Weitfle. Q-BAR

This dramatic view of Denver, South Park & Pacific engine Number 112 hauling a freight train through the lower reaches of Platte Canyon was sold as a stereo card during the late 1880's by Griffith & Griffith of Philadelphia.   Q-BAR

The mammoth wooden trestle of the Colorado Midland Railway, on the east side of Hagerman Pass, as it looked when photographed in 1889. This is one of the many promotional shots made for the line. The back of this picture was imprinted with the Colorado Midland "herald" (the company emblem) and a pitch for the photographer: "J. L. Clinton, Scenic Photographer, No. 20 Pikes Peak Avenue, Colorado Springs." SHSC

A street scene in Canon City produced this view by Charles Goodman in the late 1880's. Q-BAR

Opposite, above: If you were a young athletic man in Denver in the 1880's, you could join a fire company; or, if you were more modern, get a bicycle and join a wheel club. Here, the members of the Denver Ramblers pose for an informal shot with their wheels.   SHSC

Opposite, below: Outings were a major part of the activities of the wheel clubs in Colorado during the '80's. The Denver Ramblers perhaps were the most prominent organization; one of their outings was to the top of Pikes Peak. Here, members of the Ramblers were caught on an outing to Golden in 1888.   SHSC

Bicycles were very big by the end of the 1880's. Clubs were being formed, magazines which were devoted to cycling appeared and individual champions were gaining reputations among a growing number of fans. Here, E. A. McIntyre, young champion wheelman, poses in 1889 at Sportsman Park, near the Mile High City.   SHSC

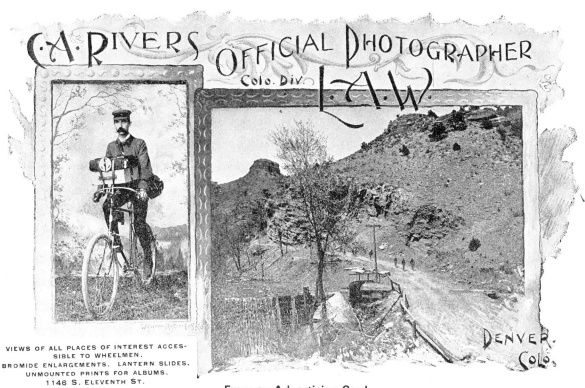

C.A. RIVERS OFFICIAL PHOTOGRAPHER Colo. Div. L.A.W.

DENVER. COLO.

VIEWS OF ALL PLACES OF INTEREST ACCESSIBLE TO WHEELMEN.
BROMIDE ENLARGEMENTS. LANTERN SLIDES.
UNMOUNTED PRINTS FOR ALBUMS.
1146 S. ELEVENTH ST.

From an Advertising Card

The pride of Denver before the turn of the century was the Arapahoe County Courthouse on Court Place in the downtown section of the city. Photographed by Alex Martin about the end of the 1880's.   SHSC

Below: Trinity Church in Greeley was the scene of this photograph. Taken during the 1880's, the occasion probably was the christening of the child in the baby carriage.   SHSC

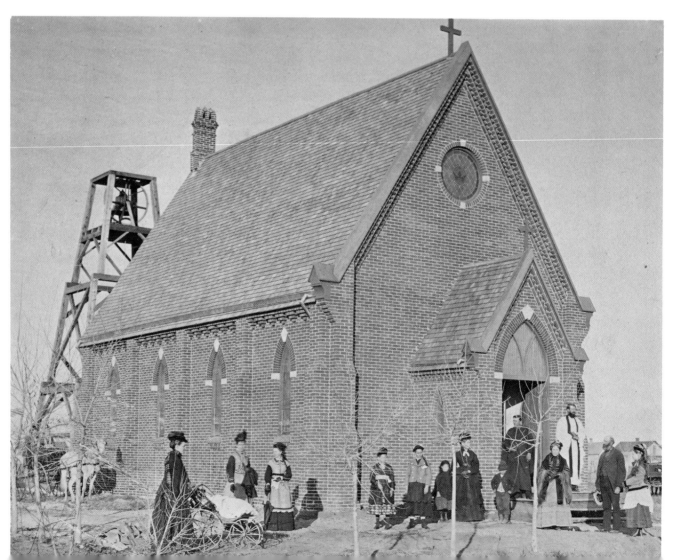

Color, Speed and Motion

IX

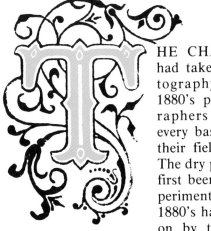

THE CHANGES which had taken place in photography during the 1880's provided photographers with almost every basic ingredient of their field in use today. The dry plates which had first been introduced experimentally during the 1880's had finally caught on by the end of that decade. It was no longer necessary for a photographer to make his own plates in the field and use them quickly before they dried. Ready-made glass plates coated with photosensitive gelatin and packed in lightproof boxes made picture taking comparatively simple. With the ready-made plates also came greatly increased sensitivity, making shorter exposures possible. With this particular improvement came problems, however. It was now imperative that cameras be equipped with shutters. The old method of removing the lens cap and counting the number of seconds for an exposure and then replacing the cap was not adequate for an exposure of less than one second.

During the 1890's, roll film much like the roll film commonly used today, was becoming popular with amateur photographers. With the new-found speed of the film, and freed from the dark tent and chemicals, photographers of the 1890's were in a position to carry the use of the camera to heights undreamed of only a decade earlier.

Harry Buckwalter was one of the most innovative of the Colorado photographers during the 1890's. It seems as though Buckwalter was interested in doing anything which had not been done before. He was photographing lightning bolts near Denver in 1890, when he made a negative of one which struck the ground, killing a man.[1] This picture of lightning, as well as many other photographs he produced, was used as the basis for illustrations which appeared in the *Rocky Mountain News*. Buckwalter has the distinction of being the first newspaper photographer in Colorado. It was not until some time later that the direct reproduction of photographs by the halftone process became common. Instead, the photographs were used to guide the men who cut the engravings. Perhaps in order to justify the use of photography in journalism, Buckwalter engaged in a never-ending search for unusual photographic opportunities. He made a series of photographs of rapid movement with comparatively rapid exposures: one of the Denver Fire Department's steam engines with horses galloping at full speed; a horse-drawn omnibus on Seventeenth Street—anything which was too quick for an artist to capture with a sketch pad. He made several night views as well, including one of the Denver City Hall fire.

One of Buckwalter's most imaginative and daring feats involved an idea he hit upon in August of 1894. Ivy Baldwin, a pioneer in Colorado ballooning, had made a series of flights from Elitch Zoological Gardens in his balloon, "The Spirit of Denver." His ascensions had created wide interest in flying and Buckwalter was just the man to show the public what it was like looking down from a balloon.

On Sunday morning, August 12, Mr. Baldwin and Mr. Buckwalter arrived at the gas company plant near the edge of town, and not far from Elitch Gardens. The balloon was filled with something approaching 50,000 cubic feet of highly flammable gas, manufactured by the gas company. When tests proved that the balloon would not lift even a bag of sand, the two men demanded satisfaction from the company. As the gas company had charged $50.00 for the gas, the two would-be flyers were understandably annoyed.

The gas generator was started again and the

During his career as Colorado's first newspaper photographer, Harry Buckwalter captured many spectacular events on glass-plate negatives. Above is his shot of the Denver City Hall as it burned the night of December 1, 1901.   SHSC

company manufactured more gas which was fed into the balloon, and this time it proved to have sufficient lifting capacity to do the job. The balloon was walked to the launching area from the gas works. During the trip to Elitch Gardens, however, the balloon was blown into a tree limb and was torn by it. The tear was repaired before much of the gas had escaped, but when the men stepped into the basket, the balloon refused to rise. After dumping all the ballast, the craft hovered only a few feet off the ground. Mr. Baldwin turned to Buckwalter: "Well, what'll we do?"

"Will you trust the balloon in my hands?" Buckwalter suggested.

"Certainly, if you'll risk the trip."

"All right, get out of the basket and give me the camera."

With that, Baldwin stepped out of the balloon and—handing the camera to the photographer—gave him his first flying lesson: "Don't pull the valve cord until you strike. She won't lift over two miles and when she strikes, you will probably get dragged a little, but that won't hurt you much."[2]

As the balloon began to rise, Buckwalter leaned out of the basket and shouted to the 5,000 people gathered at the gardens: "You will read all about it in the *News.*"[3] As good as his word, he penned the following account of his adventure for the Sunday readers of his paper:

After the balloon had gone up out of danger from striking buildings or trees the rope was left free and the balloon and its passenger shot up rapidly. The rope was trailing on the ground and from above, it looked as though some of the people would become entangled and killed. Suddenly the end wrapped around a woman. It seemed as

H. H. Buckwalter continually searched for new possibilities for his camera. His search for speed led him to pioneer in stop-action rodeo photography and to make shots like this one of a Denver Fire Department exhibition, C. 1898.   SHSC

though she would not escape, but luckily the rope jerked loose and left her free. Then with a jerk of the balloon and basket, the end of the rope caught an electric light wire. After breaking the thermometer and shaking the basket quite violently, the balloon was freed from the earth and soared away upward.

The sensation was that the earth was falling away from the balloon which seemed not to move. It was interesting to look at the big animal house and theater in Elitch Gardens and see them apparently shrink in size. The crowd which for a few seconds could be seen so easily that each particular face could be distinguished, seemed to

shrink and finally blended into a single mass of colors. The view of the gardens was grand, but a photograph was out of the question on account of pulling up the long anchor rope, which took about five minutes. Cheering could be heard long after it was possible to distinguish individuals in the crowd. Several times the pulling-in of the rope was stopped to wave a hat in response to the cheering.

After the anchor rope was taken in, a long breath of relief was taken. It was then certain that the rope could not catch if the balloon came down suddenly and upset the basket. But right 'here a mistake was made that came near being costly to the occupant of the car. Instead of at once fasten-

Ivy Baldwin's balloon was being inflated when Harry H. Buckwalter recorded
this view.

ing the anchor to the rope, so as to be ready at a
moment's warning, that part was neglected and
forgotten. Next time it will be remembered and
attended to at once.

At 5 o'clock the aneroid registered exactly
11,000 feet above sea level, or exactly 5,000 feet
above the starting point. It was then discovered
that the thermometer had been broken, but it was
not uncomfortable to sit in the basket without a
coat on. The temperature was probably 55 or 60
degrees. The cheers from the garden had become
very faint a minute or two before. A few negatives
had been made and the view was getting grander
every moment.

. . . The higher the balloon went, the more
saucer-shaped or concave the earth seemed. The
falling away seemed to be greatest, of course,
immediately under the balloon. Pikes Peak came
closer and closer and seemed remarkably clear and
plain. The Spanish Peaks . . . were apparently
much closer than they appear from the vicinity of

Pueblo. But there was considerable haze below
that town which could be distinguished by the
pearl-colored smelter smoke.

On the west Golden seemed almost under the
basket as the balloon got higher. Range after range
of mountains came into view, but indistinct on
account of the clouds. On the north, Fort Collins
and Loveland were in sight, but north of them
there was a storm and nothing could be seen
beyond that. Greeley was distinguished by the
great bunch of trees which appeared blue instead
of green. Denver was very nearly under the basket
at one time. The streets parallel with Sixteenth
were prominent, but with the exception of the
capitol and the Equitable building, the others were
hard to distinguish. The colors were remarkably
brilliant. The higher the altitude, the more
brilliancy in colors.

Thirteen thousand feet was reached at 5:08
o'clock, 14,000 at 5:12 and 15,000 feet at 5:15.
Then the rise was somewhat slower and only a

Harry Buckwalter poses for his picture in the basket of Ivy Baldwin's balloon, the *Belle of Denver.*   SHSC

slightly greater altitude reached. Roaring in the ears and a very slight difficulty in breathing was noticed. The temperature was very little colder than at 11,000 feet. The balloon was just two miles north of the Jesuit college at 5:15 and slowly sailing towards the smelters. Just northwest of the smelters a double current of air was struck that whirled the balloon around two or three times and drew it up to a slightly higher altitude. During the whole of the trip the balloon was slowly turning, but there was no swaying or vibration of any kind.

Even moving around in the basket seemed to have no effect on the balance or steadiness.

During the whirling of the balloon, The News man looked straight below and the effect was to cause slight dizziness, but only for a moment. The effect of rising or sinking could not be noticed except by the aneroid or "snow" papers. A handful of these thrown out would at once indicate any rise or fall. If the papers sank below the basket, the balloon was rising, and if the papers went upward or remained floating in the air, apparently the

Clear Creek looked like this from Ivy Baldwin's balloon. Photographed August 12, 1894, by H. H. Buckwalter.

balloon was falling . . .

At the higher altitude, the quietness was noticeable. Only the whistle of a Colorado Central engine just below was heard for several minutes. The usual sounds of the city were entirely out of hearing and even the noises of the smelters were unheard. As the balloon struck different currents of air, there was a slight noise from the straining of the netting over the cloth forming the bag.

Handfuls of "snow" were thrown out very frequently. In fact, there was considerable comfort in knowing just what the balloon was doing. About 5:30 the raise had stopped and the bag was coming down. There was a slight noise from the top and the occupant of the car looked through the mouth of the balloon to see what was wrong. As the bag slowly swung around, daylight was seen through the top. The gas could be heard escaping and the impression was that there was a rip in the top. And this impression was believed to be a fact until Mr. Baldwin explained what was wrong. When the balloon left the gardens, the valve cord hung loosely in the basket and when the big anchor rope was taken into the basket, it was coiled on the free end of the valve rope and held it. As the balloon swelled, the rope would not give and the valve was pulled open. The News man remembers that when he looked up and saw the daylight through the top he was leaning against the valve cord and this

pulled it open. The drop from that time became quite rapid. Horses and cattle could soon be distinguished below and after a few minutes, voices could be heard. The balloon struck a current of air that drove it almost due north and towards the Westminster university building. While the occupant of the basket knew that the drop was fast, it was impossible to tell the speed. When about 1,000 feet from the ground, it became more noticeable and then it became necessary to think of ballast. To the surprise of The News man there was none in the basket to throw out and stop the rapid fall. Then he was also reminded that he had forgotten to fasten the anchor to the rope. This latter he tried to do and had some difficulty in finding the end of the rope, the coils of which had become somewhat entangled while moving around the basket. At last it was found. Then it was difficult to slip through the eye of the anchor because it was large and the end had become unraveled when it struck the electric light wire in the gardens. Just as the end was slipping through the eye, the basket struck the ground about a quarter of a mile beyond the university building, which it barely escaped in coming down. The News man was standing in the basket at the time and was thrown down and struck on a bed of cactus. It was impossible to get out of the basket at that time on account of being tangled in the rigging . . .

The balloon bounced about 100 feet in the air and crossed a wire fence, landing probably 150 yards from where it first struck. During this short trip in the air, the anchor was finally knotted fast and thrown out. After two or three bounds, the rope was drawn tight and the anchor caught in the ground. This brought the big bag to a stop with a jerk and it at once rose in the air. After getting an elevation of less than 100 feet, the anchor lost its grip and the balloon gave a quick drop again, landing the reporter in the usual bed of cactus. It seemed strange that whenever a drop was made the largest bed of cactus within reach was selected and the smooth, soft ground passed. This catching and slipping of the anchor was kept up for about three-quarters of a mile, when the reporter concluded it was time to let go and avoid being drawn through a wire fence. During the time the balloon was crossing the prairie after the first or second bound the valve cord was pulled continuously, but without effect. The valve seemed stuck, although it may have opened partly.

When the balloon hit the ground the first time the camera, plateholders and lenses began to fall out of the basket and during the journey across the fields they would fall out, leaving a trail from start to finish.

As soon as the reporter released his hold from the balloon, it shot upward at a speed double that of any previous rise. Up it went until it reached an altitude of possibly three miles above ground, and it appeared like a small speck in the clouds for at least an hour. As soon as the sun sank behind the mountains, the balloon began to fall again and first landed one mile west of Henderson, but apparently did not like the locality and again rose and went a few miles nearer the mountains.

A number of young men followed it on horseback and as soon as the anchor caught and held, they began pulling the balloon down. Just as they were about to cut it to pieces, two gentlemen drove up and took the balloon and rigging away from them and took it home. Judge Lee of Brighton afterward got a team and secured everything except the anchor and rope, which had been carried off by a couple of the people who first caught the balloon. During the time they were overhauling the contents of the basket, consisting of a coat and two plateholders, they ruined four plates which had been exposed on the city from various altitudes. They took one of the plates out of the holder and wet the others to see if a picture would develop. Their efforts at development were hardly successful.

Ivy Baldwin's balloon, the *Belle of Denver,* was being prepared for a launch on the prairie near Denver when this view was recorded. Baldwin was a friend of newspaper photographer H. H. Buckwalter, and later lent his balloon to Buckwalter who used it to make the first aerial photographs of Colorado. Q-BAR

The balloon and contents of the basket were returned to Denver on Tuesday morning. With the exception of one or two rips in the netting and several small rips in the balloon, no damage was done.

In the future, Mr. Baldwin will not depend upon the management of the gas works for his gas, but will manufacture it at the gardens. With pure hydrogen gas, such as can easily be made of iron borings and sulphuric acid, the balloon should have a lifting capacity of over 1,200 pounds, or more than double that of the gas used last Sunday. [4]

H. H. Buckwalter's most ambitious project, and his most spectacular
failure, was this attempt to photograph the Colorado Central's
Georgetown Loop from the air. In 1902 he arranged with Ivy Baldwin
to make the attempt. However, high winds made short work of the
balloon and nearly dumped Baldwin into Clear Creek.   SHSC

Opposite: Shortly before being dashed against the
rocks and torn open, Ivy Baldwin's balloon pulled
wildly at the ropes being held by the ground crew.
Photographed by H. H. Buckwalter.   SHSC

The first clinical X-ray made in Colorado was by C. E. Tennant of the Denver Homeopathic Medical College, with the assistance of H. H. Buckwalter. Here, Dr. Tennant
(right) watched the patient, a Central City marshal, as the 20-minute exposure was made
during the early part of 1896.   SHSC

A much less spectacular, but more significant
branch of photography undertaken by Buckwalter
was that new branch of science—X-Ray. The
X-Ray had been discovered in November, 1895, by
Wilhelm Conrad Roentgen. During the first week
in March of the following year, Buckwalter began
experimenting with the new ray. He worked with
Dr. Chauncey E. Tennant, a physician from the
Denver Homeopathic Medical College. They made
their X-Ray apparatus from parts gathered with
the help of technicians from the Colorado Tele-
phone Company and the Consolidated Electric
Company, both of Denver. The X-Ray tube was
manufactured locally by the Diamond Incandes-
cent Lamp Works.[5]

When the apparatus had been completed,

several attempts were made to get negatives of
various kinds. After a few preliminary attempts,
Dr. Tennant laid his hand on the plate holder
while the X-Ray tube was suspended a short
distance above it. After five minutes, the tube
became so overheated that it melted. The plate was
developed and showed the bones of Dr. Tennant's
hand with excellent clarity and detail.[6] The first
X-Ray made by Buckwalter and Dr. Tennant on
an actual patient was made shortly later. A miner
who owed a medical bill shot the judge who
ordered his wages garnisheed and the city marshal,
Mike Kelher, who attempted to carry out the
order. It was at first believed that the marshal had
been shot through the heart, but when he did not
die shortly after the gun battle, it became evident

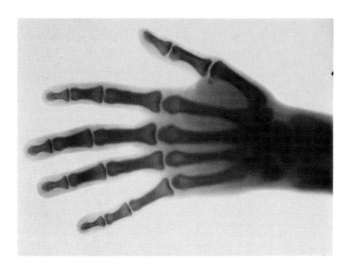

When H. H. Buckwalter and Dr. C. E. Tennant completed their experimental X-ray machine in March, 1896, Dr. Tennant laid his hand upon a plate holder. After five minutes, the X-ray tube melted. When the plate was developed, they had their first successful X-ray. **SHSC**

that this was not the case. As Central City had no hospital, he was sent to Denver. The question was: Where was the bullet? This was just the type of case in which an X-Ray would be useful. The patient lay under the X-Ray tube for 45 minutes. When the plate was developed, it showed where the bullet was lodged in the body, but it was in such a place that it was considered impractical to attempt its removal. The patient died of complications four months later.[7]

The success of the X-Ray experiments conducted by Dr. Tennant and Mr. Buckwalter established them as authorities in the field. In December of the same year, 1896, they played a major role in the first use of an X-Ray in a court of law.[8] The case involved a complaint of malpractice which had been brought against a very prominant Denver physician, W. W. Grant. The doctor's former patient claimed that he had gone to see the medical man after falling off a ladder. Dr. Grant

One of the most interesting uses of available light photos at the turn of the century was in the area of photo-journalism. Here H. H. Buckwalter has captured a scene in Denver Juvenile Court as Judge Benjamin Bar Lindsey confers with three young defendants. Photographed during the session of 1903-1904. **SHSC**

A far cry from the lonely prospector of the gold rush, the interior of the hoist room at the Stanley mine at Idaho Springs is seen here in this 1895 photograph by H. H. Buckwalter. SHSC

diagnosed the injury as a bad sprain. The X-Ray was introduced to show that the bone had been broken. If X-Rays had been introduced in any court of law prior to this time, the Arapahoe District Court, in which the case was heard, was unaware of it. A Montana court had ruled X-Rays inadmissable[9] and in the Colorado case, counsel for the defense objected to the introduction of them.

Buckwalter was called to the witness stand where he spent several hours detailing the method used to obtain the X-Rays and the results obtained in other cases. Dr. Tennant, the physician under whose supervision Buckwalter had made the X-Ray in question, also testified.[10] The X-Ray was admitted. As a local newspaper wrote:

H. H. Buckwalter of this city, who testified as an expert in the case, was the means of winning a victory for science.[11]

The AMATEUR ENLARGING AND HOME LANTERN.
With 4 in. Condensers, Achromatic Front, Rackwork Adjustment, 3-Wick Lamp, 42/-

Opposite: A stagecoach paused on the main road from Silverton to Ouray for the camera of Harry Buckwalter, circa 1897. SHSC

H. H. Buckwalter recorded this interior view of the lobby in one of Central City's hotels, C. 1889. Notice the plethora of advertisements at the back of the writing table (right side of view).   Q-BAR

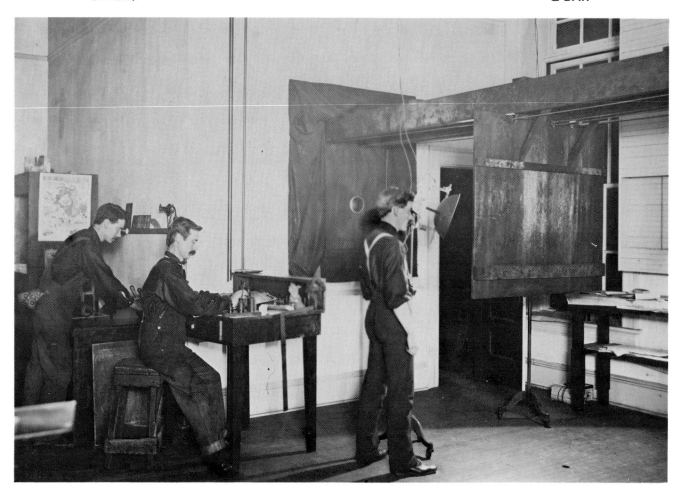

In an age less proper but more seemly, prostitution flourished in opulent surroundings. Here, H. H. Buckwalter had photographed the lower level of the Navarre in Denver, C. 1895, when it was connected to the Brown Palace by a discreet tunnel. In this setting, gentlemen of quality could meet and share dinner with ladies less constrained by Victorian sensibilities than their wives.　　　　　　　　　　　　　　　SHSC

The AMATEUR'S COMPLETE OUTFIT

Opposite, below: The development of the relatively inexpensive halftone reproduction process for newspapers, magazines and books destroyed the view business which had characterized Colorado photography since the 1860's. The halftone process camera of the *Rocky Mountain News* had been set up and was ready for use by the turn of the century — as recorded by newspaper photographer H. H. Buckwalter.　　SHSC

In addition to the many new applications of photography among the professional photographers of the 1890's, the amateur was coming into his own at that same time. Before the dry plate became popular, only the most devoted admirers of photography practiced it for recreation. With the pounds of equipment and glass, as well as the quarts of chemicals which had to be carried along with the heavy wooden camera and tripod, few were inclined to take to the field with photography in mind. When the dry plate—and later, rolled film—became available, amateur photography came of age.

This was also the golden age of pornography in Colorado. With the ability of almost anyone with a little chemical knowledge to shoot and develop his own glass plates, the prospective pornographer was freed from the scrutiny of the professional photographer. This is rather like the more recent proliferation of "art" photos which followed the introduction of cameras which produce a print in 60 seconds. Most of the models used by these photographers of the 1890's came out of the dance halls or cribs of the "red light district." In the

In a Victorian society that considered nudity wicked, photographic nudes must have been thought of as excruciatingly wicked. Sandow, the German strongman, had given private salons after his public exhibitions in flesh-colored tights. He would appear before these audiences in an abbreviated costume and allow those present to feel his muscles by turns. The two views of Sandow printed here (one above and one on the following page) were widely — if discreetly — circulated during the mid-1890's. The prints of the three women (opposite, above and below, right) were rescued from an attic wall during the demolition of a house in Denver, which had been built in the same period. The two bathers appear to be copied from a "French postcard," while the young woman with a mirror is a domestic beauty, perhaps plucked from some bordello on Holiday Street. SHSC

Developing glass plates must have provided a convenient excuse for the men and women of the 1890's to get into the dark together! Here a negative-developing party was being enacted for the benefit of the camera. A kerosene safelight can be seen on the table; the plates used during the 1890's were not sensitive to all colors of light as is modern film, and therefore could be developed with a ruby-colored light which enabled photographers to watch the image develop. SHSC

fashionable house operated by Mattie Silks in Denver, two of the girls were in the habit of posing nude for a young clerk from a drugstore who was an amateur photographer.[12] Not many of the products of these early amateur camera fans have survived and most which were spared have fallen into private hands. Public institutions rarely begin to collect pornography until it becomes almost unavailable.

For the majority of amateur photographers, however, nature photography took the form of mountains and picturesque landscapes. Camera clubs developed everywhere. The Colorado Camera Club held its first annual exhibition in 1893. Anyone interested in displaying his work was invited to take part in the exhibit. Some measure of the number of amateur photographers in the area at this time can be gauged by the fact that the number of participants was so large that it was decided that only members of the club would be allowed to display at the second annual affair which was held late the following year. At that time, there were 50 members in the club. Among the usual assortment of medals and ribbons, there

This genteel scene is a croquet party at the home of Henry C. Brown, one of Denver's leading financial magnates. The photograph was made by one of the guests, Frank Ashley, who appears in this view, fourth from right. He is holding a rubber ball in his right hand, which forced air through the tube seen on the lawn. This tube connected to a piston on the camera, which tripped the shutter. Photographed in July, 1889.   SHSC

Black infantry — stationed at Fort Logan, near Denver — passed in review during the Festival of Mountain and Plain in 1898. The troops had just returned from a tour of duty in Cuba during the Spanish American War.   SHSC

Buffalo soldiers were an important part of the military establishment on the Western frontier. Here, four black soldiers from the Buffalo Bill Wild West Show pose for an unidentified amateur during the 1890's. SHSC

The BOY'S OWN SET.

Opposite, above: During the height of the amateur craze, the thing to do was to make a photograph of a photographer photographing a photographer. In this particularly fine example, we see not only a photographer photographing a photographer, but are ourselves being photographed at the same time by the gentleman in the background. This is a Denver Camera Club photograph produced about 1900. SHSC

Opposite, below: During the 1890's, the amateur craze was sweeping Colorado. Here a member of the Denver Camera Club wades into the bullrushes and shades his lens with his hat. We are left to wonder what he was shooting. SHSC

Some of the early amateurs produced fine quality prints from their flexible nitrate negatives. This print, by an unidentified amateur, is a view of some of the summer houses at Palmer Lake. The accompanying negative envelope was inscribed with the pertinent photographic data for this shot. SHSC

Neg. No. _115_ Date _Aug 1900_
Brand of plate
Condition of light _Good_
Time of day _10_ A. M. P. M
Lens
Stop
Exposure
Developer _Pyro_
Dev. paper _____ Exposure
Subject _Farrah Cottage Palmer_
Lake Colo
Remarks
Western Trip.
Taken from any neighboring
cottage.

A black family posed before their home near the San Carlo Ranch in southern Colorado for this view. Photographed in the late 1890's by Charles Hincke, a camera artist from Denver. SHSC

also was awarded the Kirkland Prize. This prize was awarded by the Kirkland Lithium Paper Company for the best picture on Kirkland's paper.

Kirkland's lithium paper was originated shortly before 1892 by Charles Kirkland, brother of George Kirkland, whom we heard from above when he described his mountain trip with Chamberlain. This was a sort of printing-out paper which was widely used by amateurs and professionals alike. From 1892, when mass production was begun in Cheyenne, Wyoming, until 1894, when the plant was moved to Denver, the paper steadily increased in popularity. Many of the prints turned out by William H. Jackson during this period were on Kirkland's lithium paper. In a letter ordering a large amount of the paper, Jackson commented:

> The paper is now working splendidly, both with combined and separate baths, and is giving us great satisfaction, both in the facility with which it is worked and in the results obtained. [13]

Kirkland's manufacturing plant was later purchased by the George Eastman Company of Rochester, New York. It was the favorite of amateurs for years. [14]

Excursions were the principal activity of the camera clubs. On weekends or holidays, the membership would pack up and head for the mountains or the plains or almost anywhere. There seemed to be no limit to the expeditions. The Grand Junction (Colorado) Camera Club went to the World's Fair in Chicago shortly after the turn of the century. The lantern slides which they made on this trip provided the principal social occasions of the season, each showing being a major event on the social calendar. The club's most ambitious project was an extended bicycle tour of Europe. Most clubs, however, were content with this continent. Special trains were chartered, coaches and carriages rented and bicycles pressed into service to bring the photographer to the places where the best pictures could be had. The camera craze became so widespread that the *Rocky Mountain News* began to carry a regular column of helpful hints for the amateur. One article which appeared in this column in 1898 will serve to illustrate the type of advice offered. The article explains how to take indoor pictures without being killed when you explode your flash powder:

This dapper gentleman is the outstanding amateur, Charles Hincke, as photographed in Denver by his companion, L. E. Hays, 1891. Hincke was a prolific photographer whose prints show rare perception and care unusual for an amateur. SHSC

This handsome amateur is obviously a novice. Many other early camera fans probably left their fingers over the front of the lenses — at least at first. DPL

Opposite, below: The introduction of large numbers of amateurs during the period immediately after the advent of the dry plate in the mid-1880's had the effect of raising the general level of photography among amateurs and professionals alike. With the increased awareness of the graphic and pictorial potential of photographs, as well as merely recording something documentary, more and more prints appeared as objects of art. This print by Georgetown photographer George Dalgleish shows a well-muscled fireman at work on the boilers of the electric generating plant at Georgetown at the turn of the century. SHSC

The industrial expansion of the post Civil War period provided an opportunity for a favored few to accumulate great wealth. Here, three gentlemen of leisure made use of their time by shooting clay pigeons. Recorded in the late 1890's by an amateur.　　SHSC

A wind-powered handcar was photographed on the narrow-gauge Book Cliff Railway in Mesa County by an amateur member of the Grand Junction Camera Club, C. 1900.

One of the real pleasures of amateur photography is making exposures by flashlight. So universal has this become, among young ladies especially, that few informal little dinners or luncheons seem complete without taking a picture of the guests. The results, generally, will compare favorably with those secured by daylight and much better than interior exposures without artificial light. The rules to be observed are very few . . .

First it must be decided what kind of powder will be used. These may be generally divided into two kinds—the explosive and the pure magnesium. Of the former there are hundreds of varieties under different trade names, some good and most bad. The latter is divided into two or three branches, the chemically pure metallic magnesium and the more or less adulterated products containing powdered aluminum. These two metals give the light and are really the active ingredients of the explosive compounds.

For burning pure magnesium a form of lamp may be used where the powder is contained in a reservoir and is blown through a flame—usually from alcohol. This class of lamp positively will explode and do great damage if the explosive compounds are used in them. Only the pure metal and nothing else is safe. For various reasons some workers prefer this class of lamp not only on account of its safety, but also for the absence of noxious fumes, the smoke being nothing more than an inoffensive ash of the metal and almost tasteless. It has the disadvantage of not being an "instantaneous" flash, not permitting its use for portraits of nervous and youthful subjects. To offset this, it has the advantage of being continued in one long or several short flashes, so long as the supply of powder remains. . . .

In making a flashlight picture the camera is set up, leveled and focused as usual. If difficulty is experienced in getting the latter properly, a lighted

No luncheon was complete without a "flashlight photograph" to record the event. Here, the ladies of the Canon City Dickens Club concluded their repast with a print by Krueger of Canon City, C. 1908.
SHSC

match or lamp held very near the object to be photographed will give great assistance. Focus very carefully on the flame and use the largest stop in the lens. Fixed-focus lenses, of course, will not require this. To ascertain how much field the lens will take in, the match may be moved from side to side until the image just touches the side of the ground glass or finder. Vertically the same result is obtained and by looking from under the focusing cloth the exact angle can be noted.

When everything is set about the camera, the flash may be arranged. Now, in order to get depth and roundness, the main source of light should be behind and to one side of the lens. If one flash only is used, there is danger of harsh shadows, but these may be modified very much by having a large white reflector behind the powder. A better way is to use one main flash just behind and on either

JAMES FLASH LAMP, No. 2.

315

The height of fashion during the 1890's was to have your dinners or club meetings photographed with exploding flash powder. Here, the Leadville Card Club, meeting at the Harp's home, March 6, 1895, was photographed by the company of O'Keefe & Stockdorf of the same city.

SHSC

side of the lens and another smaller on top of the camera and just above the lens. It is by no means necessary to use an expensive lamp to get the best results. Really, the only advantage of a lamp is in the igniting and this is not always certain even with the best. . . . For a large room with medium-colored draperies and walls, and with lens of medium rapidity, next to the smallest stop, two or three tablespoonsful of powder may be placed in the larger pile and one in the smaller. If a parlor match is buried in the larger pile so that the business end just shows above the surface the whole affair may be safely lighted with a taper not less than 10 inches long, or another match stuck into a slit in the end of a stick 18-inches long, and when everything is ready by lighting the buried match the powder will certainly go off without burning the hands. . . .[15]

JAMES FLASH LAMP, No. 1.

316

Cage Scene Ajax Mine.
Flashlight by.
O.E. Masters.

With improvements in explosive flash powder during the 1890's, mine interiors became easier to photograph. This turn of the century view of the Ajax mine elevator was the work of O. E. Masters of Cripple Creek.   SHSC

Opposite: By the 1890's, photography had become big business in Colorado. Amateurs swelled the already rapidly increasing number of photographers in the state, and created a large demand for photographic supplies. Here, the R. M. Davis photographic supply house is seen in an 1889 photograph by an unknown photographer. Notice how the billboard sign on the building classifies cameras as "portrait, view and detective" types.

Among the palatial surroundings of the still incomplete State Capitol in Denver, Governor Albert W. McIntire posed with the officers of his elite "Governor Guards," C. 1896. The guards represented prestige and acceptance in the "upper levels" of society. Numbered among its officers were many of the notables in Colorado at the time. S. K. Hooper — famous among rail devotees as the man who originated the silver pass of the Traveller's Protective Association (to boost rail travel) — is standing at left.   SHSC

Frank Kendrick, mining engineer and entrepreneur, traveled widely among the mines of Colorado. An avid amateur photographer, he also took pictures of many of the mining properties he visited. In the view above and the one on the following page (above), Kendrick has captured the crew of the Phillips gold stamp mill at Alma, and the flotation tables at the same mill, about 1890. The kerosene lamps hanging over the tables must have provided poor lighting at best.   SHSC

With the problems in producing sufficient light for underground exposures of small areas, whole scenes such as the one at right are rather rare. This view of the "Bobtail" mine at Black Hawk was photographed in 1898 by an unknown photographer for the Keystone View Company. SHSC

In an attempt to stimulate interest in the new color reproduction process then being used on his black-and-white negatives, W. H. Jackson traveled the length of the country in this showroom on wheels, aboard the *California Limited.* This view was made enroute, probably in 1902.

SHSC

LANCASTER'S "HIERO"
WASHER,

From the earliest days of the daguerreotype, photographers had dreamed of capturing color. Tints were laboriously applied to cheeks, and soft pastel colors were applied over the delicate mercury image of daguerreotypes. Later, when ambrotypes and paper prints became available, artists were hired by the more prestigious galleries to manually supply the color which chemistry failed to produce. By the late 1890's, however, enough was known about the physics and chemistry of color to suggest that an answer to the problem of natural color photography was within the realm of possibility.

In 1907, the breakthrough came. Again, as with the original invention of photography, the discovery came from France. The Lumiere brothers, already famous for their work on the "Cinematograph" moving picture machine, introduced a process which they had evolved.[16] Based on principals which are largely unrelated to modern color photography, the "Autochrome" process, as it was called, nevertheless enjoyed 25 years of prominence as the leading color process, being used until 1932, when the Lumiere Company discontinued manufacturing the plates.

Autochromes were not paper prints—they could be produced only on sheets of glass or other transparent support material. This was a disadvantage in most respects, but immediately suggested the use of Autochrome plates in the "magic lantern." The reason that prints could not be made, is that the colored effect is due to light passing through millions of nearly microscopic grains of translucent starch which have been dyed red, green and violet-blue. These starch grains, extracted from rice or Irish potatoes, were applied in an even coat on the plate and smashed flat with a heavy roller, the area between the grains being filled with opaque pigment. This process created a glass screen on which specks of red, green and blue-colored starch were uniformly scattered over a black background. A photographic emulsion was then applied over the colored particles and the plate was ready for exposure in the camera. In order that light striking the emulsion pass first through the colored particles, the plate had to be inserted into the camera with the glass side toward the lens, and the emulsion toward the back of the camera. The light passed through the glass and through the colored filtering particles. As the green particles will pass only green light, the image of summer foliage impresses itself upon the plate only in those microscopic areas under the green starch grains; blue sky likewise is recorded as millions of tiny dots immediately behind the blue particles; red hues, likewise, are only possible where the red filtering material allows them to pass.

By combining these three basic colors in various combinations of dots, results could be obtained which are comparable to color processes of much later periods and much greater complexity. The plates had to be exposed through a yellow filter to retard the blue end of the spectrum, and this, in addition to the fact that the plates were placed in the camera glass-side forward, considerably lengthened the exposure time and made it difficult to shoot many subjects which were comparatively easy with the black-and-white films and plates of the day.

On a well-lighted landscape, the recommended exposure in 1907 was one-fifth second at f/4.[17] This is roughly equivalent to an emulsion speed of ASA .5 in modern measurement. But the major difficulty—aside from the fact that Autochromes had to be viewed by transmitted light and therefore could not be printed on paper—was the large grain pattern built up by the lumping together of many particles of starch. Individually, the grains were too small to see, but they tended to cluster together and form a sandy-looking texture, especially when projected, enlarged upon a screen.

Colorado, with its magnificent scenery, was not long waiting for the new color process to arrive. The Lumiere factory in France had difficulty making sufficient numbers of plates to satisfy the demand during the first months of production. In December, 1907, a leading photographic magazine announced that the plates were finally available in this country at $20.00 per dozen.[18] The first batch of Autochrome plates to arrive in Colorado was secured by two amateurs in Denver, Stanley McGinnis and George Clifton. Early in 1908,[19] the two men—members of the long-established Denver Camera Club—set up a photographic laboratory in the Denver Athletic Club, of which they were members. They started immediately securing colored views of Denver, as well as the surrounding mountains and "the costumes of local society belles," as one newspaper account had it.[20]

The idea of natural color photography caught the public interest and the local Orpheum Theater decided to capitalize on the experiments in the new field. McGinnis and Clifton soon were persuaded to go on tour with their color slides. Interspersed with vaudeville acts, the Autochrome lantern slides received rave reviews from local papers as far west as Salt Lake City, where the tour opened.[21]

About 1910, the Trinidad Camera Club began experimentation with the Autochrome plates for their regular magic lantern shows, held in the gallery of the Aultman Studio, over the Branson and Griswold Hardware Company on Main Street

William H. Jackson utilized many different photographic trains over the years. This one had paused on the Denver & Rio Grande Railroad's branch line to Silverton in the 1890's, as Jackson made this exposure. In the original black-and-white version of this view, several of Jackson's party can be seen fishing in the waters of the Rio de las Animas; however, in this colored view, they were eliminated by the artist who made the original color printing plates. The renowned Needle Mountains can be seen in the distance. SHSC

in Trinidad, Colorado. Ollie Aultman, one of the prominent members of the club and the leading commercial photographer in Trinidad at the time, provided the expertise in the darkroom to guide the club into the new field of color photography. The club wandered throughout southern Colorado and New Mexico, recording for the first time in natural color, the beauty of the landscape and the works of the hand of man. Everytime the Trinidad Camera Club met to exhibit its latest efforts in magic lantern slides, the Autochromes stole the show. Even the most demanding critic, Glenn Aultman, the 10-year-old son of the owner of the studio, pronounced the Autochromes first-rate. [22]

53131. Colorado. Snow Shed and Snow Plow, Hagerman, F... Copyright 1899 by Detroit P...

This rotary snowplow was emerging from the snowsheds on Hagerman pass, along the Colorado Midland Railway. This view was published in 1899 by the Detroit Publishing Company in a colored version of W. H. Jackson's original. SHSC

The EXCELSIOR LANTERN,

The Empire State Photographic Outfit.

WITH COMPLETE DEVELOPING, FINISHING AND MATERIAL OUTFITS.

EVERYTHING NEEDED for the **BEST AMATEUR OR PROFESSIONAL WORK** ....

A $52.00 OUTFIT for $34.65

RAPID RECTILINEAR LENS, DOUBLE VALVE UNICUM SHUTTER.

3 Sizes:

5 x7
6½x8½
8 x10

THE SPECIAL ADVANTAGES of the EMPIRE STATE CAMERA are many, as it is capable of any class of work that can be done with any View or Portrait Camera. It is constructed throughout from thoroughly seasoned Honduras mahogany, and all metal parts are of polished brass. **FOCUSING** is accomplished quickly and easily by a fine rack and pinion movement. The bed is hinged and folds completely under the camera, thus permitting the use of very short focus or Wide Angle Lenses, if desired. **THE FRONT** has a rising and falling movement, enabling the operator to regulate the relative amount of sky or foreground at will. **THE SWING BACK,** which is pivoted at the center, can be quickly adjusted to any desired angle and securely clamped into position by turning a milled head screw. **THE BACK is reversible,** and may be changed instantly from upright to horizontal pictures, without disturbing the camera. The holder is inserted between the spring actuated ground glass and the camera back, and the slide may be drawn from either side, top or bottom, a great advantage when working in confined situations. **THE LENS** is our Double Rapid Rectilinear, possessing great depth of focus, giving the finest detail and the most brilliant definition. As it is perfectly rectilinear and works very rapidly, it is splendidly adapted to **instantaneous work, groups and portraits, and is unexcelled for landscapes or buildings.**

The Empire State Camera.

The Unicum Shutter
is one of the features of this outfit, being a wonderfully ingenious piece of mechanism. It is constructed of bronze metal, **practically dustproof,** and the shutter blades are made of thin, hard rubber, thus avoiding the danger of rust to which metal blades are subject. **THE IRIS DIAPHRAGM,** with which this shutter is provided, is also made from thin sheets of hard rubber, of the most perfect construction, and affording the best known means for regulating the size of stop or diaphragm. With one pressure of the bulb the Unicum Shutter gives automatic exposures of from $\frac{1}{100}$ of a second to 1 full second. With the indicator set at "B," a pressure of the bulb opens the shutter which remains open until the pressure is released, a very convenient and accurate method of making short time exposures. With the indicator set at "T," the first pressure of the bulb opens the shutter and it remains open until the bulb is again pressed, the best known method for long time exposures.

The Unicum Shutter.

THE COMPLETE EMPIRE STATE PHOTOGRAPHIC OUTFIT CONTAINS:

1 Empire State Camera, with double Rapid Rectilinear Lens, Double Valve Unicum Shutter, Sliding Tripod, one Double Plate Holder, and Canvas Carrying Case.
1 Heavy Printing Frame.
1 Cone Shaped Graduate for measuring liquids.
1 Print Roller for smoothing down prints.
1 Heavy 2-inch Paste Brush.
1 Dozen Dry Plates.

1 Fine Metal Dark Room Lamp, with oil burner.
1 Compressed Fiber Tray for developing.
1 Compressed Fiber Tray for toning.
1 Compressed Fiber Tray for fixing.
2 Dozen Sensitized Paper.
25 Card Mounts.
1 8-oz. Bottle Concentrated Developer
1 8-ounce Bottle Concentrated Toning and Fixing Solution.
1 8-ounce Bottle Intensifier for weak negatives.

1 Package Hypo for fixing negatives or prints.
1 Jar Photo Mounting Paste.
1 Fine Gossamer Focus Cloth.
1 Copy "Complete Instruction in Photography."

Taking the 5x7 size as an example, the Camera alone, if purchased at retail, would cost $17.00, the Lens $15.00, the Shutter $9.00, the Tripod $2.25, and the Developing, Finishing and Material Outfit about $8.80, making the total retail value of the entire outfit over $52.00.

OUR SPECIAL PRICES

No. 18750 The 5x7 Empire State Photographic Outfit, consisting of camera, rapid rectilinear lens, unicum shutter, tripod, plate holder and complete outfit, as described above.................**$34.65**

No. 18751 The 6½x8½ Empire State Photographic Outfit, consisting of camera, rapid rectilinear lens, unicum shutter, tripod, plate holder and complete outfit, as described above...........**$43.50**

No. 18752 The 8x10 Empire State Photographic Outfit, consisting of camera, rapid rectilinear lens, unicum shutter, tripod, plate holder and complete outfit, as described above....................**$49.75**

No. 18756 Empire State Outfits without Shutter. If desired, we can furnish the complete Empire State Outfits, just as described above, **without shutter,** but fitted with our famous Seroco Double Rapid Rectilinear Lens, at the following prices:
5x7, $27.50; 6½x8½, $34.95; 8x10, $41.50.

No. 18757 Empire State Outfits with Single Lens. For the benefit of those who do not desire to invest in the complete outfit with rectilinear lens and unicum shutter, we can furnish the Empire State Outfits, just as described above, without shutter and with our Monarch Single Achromatic Lens, instead of the double rectilinear lens, at the following prices:
5x7, $23.25; 6½x8½, $28.50; 8x10, $32.25.
From the profits made with the outfit, the Double Rapid Rectilinear Lens and Unicum Shutter can be easily added later.

No. 18760 Empire State Cameras without Lens, Shutter or Outfit. Empire State Camera, with canvas carrying case and one double plate holder, but without lens, shutter or outfit:

Size of View	Weight of Camera	Single Swing	Double Swing
5 x7	5 lbs.	$14.45	$16.25
6½x8½	5¾ lbs.	17.00	18.70
8 x10	7¾ lbs.	18.70	20.40
10 x12	8¾ lbs.	23.80	25.50
11 x14	11¼ lbs.	27.20	30.60
14 x17	23¾ lbs.	36.00	38.25

$52.00 WORTH OF GOODS

FOR

$34.65

EXTRA PLATE HOLDERS. No. 18761 The Plate Holder used with the Empire State Camera is beyond question the most efficient, most easily handled and best made holder on the market. In fact, it is one of the features of the outfit. We advise the purchase of a number, as the more holders you have the more plates you can carry at a time.

Size	Price	Size	Price
5 x7	$1.06	10x12	$2.55
6½x8½	1.37	11x14	3.40
8 x10	1.57	14x17	6.37

OUR MOVING PICTURE DEPARTMENT.

OF ALL FORMS OF PUBLIC ENTERTAINMENT
THERE IS ONE WHICH LEADS
ALL OTHERS FOLLOW.

WE REFER to the projection of moving, animated pictures, an effect which is so realistic, so lifelike and so true to nature, that it never fails to charm an audience, whether it is within the walls of a huge metropolitan auditorium, or confined within the comparatively narrow limits of the little red school house.

THE CHARM OF NOVELTY IS THERE.

Outside of the big cities only a small percentage of the people have been privileged to witness a good moving picture exhibition. All, however, have heard of it and almost all are anxious to see it.

THE MOVING OR ANIMATED PICTURES

are not only just as popular as ever, but a great deal more so. This is accounted for by the steady improvement which has been made in the machines by which the pictures are projected and the films containing the pictures which are thus shown. Enterprise also has greatly developed the art of taking the pictures themselves, and competition is responsible for the fact that new and more interesting scenes are each day photographed and depicted.

THE APPARATUS

is used in combination with the stereopticon, but must not be confounded with it. The magic lantern or stereopticon shows merely the stationary pictures. The moving picture machine is of comparatively recent invention, and projects moving pictures lifelike and of life size upon a screen or canvas. It undoubtedly represents the highest branch in the art of photography and illuminated picture projections and brings before the eye an exact and life size reproduction, with all the accompanying effects of light, shadow and expression. We have always been in the forefront of dealers in handling this type of outfit. We have made a study of this branch of the exhibition business. For the past three years the manager of this department has come in personal contact with more exhibitors, has corresponded with a larger number of successful operators than probably any man in the United States. We know what is needed to build up a successful exhibition. We place our knowledge and our experience at the disposal of any purchaser or prospective purchaser absolutely free of charge. We advise him to the best of our ability whether he does or does not purchase an outfit, and we are able to assist him in his final selection by pointing out to him outfits which will make his success certain, and subjects for his exhibition which will insure him an audience wherever he advertises, and guarantee him in successfully entertaining them.

WE GUARANTEE EVERY MACHINE,

every outfit which we send out. We have an established reputation in this line to support. Those who have dealt with us do not require any assurance of this, but to those who have not, we say, that any outfit sent out by us can be thoroughly tested, tried and examined at the customer's house and if not exactly as represented, up to standard and capable of the most effective work, we not only permit but we ask that you return it to us within a reasonable time from its receipt and we will refund whatever money you have paid for it.

THE OUTFIT

may be shortly described as made up of three principal items outside of the small and less considered accessories; these are, first: The moving picture machine or apparatus itself, upon which the most depends and in the choice of which the frankest and most careful advice is offered to our patrons, and an absolute guarantee given with the machine. Without a high grade projecting instrument, such as we furnish, the most talented operator can do nothing, and the small amount saved by purchasing an inferior or lower grade machine is money worse than wasted; it is not only thrown away, so far as the moving picture outfit is concerned, but tends to bring the entire exhibition into disrepute owing to its inferiority.

THE FILMS, which come usually in lengths of 50 feet or longer, containing from six hundred pictures upwards, each taken from the same subject in slightly different pose, and the combined effect of which when thrown on the screen by the Optigraph is to give the result of a single picture apparently with all the movements of life. Every movement and every detail is clearly defined.

THE LIGHT for projecting and illuminating the pictures upon the screen. For first class results either electricity or the oxy-hydro light, sometimes known as calcium, must be used. Where there is an electric light current, and where the place of entertainment is wired for the purpose, electricity is the best. This, however, can only be obtained in the larger towns and cities; and for ordinary traveling purposes, calcium or oxy-hydro light is used. The gases required for this light can be procured in any large city, compressed in tanks; or can be generated by the operator with his own gas making outfit, which is described on the following page, No. 21T428.

WHAT IS THE BEST MOVING PICTURE MACHINE FOR GENERAL USE?

Is a question that we are asked daily. The answer is simple. First, a machine that will give the FINEST RESULTS; will project a life size picture on the screen without flickering and unsteadiness, so that it may be clearly and distinctly seen in every part of the hall. Second, LEGALITY. Make sure that it does not interfere with or infringe on any conflicting patents, and last but not least, THE COST.

THE FIRST TWO QUALIFICATIONS ARE COMBINED IN THE MACHINE
WE HANDLE AND THE PRICE WILL SPEAK FOR ITSELF.

THE OPTIGRAPH
IMPROVED 1902 MODEL.

WILL PROJECT PICTURES OF ANY SIZE AND AT ANY DISTANCE, AND IS GUARANTEED TO DO ANY WORK THAT ANY OTHER MOVING PICTURE MACHINE WILL DO.

PORTABILITY. We are pleased to call the attention of our customers to the many points of excellence possessed by this machine. It is portable, and even when combined with the Enterprise Stereopticon weighs less than 25 pounds and will only occupy a comparatively small space in any ordinary trunk.

SIMPLICITY. The machine is easily set up and operated, every instrument is accompanied by full directions. An amateur can operate it as well as a professional.

DURABILITY. Every part is thoroughly well made of the best material, under the immediate supervision of the inventor. It includes many devices, many improvements, which until the present year were entirely unknown.

ACCURACY. Every detail has been so carefully planned that the result is a steady and brilliant picture and any scratching or injury to the films is reduced to a minimum, there being an entire absence of friction on the picture, something which has never been attained before.

NOISELESSNESS. The Optigraph works with a motion so smooth, easy and perfect that no noise is perceptible. This can be said of no other moving picture machine on the market.

SIZE OF PICTURE. It will project a picture of any size and at any distance, and is equipped at purchaser's option with any one of three ranges of lens, so that the size of the picture is practically controlled by him.

NO FEAR OF HARASSING LITIGATION. A word about litigation. The United States Court has handed down a final decision that the basic principles of moving picture machines is open to the world. The special advantages possessed by the Optigraph are carefully covered by patents; outside of these, however, the market is open and the purchaser of an Optigraph can be assured that he is fully protected and guaranteed in using his machine and in doing so he cannot be interfered with by any person, company or corporation in the United States.

COST. The purchase of a very large number of these machines has enabled us to make the above prices the lowest ever made upon a high grade, reliable combined outfit capable of the best work in either stationary or moving pictures. We place the 1902 Optigraph, admittedly the most practical, the most simple, the most portable and the most durable moving picture machine on the market, within the reach of anyone who contemplates embarking in this most profitable field of labor.

FILMS FOR PROJECTION OF MOVING PICTURES. Next to the instrument for projecting moving pictures, the film, which contains the pictures themselves, is the most important item. It is a long celluloid tape, usually about fifty feet, with a series of photographs taken at the rate of forty every second, the animated movement being obtained by passing the same film rapidly before the projecting lens of the Optigraph at the same rate of speed, thus reproducing all the movements which were in view when the picture was taken.

THE NEW MODEL 1902 OPTIGRAPH MOVING PICTURE
MACHINE.

HIGHEST QUALITY.   LOWEST COST.
DISTINCT AND STEADY PICTURES WITHOUT FLICKER.
DURABLE, COMPACT, PORTABLE AND EXCEEDINGLY SIMPLE.
NOT LIABLE TO GET OUT OF ORDER.

Change from moving to stationary pictures can be made instantly.

Runs the films either backward or forward with equal ease and facility.

The above illustration, taken from an actual photograph, shows the New Model Optigraph attached to our regular Enterprise Stereopticon for the projection of moving pictures as well as the ordinary stereopticon views. We usually furnish this combination, but the Optigraph alone can be attached to and used with any regular stereopticon or magic lantern.

No. 21T400 New Model 1902 Optigraph, used for attaching to any regular magic lantern or stereopticon, either single lantern or double stereopticon, including sliding device for change from moving to stationary pictures...................................... **$35.00**

No. 21T402 Combined Enterprise Stereopticon with 1902 Model Optigraph, fitted with either electric arc lamp or calcium burner..................................... **64.00**

FOR EACH SUBJECT A SPECIAL FILM IS NECESSARY.

THE FILMS which we handle are of the finest grade. A complete revolution in the printing and development departments, the employment of an entirely new process, and the care exercised in scrutinizing and inspecting every film before it is sent from the factory, has resulted in a clearness of definition and a mellow tone, which, although long sought for by leading exhibitors, has never been obtained before. We have not space to give here a detailed list of our entire stock of films. We publish, however, a complete list containing names, lengths and descriptions of the latest films. We supplement this list with monthly statements of all new films as they are taken, and upon receipt of a postal card we will send free of cost our latest list of films and will place customers' names on our mailing list so that they may keep posted regarding the latest subjects. Our present list, which will be forwarded on application, includes over 300 subjects, classified under the following headings: **War Films, Civic and Military Parades, Fire Films, Mythical and Mysterious Subjects, Comic Subjects, Railway Scenes, Dances and Miscellaneous.**

AUTOCHROME COLOR VIEWS

Autochrome plates, introduced into Colorado early in 1908, provided the first practical method of producing natural-color photographs. The plates reproduced here span the years from 1910 to about 1922 — the period during which Autochromes were most popular. From the collection of the State Historical Society of Colorado and the Aultman Collection.

Among the most famous landmarks of southern Colorado is Fishers Peak, seen here in an Autochrome produced by the Trinidad Camera Club circa 1910.　　AC

Reflection, by O. E. Aultman, is an Autochrome lantern slide, made about 1910. The subject is Stonewall, about 35 miles west of Trinidad.　　AC

This Autochrome was entitled, *Hayfield,* and was photographed by W. Dearden of the Trinidad Camera Club, C. 1910. In the distance, the Stonewall formation can be seen.　　AC

A Pleasant Valley was photographed by W. Dearden, member of the Trinidad Camera Club. This scene — recorded on Autochrome lantern slide plates about 1910 — shows the Stonewall area on the road to Monument Lake, near Trinidad.　　AC

George L. Beam, the indefatigable photographer of the Denver & Rio Grande Railroad, had two great interests: Indians and Mesa Verde. Here we see a large-format Autochrome plate he made in the Mesa Verde area of southern Colorado and northern New Mexico. A group of Indians posed outside their dwelling for him. This picture is reproduced in actual size from a colored glass original made about 1920.   SHSC

Native American pottery, with its deep earth colors, was a natural subject for the new color process. The view above is from an Autochrome lantern slide plate made in 1915 by an unknown photographer.   SHSC

This Autochrome plate shows an unidentified woman with her bouquet of "mums" — probably taken during the fall of 1908 by McGinnis & Clifton of Denver. SHSC

OUR FILM LIST

is as complete as the greatest care in selection and liberality in buying can make it. We carry a full stock of every film which we list and can fill orders at an hour's notice. We list films in lengths of 25, 50, 100 and 150 feet.

New Special $4.00 Films for Moving Picture Machines.

We have made special arrangements for a very large quantity of moving picture films, by which we are enabled to offer the following subjects at the heretofore unheard of low price of $4.00 each.

These films are first quality, are made from the Eastman Co.'s stock, which is the best there is to be had, and they are finished in the most thorough manner, so that the picture comes out on the screen clear and sharp.

We advise every exhibitor to take advantage of this rare opportunity and secure this set of special films. Some of them run a little over and others a little under 25 feet in length, depending on the nature of the subject, but we would say for these special films that the most entertaining part of the pictures would be of no greater length in the longer films.

These are not only made specially for the Optigraph Moving Picture Machine, but are made to fit any standard moving picture machine on the market.

No. 21250 Serpentine Dance. This is a very beautiful scene, showing this well-known dance to its best advantage, and it is one of the best subjects for moving picture machines.

No. 21251 Union Stock Yards, Chicago. This film is of great interest, showing the entrance to the Union Stock Yards, Chicago, time chosen being noon, when teams, men and horses are coming through the gateway in streams. A characteristic and most lifelike scene.

No. 21252 Cheyenne Indians Riding Through Cheyenne Canyon, near Manitou, Colo., at full speed. Full of animation and a scene which is much appreciated.

No. 21253 State and Madison Streets, Chicago. Two of the most crowded streets in this immense city of nearly two million inhabitants, showing Chicago's famous character, "Old Sport," crossing the street. Full of action and very interesting.

No. 21254 Racing Scene, Lexington, Ky. Showing the finish of a good running race with clouds of dust rolling up behind. Very lively and exciting.

A scene that is good for an encore every time.

No. 21255 Kissing Scene. This is a burlesque on John Rice and May Irwin's famous kissing scene. This we consider one of the greatest side splitting scenes ever thrown on a canvas.

No. 21257 Bicycle Parade on Washington Ave., Chicago. Showing both lady and gentlemen riders in regular riding costume. Full of animation and very interesting.

No. 21258 Watermelon Scene. Showing colored boys scuffling over a watermelon, which they have taken from an old colored man. A very exciting and interesting scene.

No. 21259 Cavalry Horses fording Stream in Santiago de Cuba. The best 25-foot film we have, and an exceptionally fine and realistic subject. The horses are ridden to the edge of the stream where they immediately plunge in and, with their riders, are plainly seen swimming across the river.

No. 21260 Street Scene, Lexington, Ky. This is a very fine scene and full of animation; the street is crowded with vehicles and pedestrians.

No. 21261 Wash Day in Camp Alger, showing soldiers out in the stream washing their clothes.

No. 21262 Cock Fight, or Soldiers' Sport, shows one of the amusements of the soldier boys when they are not in action and have a little time for lighter occupations.

No. 21263 Initiating a New Recruit, shows a crowd of soldier boys, many of whom are holding a blanket by the edges and tossing high in the air the victim of their sport.

No. 21264 Off to the Front is a magnificent marching scene, showing the soldier boys as they march from camp to board the train for the front and take an active part in the war.

No. 21265 Bathing Scene, with High Diving, a most interesting scene and one that is full of life and animation.

No. 21266 Cake Walk. Very clean and bright.

This set of sixteen films **comprises all we are able to furnish in lengths of 25 feet.** Our list of 50-foot films is far more extensive, and there is so much greater space within which to show the life and active motion of the various subjects represented.

Regular 50-Foot Films. Special Price, $7.50 Each.
PRICE REDUCED FROM $8.00.

These Films are of the regular length (50 feet) as used on all standard moving picture machines. They are made on regular **Eastman stock of the No. 1 quality,** and are finished in the best possible manner. We have carefully selected from a very large list the following subjects, all of which will be found to be first class in every respect. **Other concerns charge $10.00 to $15.00 for films of this grade.** These films must not be compared with the copied films that are made on inferior stock and sold by some concerns.

No. 21280 Unveiling of the Logan Monument at Chicago. Showing the flag as dropped at the unveiling. This is the only picture of this subject taken for moving picture machines.

No. 21281 Logan's Old Regiment marching past before the unveiling of the Logan monument. Full of action and very interesting.

No. 21282 First Regiment, Illinois National Guard, as they marched in the Logan Day parade before the unveiling of the monument. This represents Illinois' finest regiment. It is a beautiful subject and full of life.

No. 21283 Knights Templar Marching in the Logan Day Parade. This is the only Knights Templar picture on the market and a very desirable subject.

No. 21284 The Magician. Sleight of hand always pleases old and young, and this film is one that is always successful. The Conjuror removes rabbits and other things too numerous to mention from an empty hat and afterwards causes them to disappear in a manner equally mysterious.

No. 21285 Rescue from Drowning. An exclusive film taken for us at the Omaha Exposition and showing the Life Saving Crew rescuing from the water a man who has fallen in and would otherwise be drowned. So thrilling and exciting that your outfit is incomplete without it.

No. 21286 Watermelon Scene. The best and most amusing street scene that can be shown and brings the house down every time. A lot of street "gamins" fighting and scuffling for a watermelon that has fallen from an old colored man's basket. Two dogs take a hand and the fun becomes fast and furious.

No. 21287 Kiss Scene. A burlesque on the osculatory performance of John Rice and May Irwin. An encounter by two colored people in which a mutual good time is certainly enjoyed. One of the funniest views on the market.

No. 21288 Bicycle Parade. Showing a cycle parade on Washington boulevard, Chicago. A number of the best riders in Chicago in line; showing both ladies and gentlemen. A very fine subject and a good picture.

No. 21289 Shooting the Chutes. A lively Chicago scene, showing tobogganning down the water chutes and the arrival of the boats, which splash into the water in the most lifelike and realistic manner that can be imagined.

No. 21290 The Overland Flyer. Showing the arrival of the Overland Flyer, owned by the Santa Fe R. R. Co., at La Junta, the alighting of the passengers, and the general bustle raised about the railway station. Full of animation and a very fine scene.

No. 21291 Freight Train in the Royal Gorge, Colorado. Showing a freight train on the Denver & Rio Grande railway passing through the Royal Gorge and over the swinging bridge. A very fine picture, surrounded by royal scenery.

No. 21292 Bathing Scene. Showing swimming pool at Glenwood Springs, Colo., with fountain playing, and bathers sporting in the water

No. 21293 Horse Scene. Showing the famous stallion Hanover at McGrathiana farm, Ky. Senator Blackburn and others standing about discussing the horses. A very fine picture.

No. 21294 A Spanish Bull Fight. Enraging the Bull. This is one of the most intensely interesting and exciting films ever prepared. This and the companion film, No. 21295, are the two best selected from the entire series. No. 21294 shows the matadors exciting and enraging the bull in the cruel manner usual at Spanish bull fights; the representation given by these films shows all the more than animated action, the daring encounters and the narrow escapes without the debasing cruelty attendant upon the actual witness of the fight.

No. 21295 Spanish Bull Fight. Death of the Bull.

No. 21296 Water Toboggan Slide. Very animated and amusing.

No. 21297 Union Stock Yards, Chicago. This film is of great interest, showing, as it does, the entrance to the great Union Stock Yards in Chicago, the most wonderful in the world, the time chosen is noon when teams, men and horses are coming through the gate in streams. A characteristic and most lifelike scene.

No. 21298 Streets of Cairo. A true oriental scene, showing natives with camels, etc., of most intense interest, transporting the audience in imagination to these far-Eastern climes, and sure to be hailed with delight wherever shown.

No. 21299 The Rival Bill Posters. A fight between two bill posters, who both wish to decorate the same space with their literature, it ends in a "free-for-all" fight in which one of the men extinguishes the other with the paste pot. The funniest film ever shown.

No. 21350 Annabelle Serpentine Dance. One of the prettiest and most popular dance subjects ever made.

No. 21351 Washing Streets of Algiers. Is another unique oriental scene, describing the manner of washing down the streets in that far country. Most interesting.

No. 21352 Black Diamond Express. This scene represents the fast Lehigh Valley Flyer running at full speed, the section gang in the foreground, engaged in repairing track, wave their hands to the engineer, who is leaning out of the cab. The porter is shaking the tablecloth from the platform of the dining car. The Black Diamond is classed as one of the handsomest and fastest trains in America, and was running at the rate of nearly 70 miles an hour when the picture was taken.

This page from a Sears catalog for 1899 lists two motion-picture films produced in Colorado.

SHSC

NORTH ON CURTIS FROM SIXTEENTH STREET.

Colorado's motion picture industry was born in the billiard parlor, which was indicated by the circular sign at the curb to the left of this picture. This is the Brightman & Company cigar store, where the first Edison Kinetoscope to arrive in Colorado was set up.
SHSC

November 10, 1894, is a red letter day for the history of photography in Colorado. On that wintery Saturday, a box containing 100 posters left the Edison Kinetoscope distributor's warehouse in the East and began its trip by railway to Denver. The Kinetoscope—Edison's newest wonderful invention[23]—consisted of an oak box about four-feet tall and 18 inches wide, with a hole in the top. If you put your eyes to the hole and a nickel in the slot, you could see moving pictures. With this ingenious device, it was possible to photograph subjects while in motion and to counterfeit that motion with the instrument later. What a startling invention! Soon the posters were plastered on every barn and telegraph post in Denver. The curiosity

of many was raised, but this novelty was not taken seriously by most. The common consensus of opinion was that it was interesting, but that little could be done with only 20 or 30 seconds of movement—moving pictures obviously had no potential!

Undaunted by the disinterest of some, the Western agent for the Kinetoscope, Peter Bacigalupi, continued his preparations for the installation of the machine in Brightman and Company's cigar store at 1607 Curtis Street. One week after the posters were shipped, two "first run" films followed. These two titles—*Gaiety Girls* and *Alcide Capitaine*—were both filmed on November 1, less than three weeks before they arrived in Denver.[24]

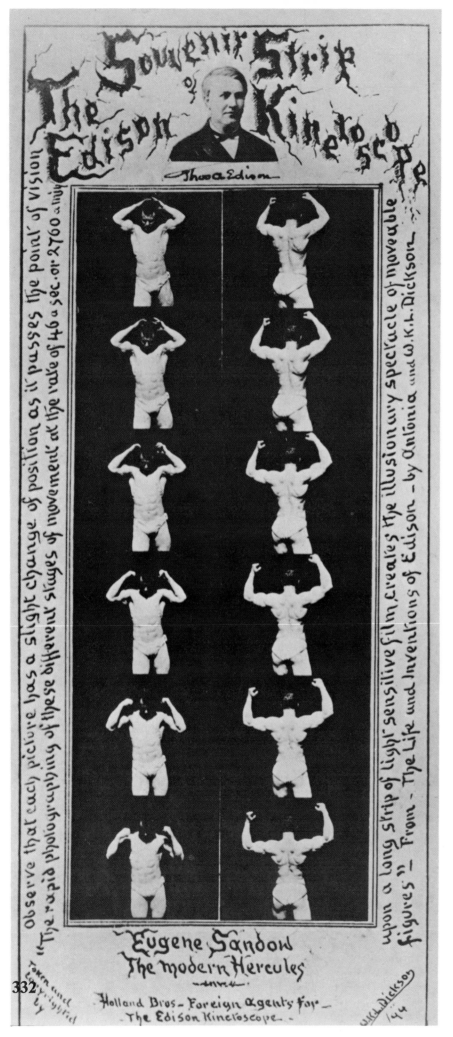

Sandow, the Modern Hercules appears on this handout, advertising the Edison Kinetoscope. One-hundred copies of this broadside were shipped to Denver on November 10, 1894, as advance publicity for the new Kinetoscope peep show machine, which was soon to arrive in Denver. Sandow also had the distinction of being one of the first film subjects ever projected on a screen, when Mary Elitch Long showed the strongman stripped to the waist and flexing his muscles at her theatre in Elitch's Zoological Gardens during 1896. Many of the early projected films had originally been made for the "nickel - in - the - slot" machines. NPS

LIMBS AND LENSES.

A GATHERING OF LONDON GAIETY GIRLS INVADE WIZARD EDISON'S LABORATORY AT ORANGE, N. J., AND GIVE AN EXPOSITION OF THEIR DANCES BEFORE THE KINETOSCOPE.

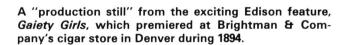

A "production still" from the exciting Edison feature, *Gaiety Girls*, which premiered at Brightman & Company's cigar store in Denver during 1894.

Alcide Capitaine, the talented and popular acrobat, was the star of one of the first two films ever shown in Colorado. Her thrilling performance could be seen by anyone depositing a nickel in the Kinetoscope set up in the Brightman & Company cigar store at 1607 Curtis Street, Denver, after November of 1894.

As Lillian Hurd, queen of the Festival of Mountain and Plain for 1897-98, was drawn past the reviewing stand by four matched horses; the kinetographing staff of Thomas A. Edison can be seen (at left behind their sign) making a moving picture of the event. This probably was the first expedition of film makers into Colorado and the occasion for several stunning titles, which later showed up in the Sears and Montgomery Ward catalogs. Several of these films have survived and give an interesting glimpse of Colorado in the last century.   SHSC

Gaiety Girls was then playing on Broadway in New York, and so was especially timely. Capitaine was a popular trapeze artist and performer. With these two films, and probably with two machines removed from the Bacigalupi Kinetoscope Parlor in San Francisco,[25] Brightman's cigar company brought the movies to Colorado.

This was a rather quiet beginning for what was to become a multi-million dollar industry—to be shunted into a corner of a cigar store, between the billiard table and the tobacco counter—but the "novelty" paid off. More films were added, and soon other locations boasted Kinetoscopes. By January of the next year, Trinidad had its own moving pictures, with the debut of *Carmencita*, the motion picture with the dubious distinction of being the first film ever censored.[26] The companion feature was another spicy number, *Carnival Dance*. Together, these two films cost the proprietor $25.00, quite an initial investment in 1895, but at five cents a shot, the capital was probably quickly recovered.

One of the major deficiencies of the Kinetoscope was the short duration of the films, less than half a minute in most cases. This limitation was first the result of the crude camera which would not operate for much longer than that without jamming or sprocketing the film. Later, when the camera was able to run for longer periods of time, new problems arose. In the Kinetoscope, an endless loop of film was wound up and down through rollers within the body of the machine. As films became longer, there was not enough space in the cabinet to coil them. In order to solve this problem and to give the Kinetoscope industry added impetus—which it needed as the initial novelty was beginning to wear thin—Edison announced a "new, improved Kinetoscope." The film was still coiled as in the earlier models, but the cabinet had been expanded to accomodate the extra rollers and loops of film. The subject which was chosen for the new apparatus—or probably the subject which prompted the development of the new apparatus—was *boxing*. What more natural topic for a machine which as often as not ended up in a pool hall or cigar store?

As early as June, 1894, a fight between Mike Leonard and Jack Cushing had been filmed by the Edison camera. The pinnacle of prize-fight films during the Kinetoscope era, however, was the battle between Gentleman Jim Corbett, the world's heavyweight champion, and Peter Courtney. Such interest was aroused by this film that in early August, 1896, the Tabor Grand Opera House installed four machines in its lobby, each showing one round of the fight.[27] Fight fans could see each

During the 1890's, boxing emerged as a major spectator sport. Banned in many states during the period, it never-the-less achieved wide popularity. Prints of famous boxers were collected and traded — as baseball cards came to be, half-a-century later. This is a card published by the *Police Gazette* and was widely distributed throughout Colorado.   SHSC

round for a nickel, or 20 cents for the entire fight.[28]

Not even such grand productions as this could sustain Colorado moviegoers' interest in the Kinetoscope in the face of an even more unbelieveable wonder—lifesize moving pictures! On Friday evening, August 14, 1896, Mary Elitch Long invited a select group of friends to her theater in the Elitch Zoological Gardens at Denver, to witness for the first time in Colorado, the Edison "Vitascope." In the Vitascope, the pictures move as in the Kinetoscope, but they are projected on a screen, as in the magic lantern. Mrs. Long favored her audience with numerous short subjects, largely drawn from the catalog of films made for the

Harry H. Buckwalter stood behind his movie camera as a stagecoach thundered past — during the filming of his epic feature, *The Robbery of the Leadville Stage,* produced at the turn of the century. SHSC

Kinetoscope. The first film presented at this film premiere was *Leigh Sisters' Umbrella Dance*, then *The Breaking of Waves on the Sea Shore.* Commenting on this film, the *Denver Republican* reported:

> . . . the effect was simply marvelous, wave after wave came tumbling on the sand and as they struck and broke into tiny floods just like the real thing, some of the people in the front row seemed

to think they were going to get wet and looked about to see where they could run to in case the waves came too close.[29]

With the movies now playing in a legitimate theater, it would be only a short step to theaters being built for movies. Soon the leading theaters in Colorado were playing films between acts and before the close of the century, films were even being made in Colorado.

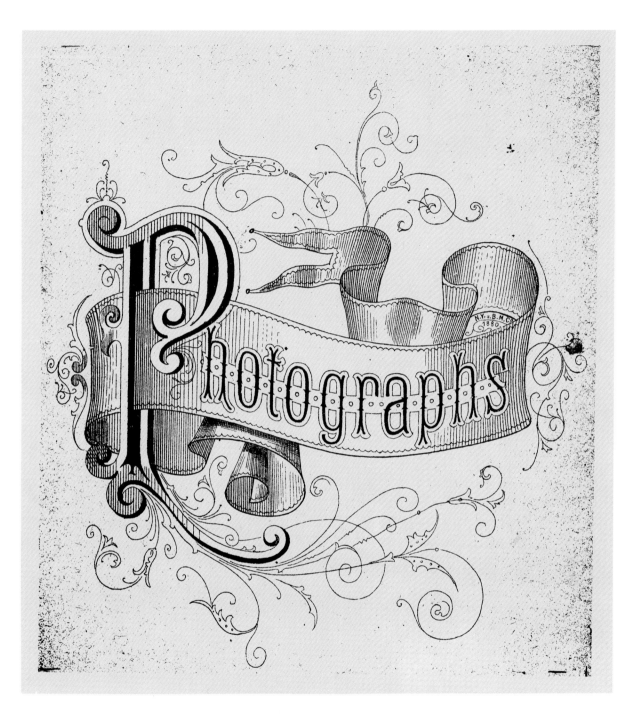

Album of the 1890's

As the native American culture began to disappear in the 1890's, more and more people became interested in it. This photograph was taken in southern Colorado during the period and shows an Apache runner re-enacting a scene from earlier days for the benefit of the photographer.

SHSC

Post   1459 Larimer St. Denver, Col.

This resolute group of musicians was assembled in the F. E. Post gallery on Larimer Street, Denver, about 1890. There they sat for this portrait, but who the members were — or how they were received by their auditors — is anyone's guess.   Q-BAR

With the help of institutions such as the Teller Institute for the Education of Indians, the native American culture largely was being suppressed by the close of the century. Here, a Ute student from that school near Grand Junction posed before the camera of Frank Dean, in his costume as a baseball player.

During the 1890's the cultural center of Lamartine Camp was run by a gentleman named McMabon. Here, the local "temperance society" gathered for an unknown photographer to record the event.

Q-BAR

Stacy COL. WM. F. CODY 5th Ave. & 9th St. Brooklyn N.Y.

"BUFFALO BILL"

Photographs made in other parts of the country were widely distributed in Colorado during the 1890's. This print of William F. "Buffalo Bill" Cody was made by the well-known New York photographer, Stacy, and was sold by the hundreds in Colorado and throughout the world.   Q-BAR

341

Here, we have a closeup view of a typical Denver & Rio Grande "standard" passenger depot, many of which were built throughout western Colorado during the 1880's and '90's. Quarters for the station agent and his family were on one side of the building, while the telegraph office was in the bay window, and a waiting room for passengers was at the right. The signal extending out from the depot tower was called a "train order board," and primarily was used to advise train crews whether or not they had to stop — or at least slow down — at the depot to pick up written orders issued from the dispatcher's office. The Garrison Brothers recorded this view of the Rifle depot — at that time on the Rio Grande Junction Railroad — about 1901.　　　　SHSC

Opposite, above: During 1895, the Denver & Rio Grande had a standard-gauge caboose specially painted white (on the outside) — Number 0870 — which ran between Pueblo and Salida. Evidently, someone in the company wanted to put special stress on "cleanliness," because the car was placed on the water track each week for the crew to clean. In this view, one can see that Conductor J. E. Duey saw to it that his office on wheels was decorated in a proper manner.　　　　SHSC

Below: S. K. Hooper's excursion train for the General Passenger Agents was photographed in the Royal Gorge during 1890. This was the first use of the Travel-ler's Protective Association silver pass, good for the D&RG, the Union Pacific, and the Colorado Midland railroads. The photographer is unknown.   Q-BAR

Officers and men of the Wells Fargo Express Company posed under the awning of the Denver Union Depot in this print from the mid-1890's.   Q-BAR

The Grand Junction terminus of the Book Cliff Railroad was the end of the line for this miniature narrow-gauge railroad. The few passengers it carried were either miners on their way to work or tourists bound for the Book Cliffs on a picnic. The bulk of the business along the line was hauling coal for the city's use. Photographed by Frank Dean.

In most people's minds, Pueblo conjures up thoughts of the great Colorado Fuel & Iron Corporation's steel mills. This rare view of a portion of their switching yards was taken about 1901. Both standard and narrow-gauge trackage served the CF&I plant, as evidenced by the three-rail tracks in this picture. The photographer is believed to be Charles R. Osgood. His family graciously donated the view above for use in this book.   OSGOOD

Engine Number 3 of the Denver & Santa Fe Railroad paused on the line near Larimer Street and Cherry Creek. This line ran from lower downtown Denver to the University of Denver area in the southeast section of the city. Photographed in the late 1890's, probably by George Beam.   SHSC

A Denver & New Orleans passenger train was pulling through Elbert on its way to Texas when Sturtevant shot this photograph about 1895.   Q-BAR

Excursions were a major part of the traffic on Western rail lines during the 1890's. The Colorado Central road was used for this convention group in 1896, as evidenced by the scene at left showing them looking over the mines at Roscoe. An interesting sidelight to the history of photography is seen here with the man at left, holding a "Kodak" camera. These amateur picture-takers were already making inroads into the once-exclusive domain of the commercial photographer, such as Henry Buckwalter, who made this view.   Q-BAR

Freighting Out-fit, Rico, Colo. — 1890. — No 8.

ON THE NEW ROAD, HAULING ORE FROM LAST CHANCE MINE TO THE CARS, CREEDE, COLO. NOV. 189

NO. 261.

Opposite, above: The commerce of the Colorado high country is symbolized in this shot of Main Street in Rico during 1890. Charles Goodman made this print at a time when ox-freighting was drawing to a close. **Q-BAR**

Opposite, below: Members of the Trinidad Camera Club ventured out from Trinidad into all parts of southern Colorado. In this print of a lunch break, ranch hands had gathered around a chuck wagon to eat. O. E. Aultman captured another man's camera as he recorded this view (see left background). **SHSC**

Getting the ore from the mines to the trains was often as difficult as finding the ore in the first place. Here, a wooden plank roadbed is used to make a right-of-way through a narrow canyon so that wagons could get up to the Last Chance mine. Photographed in November, 1892, by W. W. Crooks. **SHSC**

When winter closed in upon the high reaches of the Rocky Mountains, wheeled travel practically came to a standstill. Here, two loads of hay were being moved by sledges through Telluride during the winter of 1892 — from a print by Carpenter & Taylor.   SHSC

This interior view shows the lobby of the Hotel Colorado in Glenwood Springs, as it appeared in 1900. Recorded by C. H. Graves, a traveling photographer.　　Q-BAR

Opposite, below: Some unknown traveling photographer wandering over the High Plains of eastern Colorado came across this anonymous family and their sod house at the turn of the century. For many people, the photographers' visits were rare occurrences — and something to be looked forward to.　　Q-BAR

The work crew from the "Suffolk" mine in San Miguel County paused for this photograph by D. W. Carpenter, a photographer from Telluride, 1890-1893.   SHSC

Opposite, above: Worker dissatisfaction brought the Colorado National Guard to Leadville to protect the mine owners' property in 1896. This view is by O'Keefe & Stockdorf of Leadville.   SHSC

Opposite, below: A group of miners below the surface of a Cripple Creek mine provides us with this glimpse of working conditions at the time. Underground photography had been attempted in the West even during the 1860's, but generally the lighting problems during the collodion negative days were almost insurmountable. By the time this photograph was made in the late 1890's, the increased speed of plates and improved flashlight apparatus made shots such as this one much more common.   Q-BAR

EMMETT MINE
LEADVILLE

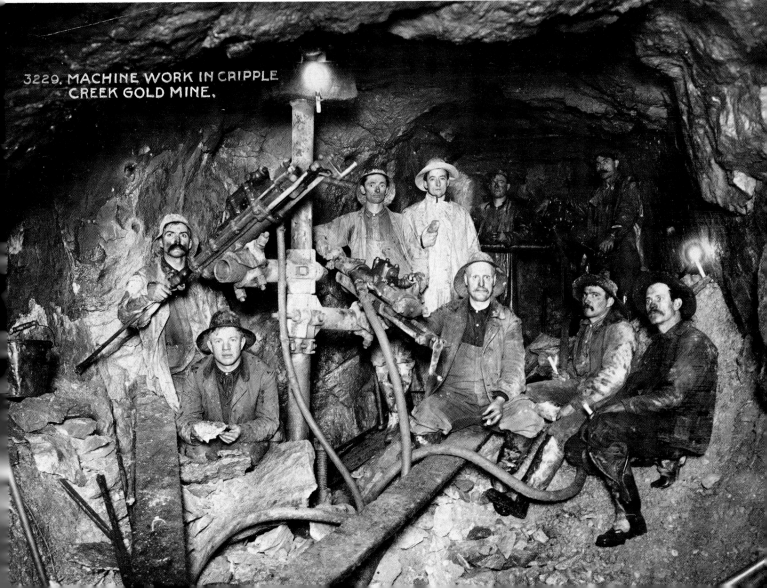

3229. MACHINE WORK IN CRIPPLE
CREEK GOLD MINE.

Before the days when child labor laws excluded boys from dangerous jobs, boys were frequently to be found among the ranks of seasoned miners. This view of miners from the Brewster mine in Fremont county was taken about the turn of the century by an unknown photographer.

SHSC

Opposite, below: A five-cent cup of coffee and a fifteen-cent sandwich was offered at this Cripple Creek lunchroom. This photograph was published by W. E. Hook of Colorado Springs in 1896-'97, but it probably was taken at least five years earlier by some other photographer.

SHSC

The fourth estate was represented in Cripple Creek by the *Crusher* during the period 1891-1895. Offices and press facilities — and the residence of the proprietor — are pictured here by W. Ira Rudy, a Colorado Springs photographer.　　　　SHSC

Mining camps sprang up so fast that it is difficult to find a photograph of one which shows a camp in its infancy. In the print above, however, the very beginnings of Cripple Creek were photographed by Horace Poley in 1892. In only a short time Cripple Creek became an important Colorado mining center.   Q-BAR

When fire raged down Bennett Avenue in Cripple Creek, people scrambled to save some of their belongings, or just to get out of the path of the fire. This scene of chaos was captured on glass in April of 1896, as the first of two disastrous fires consumed the heart of Cripple Creek.   SHSC

356

The great Victor fire of August 21, 1899, was photographed by O. I. Jones.   SHSC

It is believed that Harry H. Buckwalter burned magnesium to generate light for this underground view of a "tunnel stope" in a mine near Idaho Springs. Photographed C. 1895.   SHSC

357

The Boulder City Brewing Company plant provided the backdrop for this shot of the crew taking a break in 1896 — as photographed by J. B. Sturtevant. Notice the two cats on the window sill.   SHSC.

Penitente Desconsos, or resting places, mark the places where the penitents fall on their trek. This group of markers was photographed by O. E. Aultman, Trinidad photographer, about 1895.   SHSC

HOTEL IN BACHELOR CITY COLO.

Bachelor City, during its boom in 1892, was recorded by Charles Goodman. He was spending his time between Amethyst, Creede and Bachelor City, all within the same mining area. **Q-BAR**

Penitentes were flagelating themselves during the ceremony shown below, C. 1890. Photographs of penitent ceremonies are unusual, and the circumstances surrounding this print are unclear. It was part of the O. E. Aultman collection, but it is not likely that he took it. **SHSC**

Saint John's Church at Boulder on Easter of 1890. SHSC

Opposite, above: ". . . Erin O'Keefe . . . Eaten by Mountain Rats in the year 1879." This pious funeral scene was staged by a group of pranksters who assembled in the 1890's to "pay their respects" to the fictional martyr of the summit of Pikes Peak.   Q-BAR

Mortuary photography was highly popular in an age when photographs were much more rare than they are today. Bodies were sometimes posed with their families when no pictures of the deceased had been made prior to his death.   Q-BAR

MEDICAL WARD

Down at the old swimmin' hole! In this case, the locale was near Denver, but it could have been near almost any town in the state during the period. Photographed by an amateur, about the turn of the century.   SHSC

Opposite, above: For families on remote ranches in western Colorado, the arrival of a photographer was an infrequent and important occasion. If the opportunity was missed, it was likely to be a long time before another chance came along. It appears that this family had lost a child shortly before Fred Garrison drove his photo wagon down their lane. In order not to miss an opportunity for the family to be photographed — but also to observe the occasion in appropriate solemnity — the vacant highchair was decorated with a black crepe bow and an iron horse (probably the infant's favorite toy) was put in the seat. Victorians made much of such displays of symbolic mourning.   SHSC

Opposite, below: Lighting interiors evenly was no easy task at the turn of the century. Here, Louis Regnier, a Denver photographer, has taken the main ward of Arapahoe County Hospital, using available light. By the time this photograph was made in the late 1890's, the hospital had installed half-gas and half-electric lighting fixtures, apparently uncertain as to which type would prove more serviceable.   SHSC

This photograph by H. H. Buckwalter was of the Black Wonder mill and store, located at the foot of Cinnamon Pass between Lake San Cristobal and Animas Forks. The photo was taken in 1895.   Q-BAR

Opposite, above: Theodore Roosevelt, fresh from his experiences in Cuba during the late war, was the Republican nominee for vice-president during the election of 1900. Portraits of Roosevelt and the presidential nominee, William McKinley, decorated the front of the Pitkin County Republican headquarters during the victory celebration after the election.
                                                                                                                SHSC

Opposite, below: On October 13, 1896, an attempt was made to rob the bank of Meeker. Here, Jim Shirley lies at the edge of the boardwalk, felled by five bullets fired by townspeople. Photographers could rely on doing a brief, but active, business with such views as this.
                                                                                                                SHSC

The capitol building in Denver was planned as a monument to the wealth and development of the state. An extravagent building by the standards of the day, granite, marble and alabaster were lavishly used to make it the premier building of Colorado. In the view above, taken by an unknown photographer, the iron skeleton of the dome was rising above the granite walls of the empty structure.   SHSC

This view was made from the top of the uncompleted state capitol during the late 1890's. The Capitol Hill residential district stretches south in this view from the corner of Fourteenth and Lincoln streets.   SHSC

Opposite, below: Mrs. Wynn's Class is shown here at the Colorado School for Deaf and Blind in 1891.   SHSC

The following three pages are from an album called, "Our Home," which was produced in 1894 for William Church to commemorate the completion of his new home at 1000 Corona in Denver. The ornate Victorian opulence of the era's well-to-do is graphically illustrated in these views.

SHSC

"Our Home"

"Our Home"

In 1894, a dispute over office tenure arose between the governor of Colorado, Davis Wait, and the officials of the Denver city government. When the problems developed into a showdown, the governor sent the Colorado National Guard to Denver city hall to evict the occupants and install new officers. In the accompanying photograph, as an anarchistic crowd gathered in front of the city hall, observers on the roof reported developments to those inside the building. SHSC

Whole forests were destroyed to produce the building materials for the mining boom in Colorado. Here, the Wapiti Saw Mill at Bull Creek was turning out timbers for mine shoring and beams for heavy construction, circa 1895.　　　　SHSC

Opposite, above: Lumber was being turned out for the building boom in Leadville when this picture was shot. Crawford's Saw Mill was photographed by Howard & Company, about 1892.　　　　SHSC

Opposite, below: During 1890-1891, some proud owner brought this pet into Payne & Stockdorf's studio on Harrison Avenue in Leadville.　　　　Q-BAR

Payne & Stockdorf,
413 HARRISON AVENUE,
LEADVILLE, COLO.

Charles Price, a turn of the century amateur, captured this homely cabin interior in the middle 1890's.   SHSC

The "ins and outs" of a country school at the turn of the century were photographed by an amateur. Here, the Lamb school in Critchell is shown decorated for the Christmas holidays in 1901.   SHSC

By the turn of the century, 15 years of photographic work had enabled O. E. Aultman to plan and build this comfortable residence in Trinidad. Not all photographers were as successful as Aultman, however. This interior view shows the extravagance in decorating which was typical of late Victorian homes owned by persons of some means. SHSC

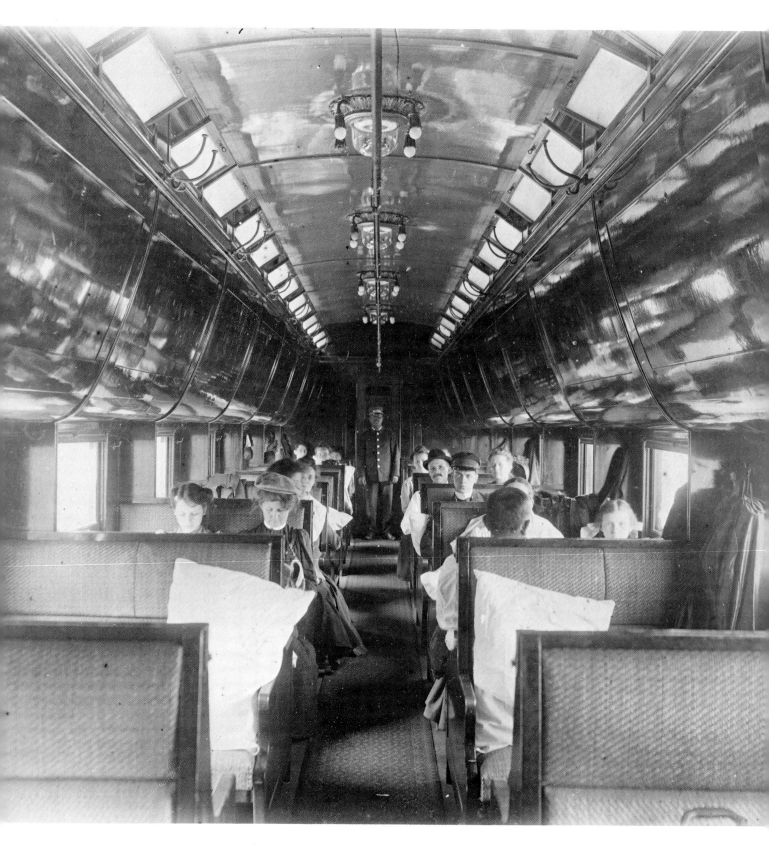

This interior view of a Colorado Midland tourist sleeping car apparently was photographed about the turn of the century for advertising purposes. Rattan (wickerwork) seats certainly could not have been very comfortable, as evidenced by the many pillows in use. The name of the photographer is unknown.

SHSC

PHOTO. BY GEO. L. BEAM, DENVER

SCENES ALONG THE LINE OF

THE DENVER & RIO GRANDE RAILROAD

PRESIDENT ROOSEVELT AND PARTY IN ROYAL GORGE

May 8, 1905

One of the many publicity photographs produced by D&RG company photographer, George L. Beam. SHSC

377

The industrial revolution made an important impact on farming in Colorado by the turn of the century. Here, an unidentified photographer captured a harvest scene

on the eastern plains of the state. The harvesters were using a steam tractor and belt-driven thrashing machine to assist them in their work. SHSC

SUMMIT OF PIKE'S PEAK 299
Altitude, 14,336 feet. 22·7·7

Hook Photo.

A crust of bread was just the thing to catch the attention of a reluctant model atop 14,110-foot Pikes Peak — photographed by W. E. Hook during the mid-1890's. SHSC

The McVey children lined up for a photographer at the turn of the century. SHSC

Denouement

ITH THE advent of motion pictures, the evolution of photography in the period covered by this book is complete. In 1853, when Solomon N. Carvalho brought photography to Colorado, picture taking was strictly a professional undertaking. The primary enterprise of many galleries was the "view" business. Generally speaking, a view was anything which was not a portrait. Pictures of Indians, buffalo, mountains—anything that could be sold to the general public, which had no direct connection with the picture, was a "view." They usually were made up by the dozens and sold at low cost. By the 1890's, this was beginning to change. As one pioneer Denver photographer, Alexander Martin, put it:

> We photographers did a wonderful business in those days selling views, which brought prices far exceeding . . . prices of today. Then the news-papers began to install machinery by which photographs could be reproduced successfully by the halftone process, and the business began to decline. When the picture postcard, produced by the hundreds of thousands at a cost infinitely less than photographic prints, became popular, the view business, so far as the photographer was concerned, became almost of no value. Most of the photographers then began to limit themselves to portrait work.[1]

With the loss of the view business, many photographers turned their entire attention to portrait work, while others went into special fields. A few of the men displaced by the invention of halftone reproduction of photography got onto this new bandwagon—men like H. H. Buckwalter, who became Colorado's first newspaper photographer. Not only were views no longer in large demand, but people no longer came into town to get the photographer to take a picture of their new barn or their prize hog. People were fast learning to be independent: now when someone wanted a picture taken, he could take it himself. Perhaps photographers were compensated in some measure by the recent invention of moving pictures—something which would remain almost the exclusive property of professionals until the 1930's.

Almost every photographer attempts a self portrait sooner or later — with greater success in some cases than in others. This is Meeker photographer Henry Wildhack's attempt, 1886. SHSC

Self portraits of photographers often revealed how they saw themselves more emphatically than how they may have actually looked. Here, O. E. Aultman, an **aspiring Trinidad bank clerk who became a photographer** due to the foreclosure of a loan he had made to J. F. Cook, posed in his newly acquired studio in 1889 — looking more like a banker than a photographic artist. SHSC

Opposite, above: Charles Goodman, one of the pioneer photographers of the western slope, is seen here in a self portrait — made C. 1880, the year he moved to Colorado from his home in Wisconsin. Q-BAR

Opposite, below: Frank Dean was passionately interested in portraiture. Heavily influenced by Sarony of New York and always trying for a "Rembrant effect," Dean considered his portraits to be so much more important than his commercial work that when he retired from business he discarded the glass plates of scenes and events he had made over the half-century he had been in business and kept only his portraits. In this unusually stark portrait, Dean has captured another early western slope photographer, D. N. Wheeler.

Frank Dean, early western slope photographer, made this self portrait during his first years at Gunnison, C. 1882. Dean was only 18 years old at the time.   SHSC

George Mellen's photographic party breakfasting near Gunnison during the mid-1880's.   SHSC

Byron H. Gurnsey, Colorado Springs photographer, as he sat before the camera, about 1875.

Pioneer Museum, Colorado Springs

This unusual "piece of photographic equipment" was used by Alex Martin during his trip to the top of Grey's Peak in 1884. Often, more than one pack animal was needed to carry cameras and plates if more than one size of picture had to be made.   Q-BAR

THE COLORADO "SHIP OF THE DESERT" AT ANCHOR ON THE SUMMIT OF GREY'S PEAK

Appendix

Basically, photographic renderings of camera images rely on the property of certain silver compounds to change chemically when struck by light. After a certain amount of change has taken place, the unaffected silver is removed so that the entire sensitive surface does not turn black. These two operations are accomplished variously in the several types of photographs used in Colorado during the Nineteenth Century.

Daguerreotype — In this, the first method of photography perfected, the silver is in the form of pure silver, plated onto copper. It is easy to identify a daguerreotype because of the characteristic mirror-like surface. If you see yourself on the polished silver surface, as well or even better than the object which was photographed, you have a daguerreotype.

A well-made daguerreotype has a delicacy and beauty of tone which has never been matched. Their handsome book-like cases make them quite attractive. They are quite permanent, and should they darken, they can often be restored to something like their original beauty and intensity. This is a delicate undertaking, however, and photographs of historical value should be given to museums whose staffs are experienced in the restoration process. If the cover glass is removed from a daguerreotype, care should be taken not to let anything touch the surface, as the image—which is composed of particles of mercury—will wipe away like so much dust. This process flourished in Colorado from 1853 until about 1860 or slightly later.

For information on the restoration of daguerreotypes see: *The Daguerreotype in America*, by Beaumont Newhall. For dating daguerreotypes by the type of case see: *American Daguerrean Art*, by Floyd Rinhart, *et al.*

Ambrotype — These are often mistaken for daguerreotypes because they are usually found in cases similar to those of the earlier type of photograph. The ambrotype is an underexposed glass negative painted on the back with black paint or backed with velvet of a dark color. They were used in Colorado from 1859 until about 1865. Because of their somewhat dark appearance, the ambrotype is often mistaken for the more common "tintype."

The most certain method for distinguishing the two is to remove the photograph from the case. If it is on a piece of glass, and when held up to the light, it appears as a negative, it is an ambrotype. The appearance of a positive picture is produced by the dense areas of the negative reflecting light while the more transparent areas allow the black backing to show through. If the black paint on the back of the glass is peeling, it will give the effect that the photograph is disintegrating. This can be easily remedied, however, by carefully removing the old paint and substituting a piece of deep black paper. Care should be exercised, however, as occasionally the paint was applied on the emulsion side of the glass. This was the practice of George Wakely and is usually the case when the scene being photographed included signs or other objects which could not conveniently be viewed reversed from left to right. In this case, there is no cover glass and the picture is viewed through the glass to which it is adhered. The black paper can be put in back of the glass. Anyone not thoroughly familiar with this type of work should only undertake to remove or repair the backing on an ambrotype of the latter sort when they have specimens which are expendable.

Tintype — These are actually ambrotypes on sheets of iron, covered with black lacquer. The finished picture is the same material which was in the camera, as is the daguerreotype and the ambrotype, each one is unique. This style was popularized during the Civil War and continued to be used for at least 20 years. This same process was used on black leather during the Colorado gold rush to produce pictures which could be sent through the mail. The process can be used to create a picture on almost any black surface.

Paper Photographs — Photographs on paper are produced from a negative image on glass or film. They were coming into wide popularity by 1859 and represent the overwhelming majority of photographs taken in Colorado. The early prints have a characteristic tone, but it is impossible to give guidelines which the inexperienced collector can follow. The easiest way to date a paper print is by the name of the photographer. Frequently the

385

name of the gallery or photographer will be found on the reverse side or at the bottom of a print. *Photographers and the Colorado Scene 1853-1900,* by Opal Harber, which was published by the Denver Public Library in 1961, is a directory of Colorado photographers and their dates. If a photograph bears the name, "William H. Jackson, 413-414 Larimer," the book will show that Jackson was at that address between 1880 and 1886. This is undoubtedly the best tool for dating pictures generally available for all of Colorado. It shows, however, the necessity of recording all information when copying a photograph. The name of the photographer alone —using Jackson as an example again—would place the date between 1870 and 1897, approximately, whereas with the address, the date becomes much more precise. It should be remembered, however, that most photographers kept their negatives for at least some time after they were taken. Therefore, while a picture bearing the 413-414 Larimer address was taken not later than 1886, it could represent a much earlier negative.

Another interesting aid to dating can be found in the tax stamp which was required by Federal law on all photographs sold between September 1, 1864, and August 1, 1866. If you have a photograph with a stamp on the back, this will date it approximately. The cancellation, if any, of this stamp will date it exactly.

Another clue in dating photographs is format.

The *carte de visite* was a French style photograph about the size of a calling card (approximately 2-1/2 x 4 inches). They were introduced into Colorado in 1862 and continued to be popular for some 20 years. Generally speaking, the card photographs which exist of Colorado subjects were made during the 1860's and early 1870's, although this is open to exception. The cabinet photograph came next. It was introduced about 1865, but did not become popular until about 1870 in Colorado. These were about 4 x 5-1/2 inches. The old ones (1865 through the early 1870's) have the pronounced grain characteristic of the card photograph. By the late 1880's they were generally smooth-finished.

It is important when documenting photographs to include three things: (1) the photographer (and address if known), (2) the subject, and (3) the date. These three things sound simple, but there are no surviving daguerreotypes which have been proven to have been taken in Colorado, and only one photograph taken in 1859 which is thoroughly documented. The Wakely ambrotype of the tight-rope walker is the only ambrotype which is completely documented. There are dozens of *suspected* Colorado daguerreotypes and ambrotypes, but the practice of precise documentation was not sufficiently widespread in the past to establish many of them for certain. In some cases, the subjects prove conclusively that they are of Colorado, but by whom or when, it is impossible to say.

SEROCO B Cycle Folding Camera Open.   Camera Closed.   Carrying Case.

Footnotes

Chapter 1

1. John Charles Fremont, *Memoirs of My Life* (New York, Belford, Clarke & Co., 1887), page i.
2. Solomon Nunes Carvalho, *Incidents of Travel and Adventures in the Far West* (Philadelphia, Jewish Publication Society, 1953), p. 33.
3. Ibid., p. 321.
4. Beaumont Newhall, *The Daguerreotype in America* (New York, New York Graphic Society, n.d.), p. 141.
5. Ibid.
6. Carvalho, op. cit., p. 83.
7. Robert Taft, *Photography and the American Scene* (New York, Macmillan Co., 1938), p. 263.
8. Carvalho, op. cit., p. 80.
9. Ibid., pp. 92--93.
10. Ibid., pp. 128--129.
11. Ibid., pp. 102--104.
12. Ibid., p. 126.
13. Ibid., pp. 132--133.
14. Ibid., p. 137.
15. Ibid., pp. 143--145.
16. Ibid., p. 172.
17. Ibid., p. 200.
18. Fremont, op. cit., pp. xv--xvi.
19. Taft, op. cit., p. 490.
20. Samuel M. Schmuker, *The Life of Dr. Elisha Kent Kane and Other Distinguished American Explorers* (Philadelphia, John E. Potter & Co., 1858), p. 247.

Chapter 2

1. L. R. Hafen, "The Colorado Gold Rush," pp. 219--220, reprinted from the Kansas City *Journal of Commerce*, Arpil 6, 1859.
2. Ibid., pp. 353--354, reprinted from the *Western Weekly Argus*, June 4, 1859.
3. *Rocky Mountain News*, April 23, 1909, supplement, p. 22.
4. Kansas City *Journal of Commerce*, August 7, 1859.
5. *Trail*, volume XVII, October, 1924, p. 23.
6. *Rocky Mountain News*, April 23, 1909, supplement p. 22; Opal Harber, 1956, p. viii (the photograph probably was an ambrotype).
7. Kansas City *Journal of Commerce*, August 7, 1859.
8. *Rocky Mountain News*, June 13, 1860, p. 3.
9. L. R. Hafen, op. cit., p. 337, reprinted from the Kansas City *Journal of Commerce*, June 7, 1859.
10. *Rocky Mountain News*, October 18, 1860, p. 3.
11. Kansas Territorial Census, 1860, p. 474.
12. *Denver City & Auraria, the Commercial Emporium of the Pike's Peak Gold Regions in 1859.*
13. Melvin Schoberlin, *From Candles to Footlights* (Denver, Old West Publishing Co., 1941), pp. 22--23.
14. *Rocky Mountain News*, October 20, 1859, p. 3.
15. Ibid., July 6, 1861, p. 3.
16. *Daily Colorado Republican & Rocky Mountain Herald*, July 13, 1861, p. 3; Opal Harber, 1956, p. 51.
17. Schoberlin, op. cit., p. 69.
18. *Daily Colorado Republican & Rocky Mountain Herald*, July 19, 1861, p. 3.
19. Ibid., May 8, 1862, p. 3.
20. Ibid., June 26, 1862, p. 3.
21. *Weekly Commonwealth* (Denver), August 7, 1862, p. 3.
22. *Daily Commonwealth* (Denver), April 9, 1864, p. 2.
23. Ibid., May 1, 1864.

24. *Weekly Commonwealth* (Denver), May 25, 1864, p. 3.
25. Ibid., June 1, 1864, p. 3.
26. Opal Harber, master's thesis, 1956, pp. 56--57.
27. *Rocky Mountain News* (Denver), May 11, 1861, p. 3.
28. Ibid., June 21, 1872, p. 3.
29. *Tri-Weekly Mines Register* (Central City), November 14, 1862, p. 3.
30. *Rocky Mountain News* (Denver), October 21, 1863, p. 4.
31. Ibid.
32. Ibid., December 16, 1863, p. 2.
33. Harber, op. cit., pp. 71--72.
34. *Daily Miners' Register* (Central City), December 19, 1863, p. 3.

Chapter 3

1. *Wm. G. Chamberlain Memoirs*, quoted by Opal Harber, op. cit., p. 75.
2. Biographical information from *Portrait & Biographical Record of Denver & Vicintiy* (n.n., Chapman Publishing Co., Chicago, 1898), pp. 1175--1177, and Opal Harber, op. cit., 1956.
3. *Rocky Mountain News* (Denver), June 2, 1861, p. 2.
4. Ibid., June 15, 1861, p. 3.
5. Ibid., August 19, 1862, p. 2.
6. *Weekly Commonwealth & Republican* (Denver), August 28, 1862, p. 4.
7. Ibid., November 6, 1862, p. 3.
8. Ibid., December 11, 1862, p. 4.
9. *Daily Commonwealth*, January 25, 1864, p. 2, and *Mining Journal*, April 30, 1864, p. 3.
10. *Image of America, Early Photography, 1839--1900*, Library of Congress, Washington, D.C., 1957, p. 35.
11. *Daily Mining Journal* (Black Hawk), May 27, 1864, p. 3.
12. *Weekly Commoneath* (Denver), May 28, 1863, p. 3.
13. *Rocky Mountain News* (Denver), November 23, 1864, p. 3.
14. George Kirkland Scrapbook, a manuscript in the library of the State Historical Society of Colorado.
15. Ibid.
16. Ibid.
17. *Rocky Mountain News*, June 1, 1872, p. 4.
18. Ibid., September 17, 1874, p. 4.

Chapter 4

1. Edward L. Wilson, PhD., *Cyclopaedic Photography* (New York, Edward L. Wilson, 1894), p. 356.
2. Oliver Wendell Holmes, "The Stereoscope and the Stereograph," *Atlantic Monthly*, June, 1859.
3. Ibid., p. 746.
4. Harber, op. cit., p. 79.
5. *Mining Register* (Lake City), January 1, 1881, p. 2.
6. *Handbook of Colorado* (Denver, J. A. Blake and F. C. Willet, publishers, 1872).
7. *Mining Register*, op. cit.
8. William H. Jackson, *Time Exposure* (New York, G. Putnam, 1940), p. 236.
9. *American Journal of Science*, December, 1873, p. 464.
10. *Miners' Register*, June 21, 1886.
11. *Denver Daily*, April 4, 1867, p. 4.
12. *Rocky Mountain News* (Denver), July 18, 1868, p. 4.
13. *Colorado Chieftain* (Pueblo), August 27, 1868, p. 2.
14. Taft, op. cit., p. 309.

15. *Daily Register* (Central City), November 23, 1870, p. 4.
16. Ibid., July 16, 1872, p. 3.
17. *Rocky Mountain News* (Denver), August 22, 1874, p. 4.
18. Ibid., January 3, 1870, p. 4.

Chapter 5

1. *Rocky Mountain News,* October 20, 1872, p. 4.
2. Ibid., December 2, 1868, p. 4.
3. N. H. Miller, *Shutters West* (Sage Books, Denver, 1962), pp. 79 and 137.
4. *Rocky Mountain News,* June 9, 1868.
5. Ibid., July 27, 1868, p. 4.
6. Browne to Palmer, May 16, 1867. A manuscript in the Palmer Collection in the library of the State Historical Society of Colorado.
7. Ibid.
8. William A. Bell, *New Tracks in North America* (London, Chapman & Hall, 1869), volume I, p. xv.
9. Ibid., p. x.
10. Ibid., p. xvi.
11. Taft, op. cit., p. 279.
12. Lamberton to Palmer, July 31, 1867. A manuscript in the Palmer Collection in the library of the State Historical Society of Colorado.
13. Bell, op. cit., volume I, pp. 62--65.
14. Ibid., volume I, pp. 87--88.
15. Ibid., volume II, p. 2.
16. Ibid., volume I, p. 148.
17. Several of the prints included by Palmer in his report, which were credited to Gardner, are known to be by Bell.
18. Lamberton to Bell, October 26, 1867. A manuscript in the Palmer Collection in the library of the State Historical Society of Colorado.
19. Bell to Palmer, no date. A manuscript in the Palmer Collection in the library of the State Historical Society of Colorado.
20. *The Trail,* volume 2, number 2, July, 1909, article by Mary Bohm Haight, p. 5.
21. *Rocky Mountain News,* December 15, 1872, p. 4.
22. *Colorado Business Directory,* 1875, p. 115.
23. *The Trail,* volume 2, number 8, January, 1910, pp. 21--22.
24. *Rocky Mountain News,* January 1, 1873, p. 4.
25. *Denver Republican* (Denver), April 15, 1883, p. 3.
26. *Daily Register* (Central City), January 12, 1872, p. 4.
27. Ibid.
28. *Daily Register,* January 14, 1872, p. 4.
29. *The Denver Post,* January 1, 1940, p. 2. *Rocky Mountain News,* March 27, 1873, p. 4.
30. *Daily Register* (Central City), April 29, 1873, p. 3.
31. *Central City Register,* March 20, 1874, p. 3.
32. *The Denver Post,* July 28, 1918, p. 10.
33. *Encyclopaedia Britannica,* eleventh edition.
34. Ibid., tenth edition.
35. *Rocky Mountain News,* October 23, 1874, p. 4.
36. Ibid., December 5, 1874, p. 4.
37. Ibid., January 3, 1877, p. 4.
38. *History of Clear Creek and Boulder Valleys,* 1880, pp. 491--492.
39. Francis Rizari, *Brand Book* (Denver, The Denver Western-ers, 1955), pp. 402--404, Opal Harber, op. cit., pp. 173--174.

Chapter 6

1. *Colorado Magazine,* volume III, March 1926.
2. *First Official Visit to the Cliff Dwellings,* narrative written for the State Historical and Natural History Society by W. H. Jackson, photographer of the U.S. Geological Survey, a manuscript in the library of the State Historical Society of Colorado.
3. *Annual Report,* U.S. Geological Survey, by V. F. Hayden, 1874 (Government Printing Office, Washington, D.C., 1876), p. 372.
4. William H. Jackson, *Time Exposure,* p. 232.
5. *Colorado Magazine,* op. cit.
6. *Descriptive Catalogue of the Photographs of the United States Geological Survey of the Territories for the Years 1869--1895,* second edition, by W. H. Jackson (Government Printing Office, Washington, D.C., 1875), p. 3.
7. *Colorado Magazine,* op. cit.
8. From the original manuscript in the library of the State Historical Society of Colorado, July 20, 1874.
9. Jackson, op. cit., p. 258.
10. Ibid., p. 261.

Chapter 7

1. *Rocky Mountain News,* February 27, 1881, p. 8.
2. *Encyclopeadia Britannica,* eleventh edition, volume XXI, p. 494, and *Wilson's Cyclopaedic Photography,* pp. 23, 37 and 94.
3. *Tribune-Republican* (Denver), November 29, 1885, p. 9.
4. Ibid., August 31, 1886, p. 2.
5. *Sam Howe Scrapbook,* volume IX, number 3139, an original manuscript in the library of the State Historical Society of Colorado.
6. *Scribner's Magazine,* February, 1889, pp. 215--218.
7. Mr. and Mrs. A. G. Wallihan, *Hoofs, Claws, and Antlers of the Rocky Mountains by the Camera* (Denver, Frank S. Thayer, publisher, 1894), p. 1.
8. Mr. and Mrs. A. G. Wallihan, *Camera Shots of Big Game* (New York, Doubleday, Page & Co., 1906), pp. 5--12.
9. From an original manuscript written by A. G. Wallihan in 1932, in the library of the State Historical Society of Colorado. The paging has been altered to provide logical sequence of topics.

Chapter 8

1. Opal Harber, *Photographers and the Colorado Scene* (Denver, Denver Public Library, 1961).
2. *Rocky Mountain Herald* (Denver), June 23, 1860, p. 4.
3. Harber, op. cit.
4. *Rocky Mountain News,* October 24, 1861, p. 3.
5. Opal Harber, master's thesis, 1956, p. 135.
6. *Daily Miners' Register* (Central City), July 6, 1865, p. 3.
7. *Rocky Mountain News,* October 28, 1868, p. 4.
8. *Daily Miners' Register* (Central City), July 11, 1869, p. 1.
9. *Daily Miners' Register* (Central City), November 10, 1870, p. 4.
10. Ibid., July 30, 1871, p. 4.
11. *Las Animas Leader* (Las Animas), September 8, 1876, p. 3.
12. *Rocky Mountain News,* May 26, 1874, p. 2.

Chapter 9

1. *Sam Howe Scrapbook,* op. cit., volume XL, number 5649.
2. *Rocky Mountain News,* August 19, 1894, p. 15.
3. Ibid., August 13, 1894, p. 2.
4. Ibid., August 19, 1894, p. 15.
5. Walter W. Wasson, M.D., *Radiologic Pioneers in Colorado, 1896--1918* (1934), a manuscript in the library of the State Historical Society of Colorado.
6. *Rocky Mountain News,* March 9, 1896, p. 1.
7. Wasson, op. cit.
8. *Denver Republican,* December 3, 1896, p. 9; *Rocky Mountain News,* December 3, 1896, p. 7; *Denver Republican,* December 6, 1896, p. 13.
9. *Rocky Mountain News,* December 3, 1896, p. 7.

10. The transcript of the testimony has been lost by the court or State archives since Dr. Wasson used it in 1934.

11. *Denver Republican,* December 4, 1896, p. 4.

12. *Denver Times,* March 7, 1892, p. 1.

13. *Wilson's Photographic Cyclopaedia,* op. cit., p. 492.

14. *Rocky Mountain News,* August 21, 1926, p. 3.

15. Ibid., April 3, 1898, p. 27.

16. *Wilson's Photographic Magazine,* August 1907, p. 370 *passim.*

17. Ibid., November 1907, p. 487.

18. Ibid., December 1907, p. 530.

19. *Denver Republican,* March 19, 1909, p. 4.

20. Ibid.

21. Ibid., *Rocky Mountain News,* March 23, 1909; *The Denver Post,* March 23, 1909, p. 7.

22. Oral History Interview, CoHi, TWmM--Glen Aultman.

23. Largely the work of one of his assistants, W. K. L. Dickson.

24. Gordon Hendricks, *The Kinetoscope* (New York, Theodore Gaus' Sons, 1966), p. 82.

25. This is largely conjecture from what Hendricks says in his book, *The Kinetoscope.*

26. Hendricks, op. cit., p. 77.

27. There were actually six rounds filmed.

28. *The Denver Post,* August 15, 1896. Don Block, "Flickerama for Denver," *Brand Book,* (Denver, The Denver Westerners, 1948), p. 156. This gives an excellent and reliable account of early projected moving pictures in Colorado. He did not have access to Hendricks' research and is sketchy, therefore, in his treatment of the Kinetoscope.

29. *Denver Republican,* August 16, 1896, p. 24.

Denouement

1. *The Denver Post,* January 19, 1919, section II, p. 11.

JAMES FLASH LAMP, No. 1.

Bibliography

American Journal of Science (New Haven).

Annual Report, V. H. Hayden, U. S. Geological Survey, 1874 (Washington, D.C.: Government Printing Office, 1876).

The Atlantic Monthly (Boston).

Camera Shots of Big Game, Mr. and Mrs. A. G. Wallihan (New York: Doubleday, Page and Company, 1906).

Central City Register (Central City).

Colorado Business Directory, 1875 (Denver).

Colorado Chieftain (Pueblo).

Colorado Magazine (Denver).

Cyclopaedic Photography, Edward L. Wilson, Ph.D. (New York: Edward L. Wilson, 1894).

The Daguerreotype in America, Beaumont Newhall (New York: New York Graphic Society).

The Daily Colorado Republican and Rocky Mountain Herald (Denver).

Daily Commonwealth (Denver).

Daily Miners' Register (Central City).

Daily Mining Journal (Blackhawk).

Daily Register (Central City).

Denver City and Auraria, the Commercial Emporium of the Pike's Peak Gold Regions in 1859.

Denver Daily (Denver).

The Denver Post (Denver).

Denver Republican (Denver).

Denver Times (Denver).

Descriptive Catalogue of the Photographs of the United States Geological Survey of the Territories for the Years 1869-1875, second edition, W. H. Jackson (Washington, D.C.: Government Printing Office, 1875).

Diary, W. H. Jackson. An original manuscript in the library of the museum of the State Historical Society of Colorado.

Encyclopedia Britannica, tenth and eleventh editions.

First Official Visit to the Cliff Dwellings, W. H. Jackson. An original manuscript in the library of the museum of the State Historical Society of Colorado.

From Candles to Footlights, Melvin Schoberlin (Denver: Old West Publishing Company, 1941).

George Kirkland Scrapbook. An original manuscript in the library of the State Historical Society of Colorado.

Handbook of Colorado (Denver: J. A. Blake and F. C. Willitt, publishers, 1872).

Hoofs, Claws, and Antlers of the Rocky Mountains by the Camera, Mr. and Mrs. A. G. Wallihan (Denver: Frank S. Thayer, publisher, 1894).

Image of America, Early Photography 1839-1900 (Washington, D.C.: Library of Congress, 1957).

Incidents of Travel and Adventure in the Far West, original edition, Solomon Nunes Carvalho (New York: Jewish Publication Society, 1954).

Journal of Commerce (Kansas City).

Kansas Territorial Census, 1860.

Las Animas Leader (Las Animas).

The Life of Dr. Elisha Kent Kane and Other Distinguished American Explorers, Samuel M. Schmuker (Philadelphia: John E. Potter and Company, 1858).

Master's Thesis, "The Early Photographers of Colorado, 1853 to 1876," Opal Harber (Denver: The University of Denver, 1956).

Memoirs of My Life, John Charles Fremont (New York: Belford, Clarke and Company, 1887).

Miner's Register (Central City).

Mining Register (Lake City).

Photographers and the Colorado Scene, Opal Harber (Denver: Denver Public Library, 1961).

Photography and the American Scene, Robert Taft (New York: Macmillan Company, 1938).

Radiologic Pioneers in Colorado, 1896-1918, Walter W. Wasson, M.D., 1934. A manuscript in the library of the State Historical Society of Colorado.

Rocky Mountain Herald (Denver).

Rocky Mountain News (Denver).

Sam Howe Scrapbook, an original manuscript in the library of the State Historical Society of Colorado.

Scribner's Magazine (New York).

Shutters West, Nina Hull Miller (Denver: Sage Books, 1962).

Southwest Historical Series, Colorado Gold Rush, L. R. Hafen (Glendale: Arthur H. Clark Company, 1941).

Time Exposure, William H. Jackson (New York: G. P. Putnam, 1940).

The Trail (Denver).

Tribune-Republican (Denver).

Tri-Weekly Mines Register (Central City).

Wallihan's Account, A. G. Wallihan, 1932, an original manuscript in the library of the State Historical Society of Colorado. The paging has been altered to provide logical discussion of topics.

Weekly Commonwealth (Denver).

Weekly Commonwealth and Republican (Denver).

The Western Mountaineer (Golden).

Directory of Early Photographers

1853 THROUGH 1900

Compiled by Mrs. Opal Harber
with additions by the author

KEY TO SYMBOLS

A—Aspen City Directories, 1889—1890, 1892

B&RR—Business Directory & Railroad Gazeteer of Utah, Idaho, Montana, Wyoming, Colorado, etc., 1879-1880

BCo—Boulder County, 1892, 1898

C—Colorado State Business Directories, 1875—1901

C Illus.—Colorado Illustrated Business Directory, 1889

CC—Cripple Creek City Directories 1894—1895, 1897, 1898

CC&G—Clear Creek and Gilpin County, 1892

CC—VMD — Cripple Creek—

Victor Mining District Directory, 1895

CCC—Clear Creek County, 1898

CG—Colorado Gazeteer, 1871

C,NM—Colorado, New Mexico, etc. Gazeteer, 1884—1885

CS—Colorado Springs Directories, 1890, 1892, 1896, 1898, 1900, 1901

CuC—Silver Cliff and Custer County Directory, 1880

D—Denver City Directories, 1873—1901

Del—Dellenbaugh, Fredericks. *The Romance of the Colorado River*, New York, Knickerbocker Press, 1902

L—Leadville City Directories, 1879—1901

LCor—Leadville, Corbett, 1880

McKBD— McKenney's Business Directory of the principal towns of Utah, Wyoming, Colorado and Nebraska, 1882

N—Newhall, Beaumont. "Early Western Photographers", *Arizona Highways*, Vol. 22 (May, 1946) pp. 4—11

O'H—O'Harra, C.C. "Custer's Black Hills Expedition of 1875", *Black Hills Engineer*, Nov. 1929

P—Pueblo, 1886, 1891, 1897

S&B—Schmitt, Martin, and Brown, —. *Fighting Indians*

of the West, New York, Charles Scribner, 1948

SHSC—State Historical Society of Colorado

T—Directory of Trinidad, Colorado, 1888

Ta—Taft, Robert. *Photography and the American Scene*, New York, Macmillan Co., 1938

UHS—Utah Historical Society

W—Watson, Elmo Scott. "Photographing the Frontier", Westerner's *Brand Book* (Chicago) 1866—1891, Vol. 4. No. 11, Jan. 1948

WHD—Western History Dept., Denver Public Library

A

Abbott, C. L.
1880(C) — Alamosa

Abel, Mrs. Dola
1901(C) — Denver
135 Broadway

Abraham & Isaacs
1868 — Denver
(Represented themselves as photographers but bilked their customers.)

Abrahams, J. H. & Company
(see Abraham & Isaacs)

Achleitner, Otto
1897(D) — Denver

Acme Gallery
1232 Larimer Street, Denver

Adams, E.
1892(C) — Silverton

Adams, Frank C.
1897-1898(C) — Pueblo
6th and Santa Fe

Adams, F. S.
1897(P) — Pueblo
4th and Santa Fe

Adams Brothers & Company J. R.
1900-1901(C) — Goldfield

Allen, C. F.
1860's — Denver

Allen, Edwin S.
1875-1876(D) — Denver
(with W. G. Chamberlain)

Allen, Increase
1896(CS) — Colorado Springs

Allyn, Mark
(see also Rankin, Paris & Allyn)
1861 — Central City
(with Henry Faul)
1861 — Denver

Alter, C.F.
1865-1866 — Denver

Anderson & Company, Chas. W.
1889(D) — Denver (with E. N. Clements)
1893(D) — Denver
1705 Champa
1894(D) — Denver
906 - 15th
1895(L) — Leadville
219 Harrison
1896-1897(C) — Leadville
406½ Harrison

Anderson, E. W.
1898(BCo) — Boulder

Anderson, J. August
1899(D) — Denver
428 - 16th

Anderson & Leon
1893(C) — Denver
705 Champa

Appel, Gustave R.
1887-1889(C) — Central City
1890-1891 — not listed
1892-1896(C) — Denver
1529 Larimer
1897-1899(C & D)
Iron Building
1900-1901(C) — 1623 Curtis

Arrington, Ed.
1900(C) — Brush

Armanntrout, M. J. (M. I.)
(Armanntrout and Armentrout)

1897-1898(C) — Golden
1899 — not listed
1900(C) — Golden

Armington, W. R.
1897-1900(C) — Brighton

Armstrong, Miss A.
(see Harkullas, Mrs. S.)

Atkins, Massard & Company
1865 — Black Hawk

Augustine, G. W.
1886(C) — Aspen

Augustine, William R.
1885(C) — Aspen (also grocer)
1886 — not listed
1887(C) — Aspen

Aulls, (H. L.) & Cannon (O. R.)
(D) Oro City (photo in WHD)

Aultman, O. E. (A. E.)
(see also Cook & Aultman)
1891-1900 (C) — Trinidad

Avery, J. C.
1888(C) — Lamar

Avery, Julian M.
1893(D) — Denver
1740 Larimer
1894(D) — Denver
2862 Larimer

B

Babbitt, J. P.
1883(C) — Buena Vista

Babbitt & Howard
(see also Babbitt, J. P.)
1881-1882(C) — Buena Vista

Baker, Ellis W.

1888-1890(C) — Denver
6 & 7 McClellan(d) Block

Baker, F. E.
1894(C) — Greeley
1895 — not listed
1396-1901(C) — Greeley

Baker, G. G.
1890(C) — Denver
800 14th

Baker, Josiah C.
1882(D) — Denver

Baker & Johnson (S & B)

Baldwin, George
1893(C) — Denver
Iron Building

Baldwin, S. S.
1900-1901(C) — Cripple Creek
115 South 4th

Ballough, Monte George
Rico (Ca. 1895-1903, per J.C. Thode)

Balster, F. S.
1893(C) — Durango

Bangley, C. W.
1882(McKBD) — Fort Collins

Barber, John F.
1897(C) — Denver
1515 California

Barker, A. W.
1873 — Colorado Springs

Barker & Gatch
1875 — Colorado Springs

Barley (Harie C.) & Vila (Joseph)
1890(D) — Denver

16th northwest corner Platte

Barney, B. F.
1901(D) — Denver
219-200 Symes block

Barnhart (see Brubaker & Barnhart)

Barnhouse, T. E.
(see also Barnhouse & Wheeler)
1876-1885(C) — Lake City
1885(C) — Grand Junction
(also Watchmaker)
1886-1889 — not listed
1890-1893(C) — Grand Junction

Barnhouse & Wheeler (D. N.)
1877-1879(C) — Lake City

Barrett, Mrs.
1878-1879(C) — Del Norte

Barry, David F.
1880(Ta)

Barthelmess, Christian
(S&B)

Bass (see Hosier & Bass)

Bass, Lawrence P.
1890-1892(C) — Boulder
1893-1895 — not listed
1896(C) — Boulder
1897 — not listed
1897(BCo) — Boulder

Bastian, Thomas H.
1882(D) — Denver

Baston, J. A.
1885(C) — Durango
1886-1889 — not listed
1890(C) — Durango
1891 — not listed

1892(C) — Durango

Bates, William L.
(see also below)
1881-1883(D) — Denver
40, 41 & 52 Tabor Block
1884(C) — Denver
Tabor Building

Bates & Muhr
1883(C) — Denver
Larimer and 16th

Bates & Nye
1880(C) — Denver
Larimer corner 15th

Bates & Webb
1885(C) — Denver
Tabor Block

Beaman, E. O.
1871(T)
(Powell Survey)

Beatty, Frank
1890(D) — Denver
(with C. H. Wells)

Beauchamp, Levi
1860 — Mountain City

Beckner, U. S.
1890(D) — Denver
(with W. H. Lawrence &
Co.)

Beebe, Christopher K. (with
J. E. Beebe)
1887-1890(D) — Denver

Beebe, John E.
1885-1887(D) — Denver
438 or 1716 Arapahoe
1888(D) — Denver (& Bro.)
1716 Arapahoe
1889-1892(C) — Denver
1716 Arapahoe

Beecher
1896 — Dawson City (photo
in WHD)

Bell, William A.
1867 — Kansas Pacific RR
(photos in SHSC)

Bellman, W. A.
1901(C) — Colorado Springs
112 South Tejon

Bellsmith, H. S.
1891-1898(D) — Denver
1113 - 16th, 16th & Ara-
pahoe

Benecke, Robert
1873 — KPRR (RMN No-
vember 18, 1873)

Benell, Mary
1895-1896(C) — Mosca

Benford (Thomas) & Company
1883(D) — Denver
Lawrence southeast cor-
ner 15th

Bennet, Amos S.
1893-1896 — Craig
(Possibly with Wallihan
photo of rattlesnake in
WHD)

Bennett, A. E.
1889 — Leadville
15 Emmet Block
1900(C) — Leadville
502 Harrison
1900(L) — Bennett's Studio
1901(C & L) — 502 Harrison

Bennett, Lester J.
1882(D) — Denver
(with W. H. Jackson)

Bennett, William
1889(D) — Denver
(with W. H. Foreman)

Benson, O. B.
1891-1892 — Fremont

Bierstadt, Albert (Captain
Lander's Expedition)
(Ta)

Biggart, Robert
1884(D) (with H. W. Watson)

Billman, William A. (Billinan)

1896(CS) — Colorado
Springs
116 West Huerfano
1897 — not listed
1898(C) — Grand Junction
1899-1900(C) — Colorado
Springs
112 South Tejon
1900-1901(CS) — Colorado
Springs
112 South Tejon

Bingham, Robert R.
1889(D) — Denver
(with H. Rothberger)
1890(D)

Bingler, Charles
1877(D) — Denver

Bingley, Dr. C. W.
1878-1880(C) — Golden

Bishop Brothers
1896-1898(C) — Delta

Black, Mrs. Belle
1885(C) — West Las Animas

Black, C. H.
1887(D) — Denver

Blacklidge, Cassius F.
1883(D) — Denver
(with H. W. Watson)

Black Sisters
1896-1898(C) — Boulder

Blake, F. P.
1891(C) — Canon City

Blanchard, (T. E.) & Son
1900-1901(C) — Rifle

Blue, Monte
1901(C) — Rico

Blush, Edward K.
1890(D) — Denver
(with Albert E. Lickman &
Company)
1023 — 17th Street

Bohm, Charles
(see also Perry & Bohm)
1870-1885(D) — Denver
284 — 15th Street

Bohm, Mrs. C.
1886(D) — Denver
284 15th Street

Bohm, George
1877(D) — Denver

Boston, J. A.
(see also Boston and Ziegler)
1888-1890(C) — Durango
1891(C) — Denver
(Boston Studio)
906 — 17th Street
1892-1898(C) — Durango
1899(C) — Durango
(Boston Photo Gallery)
1900 — not listed
1901 — Crested Butte

Boston & Ziegler
1880(C) — Canon City

Bottomley, Miss J. B.
1895(C) — Pueblo
239 North Union
1896-1898 — not listed
1899-1901(C) — Lamar

Bottomley, T. F.
1893-1894(C) — Pueblo
239 North Union

Boyce, H. N.
1894(C) — Aspen Junction

Boyce & Fabling
1899(C) — Denver
25 - 1617 Lawrence

Boyton, Orville R.
1894(L) — Leadville
Harrison corner 4th

Bradley (see Kellum & Bradley)

Bradley
1862 — Denver

Bradley, H. C.
1900-1901(C) — Fort Collins

Brandt, Eugene (see Oldroyd,
L.K. and Gurnsey, B.H.)

Brewer (see McEwen & Brewer)

Bricker (Brecker)
1860 — Denver

Bridge, M. L.
1874 — Colorado Springs

Brisbois, Alfred (also M. L.)
1881-1892(C & L) — Leadville
501-503 Harrison

Britt, Peter (Jacksonville to
Oregon, 1852)
(Ta)

Britton, George Francis
1897(C) — Colorado Springs
1898(C & CS) — Colorado
Springs
112 South Tejon

Britton, Walter R.
1894(D) — Denver

Brohm, A. C.
1892(C) — Denver
1605 Market

Brooks, Percy E. (P. F.)
1895(D) — Denver
808 - 17th
1896-1897(C) — Denver
926 - 16th (23 Tritch Block)
1898-1900(C) — Denver
16th and Stout (Barth
Block)
1901(C) — Denver
809 16th

Brooks & Drake
1893-1894(C) — Creede

Brown, William H.
1886(D) — Denver

Brubaker & Barnhardt
1885(C) — Black Hawk

Brumfield, M.
1881 — (Gunnison) The Free
Press, December 3, 1881,
p. 3, c. 4
1882(C) — Gunnison City
1883-1891 — not listed
1892-1896(C) — Ouray
1897(C) — Silverton
1898(C) — Ouray & Silverton
1899-1900(C) — Silverton

Buckwalter, C. E. (see Buckwalter Photographic Com-
pany)

Buckwalter, Harry H.
1897(D) — Denver
713 Lincoln
1901(C & D) — Denver
713 Lincoln

Buckwalter Photographic
Company
(H. H. & C. E.) — Denver
1898-1900(D) — Denver
713 Lincoln

Buell, Mrs. J. E.
1900-1901(C) — Evergreen

Buell, O. B.
1879(D) — Denver

Bunker, Thos
1896-1898(C) — Walsenburg

Bunn & Secker
1891(C) — Fort Collins

Burdick, James M., Son &
Company
(For a panorama of 1859 of
the Gold Regions)

Burk, Edward
1899(D) — Denver

Burliss, William
1901(C) — Osler

Burnham, D.D.
1878(C) — Canon City
1879(C) — Leadville
1880-1886 — not listed
1887-1888(C) — Aspen

Burnham & Cutler
1889(C) — Aspen

Burns & Company
1893(C) — Boulder

Buttree (see Fore & Buttree)

Byles, C.W.
1893-1894(C) — Boulder

C

Cable(s), Rufus E.
1860 — Denver (West Den-
ver)
1860 — Colorado City
(Left Denver with Oliver
Case in September 1860)

Calhoun (see Hosier & Calhoun)

Campbell, Charles
1881(D) — Denver

Cannon, O. C.
1888(C) — Cortez

Cannon, Othniel R. (see also
Aulls & Cannon)
1885(D) — Denver
100 Opera House Block
1886(D) — Denver
16 Timerman Block

Cannon, W. A.
1880(C) — Denver

Carbutt, John, UPRR
1886(Ta) — Omaha

Caribou, Colorado
1871 — Photographic Gal-
lery

Carlson, Pete(r)
1897(C) — Leadville
423 Harrison
1898(L) — Leadville
(with O'Keefe & Stock-
dorf)
501 Harrison
1899 — not listed
1900(L) — Leadville
(with Frank W. Grove)
501 Harrison
1901(L) — Leadville
425 Harrison

Carlzen, S. M.
Central City after 1880 (Pic-
ture of Eureka Street in
WHD)

Carmen, Theodore (Thos.)
1895(D) — 1897(C) — Denver
1232 Larimer

Carpenter & Taylor
1890-1891(C) — Telluride
1892 — not listed
1893(C) — Telluride

Carpenter, D. W. (E. W.)
1890-1893(C) — La Junta
1894 — not listed
1895-1898(C) — La Junta

Carpenter, W. J.
1889(C) — Silverton

Carr, J. E.
1896 — Rocky Ford

Carter, C. W.
1873(Ta) — Utah

Carvalho, Solomon Nunes
1853 —
(with Fremont in Colorado)

Case, Oliver (see Cable(s), Rufus E.)

Caseman, Frederick
1890(D) — Denver
(with W. H. Jackson)

Casey (see Gilbert & Casey)

Castor, W. H.
1901(C) — Denver
30-33, 1131 - 15th, McClelland Block

Caswell, A. E.
1899-1900(C) — Cripple
Creek
255 Bennett
1901(C) — Cripple Creek
201 Lode

Catton (Cotton), Charles
1874 — Colorado Springs

Cecil, William W.
1892(C) — Leadville
425 Harrison
1893-1898 — not listed
1899(C) — Denver
rear 1635 Stout
1900-1901(C & D) — Denver
1528 Champa

Cecil & Hunter
1896(C) — Denver
1635 Stout

Central Photo Company
1894(C) — Pueblo
407 Santa Fe

Chadband, Fred J.
1882(D) — Denver
(with Benford & Compa-
ny)
1882(C) — Denver

Chamberlain, William G. (also
Walter A.)
1861-1881 — Denver
1862-1863 — Denver
1400 block Larimer
1864-1877 — Denver
Larimer northwest corner
15th
1878-1879(D) — Denver
1881(C) — Denver (& Son)
1887-1888(D) — Denver
(with W.H. Jackson)
1889-1890(D) — Denver
(with W.H. Jackson part-
time)

Chapman, J. G.
1894-1895(C) — Walsenburg

Chase (see Wheeler & Chase)

Chase,...
1899(C) — Pueblo
304 North Main

Chase, Mrs. B. B.
1898-1901(D) — Denver
916 - 16th

Chase, Dana B.
1873-1876 — Pueblo
1877 — not listed
1878(C) — Alma, Del Norte
& Garland
1879(C) — Canon City and
Trinidad
1880-1885(C) — Trinidad
1886 — not listed
1887-1889(C) — Trinidad
1890-1891(D & C) — Denver
15th southeast corner Lawrence
1892(CS) — Colorado
Springs
1893-1895(C & D) — Denver
910 - 16th
1896(C) — Denver
910 - 13th
1897(C) — Denver
916 - 16th
(see also Erie Photographic
Co., John A. Chase and
Wheeler & Chase)

Chase, E. S.
1892(C) — Silverton

Chase, H. L.
1901(C) — Holyoke

Chase, John A.
1876 — Las Animas
1877 — not listed
1878-1879(C) — Pueblo

Chase, Morton E.
1888(D) — Denver
Larimer northwest corner
15th
1889 — not listed
1890-1893(C) — Greeley
1893(C) — Lousiville
Chase & Company, M. E.
1894-1900 — not listed
1901(C) — Ouray

Chase & Swanson
1887(D & C) — Denver
1459 Larimer

Chase's Photo Gallery
1888(T) — Trinidad
(J. F. Cook, Operator &
Manager)
101½ East Main
(see also D. B. Chase)

Chester, Benjamin
1889(D) — Denver

Chew, N. I. (see Hawkins &
Chew, and Chew & Jandus)

Chew & Jandus
1877(D) — Denver
372 Larimer

Childs, Alfred R. (see Parks &
Childs)

Christensen, D. E.
1898-1899(C) — Sanford

Christopher, E. & Company
1882(D) — Denver
1883(C) — Pueblo

Christy & Son
1892-1893(C) — Colorado
Springs

Churchill, W. D.
1882-1888(C) — Brecken-
ridge

Clark, C. H.
1884(C) — Gunnison
1885 — not listed
1886-1888(C) — Salida

Clark, Charles B.
1876(D) — Denver
1876-1881(D) — Denver
(with Charles Bohm)

Clark, D. G.
1896-1898(C) — Boulder
1899(C) — Boulder
(Clark, D. E.)
1900(C) — Boulder
(Clark, D. G.)

Clark, Frank E.
1890(D) — Denver
(with Alex Lozo)

Clark, John F.
1888(D) — Denver

Clark(e), Edwin R.
1876-1882 — Pueblo
1878-1879(C) — Pueblo
1884(C) — Clark & Nims
Colorado City

Clark, Mrs. Robert A.
1870-1871(CG) — Black
Hawk

Clark & Erdlen
1889(C Illus) — Salida and
Buena Vista

Clarke, ...
Clarke & Nims
1883(C) — Colorado Springs

Clegg, H. B. (Cleggett, B.)
(also Clegg & Phillips)
1895-1898(C) — Victor
1899(C) — Victor
102 South 4th
1895(CC—VMD) — Victor
(Cleggett, B.)

Clements, Edward N.
1883-1884(C) — Leadville
Harrison southeast corner
4th
1885(C) — Leadville
105 E. 4th
1886-1887(C) — Leadville
613 Harrison
1888-1889(C & D) — Denver
1617 Champa
1898 — not listed
1899-1900(D) — Denver
1617 Champa
1901(C) — Denver
1624 Curtis
(see also Hutchinson and
Clements, Wakely & Cle-
ments and below)

Clements & Ross
1892(C) — Denver
1617 Champa

Clements & Van Horn
1881(L) — Leadville
103 East 4th
1882(C) — Leadville

Cleveland, E. L.
1900-1901(C) — Canon City

Clinton, J. L. (J. S.) (see also
Rudy & Clinton)

1888-1894(C) — Colorado
Springs
1896(CS) — Colorado
Springs

Clough, H. R.
1883(C) — Pueblo

Colby, ...
1860 — Denver and Pike's
Peak Region

Collier, Joseph M.
1871-1874 — Central City
1874-1875 Collier & Mc-
Lean
1875-1878 — Collier (Central
City)
1878-1886(C & D) — Denver
415 Larimer
1887-1901(C) — Denver
1643 Larimer

Collier, Robert
1883(D) — Denver
(with J. Collier)
1884(D) — Denver

Collins, Richard B.
1876-1877 — Boulder
1878 — Central City (C. C.
Register, February 9, 1878,
p. 4)
1879 — not listed
1880(L) — Leadville
54 Harrison
1881 — not listed
1882(C) — Durango
1883(D) — Denver
(see also Collins & Gregg)

Collins, Walter
1892(C) — Leadville
802 Harrison

Collins & Gregg
1878 — Boulder

Colorado Artotype Company
(see Williamson, H. M.)

Colpas, Thomas J.
1889(D) — Denver
(with H. M. Williamson)

Comstock, H. L. & Company
(see also Voice & Com-
stock)
1892(D) — Denver
906 - 15th
1894(D) — Denver
2100 Larimer

Concannon, Thomas M.
1884 - 1885(C, NM) — Denver
18th southeast corner
Blake

Conley & Company
1895-1896(C) — Pueblo
325 Santa Fe

Converse, H. C.
1901(C) — Denver
11 Evans Block

Cook, J. F. (see Chase's Photo
Gallery) (see below)

Cook (J. F.) & Aultman (O. F.)
1890(C) — Trinidad

Cooker, A.
1901(C) — Silver Cliff

Cooks & Miller (see Crooks &
Miller)

Cooper, H. D.
1898(CS) — Colorado
Springs
25 South Weber Street

Cornish, J. J. (I.)
1880-1888(C) — Del Norte
1889 — not listed
1890-1898(C) — Chromo

Cory, A. S.
1889(C) — Durango

Cory & Gohner
1890(C) — Durango

Cotton (see Catton, Charles)

Corrtney, O. W.
1897(C) — Telluride

Coward, F.
1893(C) — Pueblo
115 West 4th

- Cram, Ella
1899(C) — Golden

Cronyn, W.W.
1889(C) — Pueblo
523 Santa Fe
1890-1891(C) — Pueblo
6th & Santa Fe

Crookham, George
1876(D) — Denver
(with Charles Bohm)

Crooks, ...
— Gunnison (Photo in Gun-
nison Biographies of Wo-
men)

Crooks & Miller
1895-1901(C) — Monte Vista

Cross, Walter
1890(D) — Denver
(with Horace E. Hunt)

Cunningham & Company
(Alexander M.)
1884-1885(C,NM) — Colorado
Springs

Curran, Thomas J. (see Williamson & Curran)

Currier, Frank (S & B)

Curtiss, Frank
1881(C) — Pitkin

Cutler, M. L. (see also Burnham & Cutler)
1889-1890(A) — Aspen

D

Daggett, Mrs. Frances
1900-1901(C) — Fulford

Dales, G. S.
1873(D) — Denver

Dalgleish, George
1892-1901(C) — Georgetown

Dalgleish Brothers
1890(C) — Georgetown
1891 — not listed

Danielson, Frank M. (Donald-
son, Donelson)
1864 — Denver (with W. G.
Chamberlain)
1864-1868 — Central City
1868-1872 — Denver (with
George M. Sildbee in 1870,
with Charles Stimson in
1872)
1873 — not listed
1874 — Denver
377 Larimer

Dare, D. D. (S & B)

David, V. E.
1872 — Pueblo

Davis, C. L.
1889(C) — Lansing

Davis, O. T.
1893(C) — Walsenburg
1894-1897 — not listed
1898(C) — La Veta

Davis, Robert M.
1887(D) — Denver
1107 - 16th

Dayton, M.
1899-1900(C) — Brush

Dean, Frank E. (F. F.)
1883-1889(C) — Gunnison
1890-1894(C) — Crested
Butte, Gunnison & Lake
City
1895(C) — Gunnison & Lake
City
1896-1900(C) — Crested
Butte, Gunnison and Lake
City
1901(C) — Grand Junction

Delavan, W. (Delevan)
1868(November) — Denver
1868(December)-1869(February) — Central City

Demaree, Christopher
1884(D) — Denver

Demare(e), William H.
1882(D) — Denver
1888(D) — Denver
(with M. E. Chase)
1889(D) — with F. E. Post
1890(D) — Denver

Demaree, W. Harvey
1895(D) — Denver
1126 - 15th

Dennis, A. W. (Dennes)
1881-1884(C) — Canon City
1884-1885 — see below
1886-1887 — not listed
1888-1901(C) — Colorado
Springs

Dennis & Few (Dennes)
1884-1885(C) — Canon City

Denver Photo Company
1898(D) — Denver
203 Times Building

Denver Photographic Studio
1889(D) — Denver
910 - 16th
(see also Arthur French &
Lemuel C. Graves)

Desmond, D. C. (DesMond)
1892(C) — Antonito
1893 — not listed
1894-1900(C) — Trinidad

Diamond, Daniel
1897-1899(C) — Craig

Dickerman, Allen
1892(C) — Pueblo
Holden Block Number 2

Dixon, Joseph K.(S & B)

Dodge, Frank
1884(D) — Denver
(with W. H. Watson)
1888(D) —
(with Stephan, George &
Company)

Doer, George E.
1890(C) — Denver
72 Railroad Building

Drake (see Brooks & Drake
and Hoer & Drake)

Drenkel, D. R. (R)
1890-1891(C) — Aspen
1892 — not listed
1893-1895(C) — Aspen
1896-1898 — not listed
1899(C) — Aspen

Drumfield, ...
1896(C) — Silverton

Dudley, M.
1893(C) — Grand Junction

Duhem Brothers (Constant
and Victor M.)
1869-1872 — Denver
1872-1879(C) — Denver
448 Larimer

Dunton, Oscar E.
1892(L) — Leadville
233 East 6th
1893-1900 — not listed
1901(L) — Leadville
802 Harrison

Dyer, John W.
1888(D) — Denver
(with Wells & King)
1890(D) — Denver
1113 - 16th
1891 — not listed
1892(D) — Denver
2413 - 16th
1893(D) — Denver
730 - 15th

E

Eastman, C. H.
1901(C) — Gunnison

Eastman, G. L.
1880(C) — Georgetown
1881(C) — Jackson Party
Georgetown

Eastman's Photograph & Fer-
rotype Gallery
1880's — Denver

Eaton, W. H.
1891(C) — Colorado Springs

Edgeworth, Reuban M.
1880(D) — Denver
(with H. W. Watson)
1881 — Denver

Edison, Thomas Company
Kinetograph at the Festival
of Mountain and Plain
1897-1898

Edwards, Thomas
1888-1889(C) — Erie

Eichler, ...
1885(D) — Denver

Eggleston Brothers (E. M. &
Wellington K. or W. W.)
1865 — Boulder
1866-1869 — not listed
1870-1871 — Georgetown

Elite Photo Studio
1901(CS) — Colorado
Springs
425 South Tejon

Elite Photographic Gallery
(Ryan & Company, Props)
1893-1895(C & D) — Denver
16th & Curtis and Cass &
Graham Block

Elite Studio
1895(C) — Leadville
1896 — not listed
1897-1898(L) — Leadville
Union Block

Ellington, George
1894(D) — Denver
2100 Larimer

Ellingson, George
1893(D) — Denver

Ellingson, John O.
1898(C) — Telluride
1899 — not listed
1900-1901(C) — Denver
1740 Larimer

Elliot, J. A.
1883-1884(C) — Pueblo

Elliott, R. F. (Elliot), (see also
Reiff & Elliot)
1873-1876 — Georgetown
1877 — not listed
1878-1881(C) — Georgetown
1882(C) — Silver Plume
1883-1885(C) — Georgetown

Ellis, A. B.
1893(C) — Trinidad

Ellis, C(h)arleton F.
1884(C) — Denver
1885(D) — with J. E. Beebe
1886-1887(D) — Denver

Ely, W. S. (see also Hildreth &
Ely)
1897(C) — Georgetown
1898(CCC) — Georgetown

Ely & Hildreth
1898(BCo) — Longmont
1899 — not listed
1900 — see Hildreth & Ely
1901(C) — Longmont

Elze, Edward
1897(C) — Silver Cliff

Emery, Charles E.
1880(CuC) — New Photo-
graph Rooms (p. 34)
1882(C) — Silver Cliff
1883 — not listed
1884-1885(C) — Silver Cliff
1886-1891(C) — Canon City
1892 — not listed
1893-1901(C) — Colorado
Springs
18 South Tejon

Endless, ...
1895(C) — Salida

Endsley, Dave & Company
Leadville Photo
219 Harrison

Ensminger, Clara
1888(C) — Hyde
1889-1890 — not listed
1891(C) — Yuma

Ensminger, Marcella
1893(C) — Yuma

Erdlen, C. W. (Erdler)
1885-1887(C) — Buena Vista
1888 — not listed
1889(C) — Salida and Buena Vista
1890(C) — Salida
1891(C) — Saguache & Salida
1892(C) — Buena Vista, Moffat, Monarch, Saguache, St. Elmo, Salida, & Villa Grove
1893(C) — Salida
1894-1895 — not listed
1896-1898(C) — Salida

Erickson, C. A.
1891 — Ridgway
(Ridgway Herald, December 17, 1871, p. 4)
1892(C) — Montrose
1893(C) — Montrose & Ridgway
1894(C) — Delta & Telluride
1895(C) — Rico & Telluride
1896(C) — Telluride
1897-1900(C) — Florence

Erie Photograph Company
1873-1876 — Pueblo
1876 — "Photograph car" (Dana B. Chase & Henry O. Morris — Canon City, Fairplay, Lake City, and Saguache)

Eureka Gallery
1893(D) — Denver
2200 Larimer

Eureka Studio (see Edwin A. Wilder)

Evans, Albert L.
1887(D) — Denver
(with D. Lamon)

F

Fabling (see Boyce & Fabling)

Farmer, Albert E.
1890(D) — Denver

Farr, H. L.
1892(C) — Pueblo
525 Santa Fe

Faul, Henry (see below) (see also John Glendinen & Faul)
1862-1864 — Central City
1864(August—October) — Denver

Faul & Allyn (Mark Allyn)
1861 — Central City

Faul & Saint (T. G. Saint)
1862 — Central City

Faul & Waldo
1861 — Central City

Fen, W. E.
1888(C) — Montrose

Fennimore, James
(D) (Ta)

Ferris, Miss D.
1860 — Golden City

Few, William E.
1886(C) — Canon City

Finn, Charles E.
1881(D) — Denver
300 Larimer

Fisher, M. (A.)
1896(C) — Cripple Creek
2nd & Bennett
1897-1900 — not listed
1901(CS) — Colorado Springs
32 North Tejon

Fisk, Harold
1896(C) — Loveland

Fitzgibbon, J. H. (St. Louis Daguerreotypist)
(Ta)

Flach, Gustave A.
1887(C & D) — Denver
1617 Champa

Fleischer, A. H.
1875 — Denver

Foos, W. W. (Foose)
1871 — Burlington

Foote, Thomas R.
1888(D) — Denver

Fore & Buttree
1900(C) — Cripple Creek
406 East Bennett

Foreman, Walter H.
1886(C) — Denver
377 Larimer
1886(D) — Denver
(with George Stephan)
1887-1895(C & D) — Denver
1529 or 1537 Larimer
1896-1898 — not listed
1899(C) — Boulder

Foreman & Ehrlick
1900(C) — Boulder

Forsdahl, M.
1890(CS) — Colorado Springs
1891-1898 — not listed
1899-1900(C) — Greeley

Fox, H.
1870 — Denver

Francis & Griffin
Baltimore, Colorado

Fraser, W. C. (Fraser, W. A.)
(Willoughby, C.)
1892-1893(C & D) — Denver
2108 Larimer
1894-1895(C & D) — Denver
2052 or 2055 Larimer
1896(C) — Denver
2058 Larimer
1897(C) — Denver
2052 or 1527 Larimer
1898(C) — Denver
1827 Larimer

Freedman, T., & Company
1890(D) — Denver
(with W. H. Foreman)

Freeman, Alfred
1892(C) — Pueblo
117 East 4th
1892(CS) — Colorado Springs
1893(C) — Colorado Springs
1894 — not listed
1895-1901(C) — Colorado Springs
32 North Tejon
1898 — not listed
1900(CS) — Colorado Springs
32 North Tejon

Freeman, J. B.
1884(C) — Pitkin
1885-1886(C) — White Pine

Freeman, W. E.
1890(D) — Denver

French, Arthur
1889(D) — Denver
Denver Photographic Studio, 910 — 16th

Fricke & Company (Frick, Fricks, Frickle)
1892-1901(C) — Canon City

Frost, Mrs. Addie
1897(C) — Hooper

Frost, S. F. (Captain Lander's Party)
(T)

Frost Brothers
1896-1898(C) — Idaho Springs

Fry, Camillus S.
(Ta) (W)

Fullilore, H.
1898(C) — Las Animas

Furman, R. H.
1893(C) — Pueblo
325 Santa Fe

G

Galbreath, Mrs.
1885(C) — Manitou

Garbanati, Henry
1864-1866 — Central City

Gardner, Alexander (UPRR, Kansas, 1867)
(T)

Garrison Brothers
1901(C) — Rifle

Gatch (see Barker & Gatch)

Gaylord, C. W.
1899(C) — Leadville

Gem Photo Company
1901(CS) — Colorado Springs
115 East Pikes Peak Ave.

Ghormley (see Spracklen & Ghormley)

Gilbert, John E.
1883(C) — Ouray
1884 — not listed
1885(C) — Silverton

Gilbert & Casey
1893(C) — Leadville

Gill, Delancy
(T) (W)

Gille(i), Charles
1875(D) — Denver

Gillen, William J. (Gillian)
1885(D) — Denver
300 Larimer
1886(D) — Denver
326 Larimer
1887(D) — Denver
1510 Champa
1888(D) — Denver
1332 Larimer
1889(D) — Denver
(with W. H. Foreman)
1890-1891(D) — Denver
Ashland, northwest corner Gallup Avenue and Highlands
1892(D) — Denver
Golden Avenue southwest corner Morrison Road and Colfax
1893(C) — Cripple Creek
1894 — not listed
1895-1897(C) — Cripple Creek
North 4th or 116 - 1st

Gillian (Geillen), William J.
1893 — Cripple Creek
1894(CC) — Cripple Creek

Gillingham, Charles L. (Gilligan)
1882-1890(C) — Colorado Springs
1891-1900 — not listed
1901(CS) — Colorado Springs
324 East Huerfano

Gilpin, Joseph A.
1887(D) — Denver
(with W. H. Jackson)

Glem (see Harlan & Glenn)

Glendinen, John Y. (Glendenen, Glendenin, Glendinin)
1859-1860 — visited the gold regions
1862 — Central City
(with Henry Faul)
1863-1864 — Central City

Glendiner & Faul
Colorado Mining Life, September 13, 1862, p.3, c. 2

Glew (see Harlan & Glew)

Glew, Eugene E.
1900(C) — Colorado Springs
27 S. Weber
1901(CS) — Colorado Springs
27 S. Weber

Globe Photo Company
1895-1896(D) — Denver
906 - 15th

Glover, Ridgway
(Ta) (W)

Goehner, Mrs. Gustave A.
1876(D) — Denver

Goehner, Gustave A.
1876-1878 — Denver

(with Charles Bohm)
1879 — not listed
1880(B&RR) — Denver

Goehner & Company
(C) — Denver

Goehner, H.
1876(D) — Denver

Goerke & Son, Paul
1900(CS) — Colorado Springs
1901(C) — Manitou

Goff, O. S. (S & B)

Gohner (see Cory & Gohner)

Goins, James M.
1881(D) — Denver
348 Larimer

Goldsberry & Company
1897(C) — Manitou Springs

Gonner, Frank
1891-1901(C) — Durango

Gonner & Hurd
1892(C) — Durango

Goodman & Brothers
1880(C) — South Pueblo

Goodman, Charles H. (J. H.)
1882 — Pueblo
1883 — Pitkin
1887-1888(C) — Montrose
1900(C) — Silverton
1901 — Bluff, Utah

Gormer, Frank
1899(C) — Durango

Gosha & Company, C. E.
1894(C) — La Junta
1895-1896 — not listed
1897-1898(C) — Pueblo
304 North Main

Grabill, John C. H.
(S & B) (W) — Black Hills

Graham, James B.
1875(D) — Denver

Graham, S. B.
1892-1893(C) — Colorado Springs

Granger, D.
1892(C) — Loveland

Graves, Lemuel C. (Manager, Denver Photographic Studio)
1889(D) — Denver
910 — 16th

Green, John (I)
1885-1886(C & D) — Denver
Blake southeast corner 18th
1887-1888 — not listed
1889(C) — Denver
18th & Holladay
1890-1901(C) — Denver
1800 Market

Green, Robert H.
1885(D) — Denver
(with F. D. Storm)

Gregg (see Collins & Gregg and Harlan & Gregg)

Gregg, B. Frank
1879-1880(C) — Boulder

Gregg, Thaddeus
1886(D) — Denver
(with J. E. Beebe)
1890(D) — Denver

Gregory (see Neel Brothers & Gregory)

Grigg, Samuel A.
1882(D) — Denver
(with W. H. Jackson)
1889(D) — Denver
(with F. D. Storm)
1890(D) — Denver

Gross (see Kerwin & Gross)

Gross, Nicholas
1898(D) — Denver

Grove (see Smith (S. S.) & Grove)

Grove, Charles Elmore
1899-1901(C & D) — Denver
1625 Welton

Grove, Frank W. (Grove and Gore)
1873 — Las Animas
1874 — Colorado Springs
1875-1886 — not listed
1887-1888 — see below
1889-1891(C) — Leadville
Union Block or 425 Harrison
1892 — not listed
1893-1896(C) — Leadville
523 Harrison
1897(C) — New Castle
1898(C) — Leadville
Harrison & 7th
1899-1901(C) — Leadville
5th & Harrison

Grove & Helme
1887(L) — Leadville
41 Union Block

Grove & Luke
1888(L) — Leadville
Union Block 425 Harrison

Gurnsey, B. H.
1872-1875 — Pueblo
1875 — with Eugene Brandt
1872-1880 — Colorado Springs
1881-1882(C) — Mrs. B. H. Gurnsey

Gyra, Rudolph
1884(D) — Denver
313 Larimer

H

Haffner, Frank J.
1890 — Times, April 30, 1918, p. 2 (with J. E. Beebe)
1892(D) — Denver
Iron Building, 17th southeast corner Arapahoe

Hamacher (S & B)

Hall, C.
1895(C) — Elizabeth

Hamilron & Kendrick
Denver
906 - 910 17th Street

Hanna,...
1877 — Las Animas

Hanna, A. J.
1895(C) — Cortez

Hanna, O. R.
1895(C) — Mancos
1886 — not listed
1887(C) — Mancos

Hansmans (see Williams & Hansmans)

Harding, C. C.
1889-1900(C) — Telluride

Hargrave, J. J.
1880(C) — Buena Vista

Hargroves, J. J. (see Strong & Hargroves)

Harkullas, Mrs. S. (Herkules, Mrs. A.)
1876 — Trinidad
(with Miss A. Armstrong)
1877 — not listed
1878-1881(C) — Trinidad

Harlan, Andrew James
1891-1892 — Fremont
1896-1898(C) — Victor, Barry
(Walsen RR Station)

Harlan & Glenn
1893(C) — Colorado Springs

Harlan & Glew
1892(C) — Colorado Springs

Harlan & Gregg
1891(C) — Colorado Springs

Harper (see Mellen & Harper)

Harris, Henry
1891(D) — Denver

Harrison, C. H.
1875 — Golden

Hart, A. A. (UPRR & Central
Pacific RR)
(Ta)

Hartman (William F.) & Hubbard (E. W.)
1898(D) — Denver
1625 Welton

Harvey Dry Plate Company
1884(C) — Manitou

Hassell, Gilbert
1890(D) — Denver
(with W. H. Jackson)

Hassel (see Smith-Hassel Co.)

Hastings, C.
1897(C) — Colorado Springs
25 South Weber

Hathaway (see Townsend &
Hathaway)

Hathaway, Frank H.
1894-1896(C & D) — Denver
McClelland Building, 15th
& Lawrence

Havis, J. M.
1898(CS) — Colorado
Springs
South Cheyenne Canon at
Canon terminus CSRT Ry.
1899 — not listed
1900(CS) — Colorado
Springs

Hawes, M. A.
1897-1898(C) — Las Animas
1899-1900 — not listed
1901(C) — Las Animas

Hawkins, B. A.
1873-1882 — Denver
1876 — Denver
(with N. I. Chew)
1877(D) — Denver
377 Larimer

Haynes, F. J.
1875(T) — Dakotas, Yellowstone

Hayter, C. H.
1897-1900(C) — La Junta

Head, Edward J.
1884(D) — Denver

Headley (E. B.) & Morgan
1886(C) — Colorado Springs

Hein Brothers
1900-1901(C) — Canon City

Heller, Louis (S & B) (W)

Helme, William (see Grove &
Helme)

Hemenway,…
1873 — Colorado Springs

Hentig, Arthur S.
1890(D) — Denver
48 Jackson Building

Hersom, C. E.
1892-1893(C) — Manitou
Springs

Hetherington, G. H.
1899(C) — Rocky Ford

Hicks, A. W.
1899-1900(C) — Denver
45 King Block

Hiestand, J. G.
Colorado Springs (see Ute
Springs Photo Gallery)

Hiller, H. B.
(T) — Texas

Hildreth & Ely
1900(C) — Longmont

Hillers, John L. (Powell Survey)
1872-1878) (T)(D)

Hilton, E. F.
1890-1891(C) — Alamosa
1892 — not listed
1893(C) — Bachelor and
Creede
1894(C) — Creede

Hincke, Charles L.
1890 ca Parker, Colorado

1891-1897 — Parker (RMN,
December 1, 1939, p. 11)

Histelhauber, Joseph
1899(C) — Leadville
318 Harrison

Hoer, J. A. & Drake
1895(C) — Creede (City)

Hoffman, John D. (Ta)

Holt, Alex
1893(C) — Aspen

Hook, W. E. (Hook View Company)
1888-1890(C) — Manitou
Springs
1891-1893(C & CS) — Colo-
rado Springs
1894-1895 — not listed
1896-1897(C) — Colorado
Springs
509 North Tejon

Hopkins, Benjamin Sanderson
(see also Rose & Hopkins)
1886-1896 — Denver (Rose &
Company)
40, 41, & 52 Tabor Block

Hopkins, S. D.
1897-1899(C) — Florence

Hopkins, T. E.
1880-1882(C) — Colorado
Springs

Hopkins, Thaddeus E.
1878-1881 — Colorado
Springs

Hopkins & Reed
1897(C) — Coal Creek

Hopping, Charlie H.
1860-1863 — Central City

Hose, Orville L.
1882-1884 (Frank E. Dean)
(Mazzula coal mine Crest-
ed Butte)
(WHD) — RR Station, Crested Butte

Hosford, Mrs. C. H.
1895(D) — Leadville
506 Harrison

Hosier, F. H. (I. H.)
1883(D) — Denver
1884-1886(C) — Boulder
1887 — not listed
1888(C) — Boulder

Hosier & Bass
1889(C) — Boulder
1890(CS) — Manitou Springs
1892(CS) — Manitou Springs
(Proprietor, Iron Springs
Pavilion)

Hosier & Calhoun
1868 — Denver
372 Larimer
1869-1876 — not listed
1877-1880(C & D) — Denver
372 Larimer

Houghton, A. S.
1899-1900(C) — Durango

Houseworth, Thos. (Lawrence
& Houseworth) (S & B)

Hover Brothers
1891(C) — Saguache

Howard (see Babbitt, J. P. &
Howard)

Howard, E. A.
1892(C) — Canon City

Howard, M. B.
1891(P) — Pueblo
115 West 4th

Howard, W. S.
1891-1901(C) — Pueblo
115 West 4th

Howe (see Talbot, N. H.)

Howes, M. A.
1896(C) — Las Animas

Hubbard, E. W. (see Hartman
& Hubbard)

Hubbell, J. Albert

1899-1901(C) — Denver
Times Building or 1547
Lawrence

Hubbell, Royal
1896-1901(C) — Canon City
1900 — not listed

Hudson, Joseph L.
1883(D) — Denver
372 Larimer

Huerfano Photographic Gallery
(see Catton, Charles)

Huffman, L. A.
1878(Ta) (W) — Montana

Hull, Arundel C.
(Miller, Nina Hull —
Shutters West.)

Hunt, Horace E.
1887(D) — Denver
1888(D) — Denver
(with W. H. Foreman)
1226 — 14th

Hunter (see Cecil & Hunter)

Hunter, Elijah C.
1898-1901(C) — Denver
33-1617 Lawrence

Hurd (see Gonner & Hurd)

Hutchinson (William A.) &
Clements (Edward N.)
1883(L) — Leadville
103 & 105 East 4th

Hutton, J. D.
1860(T) — Missouri River,
Reynolds Expedition

Illingworth, W. H. (Bill & Illingworth)
Custer Expedition (O'H)

Imes, Lewis
1890(CS) — Manitou Springs
(with Hiestand)

Ines, Lewis
1890(D) — 1 Alkire Block

Irish (see Ogden & Irish)

Irish, Elwood W.
1891-1892(D) — Denver
523-525 Charles Building,
15th corner Curtis

Isaacs, Charles (see Abraham
& Isaacs)

Ives, Lt.
1857(T) — Colorado River

J

Jackman, Byron D.
1890(D) — Denver

Jackson, D. Lincoln
1900-1901(C & D) — Denver
16th & Arapahoe or 1113
16th

Jackson, Frederick D.
1880(D) — Denver
1881(D) — Denver
(with A. E. Rinehart)
1885(D) — Denver
(with W. H. Jackson)
1887(D) — Denver
(with W. H. Jackson)
1888-1889(D) — Denver
(with W. H. Jackson)
1890(D) — Denver

Jackson, William Henry
1870-1876 — Hayden Surveys
1880-1886(C & D) — Denver
413 or 414 Larimer
1887-1893(C) — Denver
1609-1615 Arapahoe
1894-1897(C & D) — Denver
433 W. Colfax

Jackson-Smith Photo Co.
1898-1899(C) — Denver

Jacobs, A. L.
1898(C) — Colorado Springs
309 South Tejon
1899 — not listed
1900(C) — Denver
61 Good Block

Jamerson, & Townsend
1899(C) — Denver
1617 Lawrence

James, C. (John) (William H.)
1883(D) — Denver
Room 9, Steele Block

James, C.C.
1901(C) — La Junta

James & Maull
1874 — (Aminals Around
Colorado)

James & Son
1883-1884 — Denver
Steele Block

James & Strutevant (sic)
1891(C) — Boulder

Jandus, William (see Chew &
Jandus)

Jennings, Charles H.
1884-1885(C, NM) — Denver
1885(D) — Denver
(with J. E. Beebe)
1887(D) — Denver
(with W. H. Russell)
1888(D) — Denver

Jennings & Russell
1884(D) — Denver
326 Larimer

Jenson, A.M.
1900-1901(C) — Pueblo
304 Main

Jerrel & Motz (Canon City),
1876 (CBS)

Johnson, A.P.
1899(D) — Denver

Johnson, A. D.
1898(C) — Denver
1740 Larimer

Johnson, Adolph R.
1887(D) — Denver

Johnson, Charles O.
1886-1887(D) — Denver
1888-1889(D) — Denver
1890(D) — Denver

Johnson, Mrs. C. H.
1896(C) — Del Norte

Johnson, I.M. (J.M. or M.)
1870-1874 — Greeley (also
known as Rocky Mountain
Gallery of Art)

Johnson, John P.
1882(D) — Denver
(with H. Watson)

Johnson & Woodring
1887(C) — Crawford

Jones, A.H.
1894-1895(C) — Grand
Junction

Jones, Mrs. C.H. (Johnson)
1893-1901(C) — Del Norte

Jones, Thomas
1889(D) — Denver

Jones & Lehman
1897(C) — Denver
1615 Arapahoe
1898-1899(C) — Denver
1113 16th

Jones, J. Wesley (Claims to
have photographed Rockies
1851) (Ta)

Jordon, C.
1901(C) — Denver
16-1132 — 15th

Judkins, David R.
1885(D) — Denver
(with C. C. Wright)

Judson, Fred D.
1890(D) — Denver
(with W. H. Jackson)

K

Kalischer, Max
1893(C) — Denver
16th & Curtis
1894(D) — Denver

Cass & Graham Block

Kauffman, M.E.
1896(C) — Leadville
1897 — not listed
1898 — Louisville

Kay, William
1893(C) — Georgetown

Kearney, L.A.
1901(C) — Aspen

Kelliher's Photograph Gallery
1870 — Georgetown

Kellum & Bradley
1882(C) — Pueblo

Kennady, M. A. (Kennedy,
Bert)
1887-1894(C) — Monte Vista
1888 — not listed

Kennett, R.
1890(D) — Denver
1023 17th
1891(C) — Denver
19-21 Times Block

Kepler, Mrs. V.M.
1895-1899(C) — Central City

Kerr (see Opie & Kerr)

Kerwin & Gross
1901(C) — Aspen

Kilgore, Will A.
1892-1893(C) — Longmont

King, John H.
1882(C) — Denver

King, Will (see Wells & King)
(William S.)

Kirkland, Charles D.
1901(D) — Denver
1617 Champa

Kirkland, George
1876 — Georgetown
(with R. F. Elliot)

Kirkland Brothers (Charles D.,
George W., and P. G.)
1874-1875 — Denver
377 Larimer

Kline, Joseph L.
1878(D) — Denver Printer for
Charles Bohm
1881(D) — (with J. M. Goins)

Kneeland, Ira D.
1893(C) — Denver
2200 Larimer

Knight, Fred L.
1897-1899(C) — Akron
1900 — not listed
1901(C) — Akron

Knight, H. C.
1897-1898(C) — Lake City

Knoerzer (see Way & Knoerzer)

Koonz & Son
1886(C) — Greeley

Koester, Emil
1881(D) — Denver
(with Charles Bohm)

Krueger, Carl E.
1901(CS) — Colorado Springs
24-6 East Bijou

Kuhn, S.M. (S.N.)
1873-1874 — Colorado
Springs
1875 — Del Norte

Kuhn & Wheeler
Del Norte

Kull, A.F.
1898(C) — Denver
907-17th

Kurtz (see Slack & Kurtz)

Kuy Kendall's New Gallery
(Adv.)
Southwest corner Ohio
and Emery (p.42)

Kuykendall, Frank
1880(CuC)

1881(C)-1882(McKBD) — Silver Cliff
1882-1883(C) — Maysville

Kuykendall & Whitney
1884-1885(C,NM) — Ouray

L

Lamon, David
1887(C)—Denver
1740 Larimer
1888-1890—not listed
1891-1892(C & D)—Denver
1634 Larimer

Land, Lewis G.(F.M.)
C. 1880—Bellvue, Colorado

Lang, Mary L.
1911-1912(C)—Langdon

Lanncy(3 & B)

Mr. & Mrs. Larimer (T) (W)

Larimer, William J.
1865—Denver
Larimer Street
1866 — not listed
1867 — Julesberg

Larkins, E. W.
1890-1892(C) — Colorado City

Law, Frederick
1881-1884(C)—Boulder

Lawrence, A.J.
1873-1874 — Denver
16th & Lawrence

Lawrence, C.S.
1901(C)—Leadville
219 Harrison

Lawrence, W.H. & Co.
1890(D)—Denver
1892(D)—Denver
1108-1114 16th

Laycock, F.M.
1887-1890(C)—Hygiene
(Higiene and Hygene)
1891-1892(C)—Hygiene
(Laycock, F.M. & Son)
1891-1892(C)—Delta

Laycock, Henry E.
1893(C)—Berthoud
1894-1895(C)—Hygiene
1896—not listed
1897(C)—Hygiene

Leach, J.A.
1888(C)—Akron

Leadville Photo and View Co.
1899(C)—Leadville
318 Harrison

Lehman (see Jones & Lehman and Schedlin & Lehman)

Lenard (see Lockhart & Lenard)

Leon, T. J. (see also Anderson & Leon)
1892(C) — Denver
910 — 16th

Leon & Anderson (Lion)
1893(C) — Denver
1705 Champa

Letellier, Thomas R.
1886(P) — Pueblo
19 Union, south side
1887(C) — Pueblo
19½ Union
1888-1893(C) — Pueblo
122-126 South Union

Lettle, E.
1884-1885(C,NM) — Wetmore

Levy, H.M. (M.H.)
1899-1901(C)—Pueblo
Santa Fe & 6th

Lewis, C.C.
1890(C)—Lawson

Lewis, Emma C., Miss
1880(D) — Denver
(B. E. Hawkins)

Lickman, Albert E.

1890(C & D)—Denver
1023-17 or 17th & Arapahoe

Liebholdt, Gustave
1887(D) — Denver
(with G. A. Flach)
1889(D) — Denver

L'Imperoale Photograph Gallery
1893(D) — Denver
10—13 Iron Building or 17th, corner Arapahoe

Linquist, B. A.
1886(C) — Central City

Linquist, N.
1898(C)—Julesburg

Little, Emmet
1881(C) — Ruslta
1882-1886 — not listed
1887-1888(C)—Silver Cliff
1889-1892 — not listed
1893(C)—Siloam

Loar, William H.
1876(D)—Denver

Lockhart & Lenard
1873—Longmont

Logan, Fenamore J.
1883(D) — Denver
(with H. W. Watson)

Longshore & Ward
1882(C)—Leadville

Lorenzen, Henry
1867—Central City

Lotus Photo Studio
1901(D)—Denver
15 Evans Block

Lovejoy, E.
1886(C)—Henry (formerly Lariat)

Lowe, Mrs. Minnie
1899-1900(C)—Westcliff

Lowell, N.T.
1887-1889(C)—White Pine
(also drugs and pharmacy)

Lowell, W.J.(J.W.)
1885(C)—Del Norte
1886-1887—not listed
1888-1890(C)—Del Norte

Lozo, Alex
1890-1891(C & D)—Denver
910-16th

Luke, J.W. (see also Russell & Luke)
1874-1876—Colorado Springs

Luke, Wellington O. (W. A.) &
1882-1886(C) — Leadville
41 Union Block, Harrison & 4th, 328 Harrison
1887—not listed
1888-1889(C & L)—Leadville
103 East 5th
1890(C)—Leadville
422 Harrison
1891(C)—Leadville
Hall's Corner
1892(C)—Leadville
523 Harrison
1893(C)—New Castle

Luke & Wheeler
1879-1881(C & L)—Leadville
427 Harrison or Harrison opposite Clarendon Hotel

Lundquist, N.
1893-1897(C)—Julesburg

Lundquist Brothers
1887-1889(C)—Julesburg

Lupein, Edward Real
1894-1899(D)—Denver
1898(D)—Denver
1624 Curtis

M

McBeth, Charles S.
1876(D)—Denver

McClintock, Mrs. J.A.
1899-1901(C)—Julesburg

McClure, Lewis (Louis)
1887(D) — Denver
1888-1889(D) — Denver
1895(D) — Denver
(with W. H. Jackson)
1896-1897(D) — Denver
1898 — (Standard Fire Brick Co.)
1899(D) — Denver
(on his own)

McCormick, James A.
1890(D)—Denver

McDonald, George W., & Co.
1890-1895(C)—Denver
12th & Larimer or 1206 Larimer
1896(C)—Denver
1740 Larimer
1897(C)—Denver
1537 Larimer
1899-1901(C & D)—Denver
1031-17th or Iron Building

McDonald, Robert (see also William & McDonald)
1863-1866 — Denver

McDonald, J.
1874(D)—Denver

McEwen & Brewer
1861—Denver

McGraw, E.E.
1889 1890(C)—Boulder

McGillycuddy, V.T.
(Black Hills, 1857)(Ta)(W)

McGregor, A.Q.
1878(C)—Boulder

McIntyre, S.S.
(San Francisco, 185I)(Ta)

McKee, Mrs. A.F. (A.S.)
1899-1901(C)—Montrose

McKee, T.M.
1890(C)—Montrose
1891-1894—not listed
1895-1898(C)—Montrose

Mackie, J. M.
1901(C) — Brush

McKinney, Albert S. (McKinny, McKenney, see also Reed & McKinney)
1866-1868 — Black Hawk & Central City
1868-1869 — Georgetown
1870 — Central City
1873 — not found (see Van Alstine)
1874 — Black Hawk and Central City
1875 — Georgetown

McKirahan, Andrew
1882(D)—Denver
(with W.H. Jackson)

McKirrahn(McKirhan, C.A.) & Whitter
1883(C)—Georgetown
1884-1887—not listed
1888-1889(C & L)—Leadville
506 Harrison

McLean, Lachlan
1874(D) — Denver
1875-1877—Central City
1878-1881(C)—Georgetown
1882-1883—not listed
1884(C)—Golden
1885-1886(C)—Idaho Springs
1887-1889 — not listed
1890(C)—Idaho Springs
1887-1889 — not listed
1890(C)—Idaho Springs
1891—not listed
1892-1901(C)—Idaho Springs

Macomber, Alonzo
1885(D)—Denver

Madden, T.H.
1901(C)—Fort Morgan

Maffit, L.H.
1875—Colorado Springs

Maher, Nellie, Miss
1890 (D)—Denver

Marchington, C.
1901(C)—Idaho Springs

Marsh, A.
1886(C) — Georgetown

Marsh, B.T.(B.F.)
1875-1890(C)—Greeley

Marsh, C. M.
1891-1894(C) — Greeley
1895 — not listed
1896-1900(C) — Greeley
1901(C) — Greeley (and Son)

Marshall, Edward S.
1888-1891(C & D)—Denver
1637 Larimer

Martin, Alexander (see below)
1874-1878 — Boulder
1879(C) — Central City and Denver
1880-1883 — not listed
1884(C) — Georgetown
1885-1886 — not listed
1888(C) — Georgetown
1888-1890(C & D) — Denver
1634 Larimer
1891-1892 — not listed
1893(D) — Denver
Clear Creek Avenue southeast corner Coyote
1894-1897(C) — Denver
1740 Larimer
1898(D) — Denver
53 Tabor Block
1899-1900(C) — Denver
2500 19th
1901(C) — Denver
1629 Platte

Martin, A.P.
1900(C) — Victor

Martin & Mills, M.E.
(see Mills, M.E.)
Gold Hill

Martin & Peers
1879(C) — Central City

Martindale, Mrs. C.S.
1892(A) — Aspen

Masonheimer, John
1889(D) — Denver
(with W.H. Jackson)
1890(D) — Denver

Massard (see Atkins, Massard & Co.)

Master, Mrs. G.H.
1874—Fort Collins

Masters, O.E.
1900(C) — Cripple Creek
201 West Bennett

Masters, William H.
1873-1875—Denver
372 Larimer

Masters & Taylor
1874 — Denver
372 Larimer

Matteson, S.W.
1897 — Denver

Maull (see James & Maull)

Mayes, N.M.
1885(C) — Pueblo
122½ Union
1886(C) — Denver & Pueblo
Denver—15th & Larimer
Pueblo — Union between C & D
1887(D) — Denver
6 McClelland Block
1888-1889-1891(C) — Pueblo
407 Santa Fe &
413½ Santa Fe

Mayne, W. J.
1875(D)—Denver

Mealey, Martin W. (A. W. & Co.)
1880-1884(C) — Pueblo
4th & Santa Fe
1885—not listed
1886-1889(C)—Pueblo
115 West 4th
1890-1892—not listed

Mealey, W.P.
1896(C)—Pueblo

Mealey & Phillips
1879-1881(C)—Pueblo

Mealey & Savigny
1884(C)—Pueblo

Mealy & Son

1893(C) — Pueblo
Holden Block—South Union
1894-1895 — not listed

Meille, Louis (see also Voice & Meille)
1888—Boulder
1889-1892 — not listed
(see Miele)
1889(D) — Denver
1893-1894 — see below
1895-1896 — not listed
1897-1899(C) — Boulder

Meile & Sturtevant
1893-1894(C) — Boulder

Mellen, George E. & Co.
1882-1883(C) — Gunnison
1884-1887 — not listed
1888(C) — Colorado Springs
1889(D) — Denver
(with W.H. Jackson)
1890(CS) — Manitou Springs
(with J.G. Hiestand)
1890(D) — Denver

Mellen & Harper
Photo: County Court House, Gunnison, Colorado, August 1881, Gunnison, *The Free Press*, December 3, 1881, p. 3, c. 3; *Elk Mountain Pilot*, Irwin (in town), November 3, 1881, p. 3, c. 3

Meyers, L.
1899(C)—Denver
2615 Larimer

Meyers, Roscoe H.
1887(D) — Denver
(with George Stephan)

Mickel, D. E., Miss E.
1860 — Denver

Michaelis, H.
1889(D)—Denver

Michel, J.
1888(D)—Denver

Mickey, D.E.
1896-1898(C)—Del Norte

Miele, Louis
1890(D)—Denver
(with U.A. Voice)
2100 Larimer

Miller (see Crooks & Miller)

Miller, Harry, Tramp Photographer, 1890's

Miller, R. B., Mr. & Mrs.
1893(C) — Trinidad
1894 — not listed
1895-1897(C) — Trinidad

Miller, T.C.
1881 — Alma
1882 — not listed
1883-1884 — Alma
1885 — not listed
1886 — Alma

Millon, G.
1884(C)—Gunnison

Mills, C. C. (Simpson Expedition, Utah) (Ta)

Mills, Charles H.
1889(D) — Denver
Mills Engraving Co.
1890(D) — Denver
1893(C) — Pueblo
407 Santa Fe

Mills, M.E.
1896—Gold Hill & Wall Street

Miner's Photographing Co.
1897(C)—Victor

Minton, (Ray S.) & Trask
1894(D) — Denver
343 Gallup Ave. Highlands

Mitchell, A.M.
1889(C)—Canon City

Mitchell, A.W.
1897-1898(C)—Denver
329 16th
1889(C)—Denver
505 Times Block
1900(C)—Denver

Mitchell Studio
78 Barth Block

Mitchell, D.S. (S & B)

Mitchell, Mrs. Lillie L.
1900(D)—Denver
710 Santa Fe Avenue

Monroe — Thompson Photograph Co.
1901(C)—Denver
808-16th

Moore, G.L.
1891(C)—Boulder

Moore, G.W.
1892-1893(C)—Ouray

Moore, H. C.
1889(C) — Telluride
1890 — not listed
1891-1893(C) — Rico
1894-1898 — not listed
1899-1900(C)—Telluride

Moore, Harry G.
(see Royer & Moore)

Moon, Carl (S & B)

Mooney, James (S & B)

Moorhouse, Lee (S & B)

Morgan, D. P.
(see also Headley & Morgan)
1890(C)—Longmont
1891-1893—not listed
1894-1896(C)—Cripple Creek
113-2nd
1897(C)—Cripple Creek
10 Wilbur Block

Morgan, Samuel
1900(C)—Denver
2047 Market

Morledge, C.J.(W)

Morris, Henry O.
(see Erie Photograph Company)

Morrison, E. G.
1880-1883(C) — Canon City

Morrison, Robert
RMN May 19, 1881, p. 3, c. 1
1881 — Georgetown
Rose Street
1882(C) — Georgetown

Morrow, S. J.
(Stanley Expedition, Yellowstone & Dakotas)
(Ta) (W)

Mortimer, Frank L.
1882(L)—Leadville
223 Harrison Avenue
1882(D)—Denver
(with W.H. Jackson)

Motendale, Mrs. C.S.
1892(C)—Aspen

Muhr (see Bates & Muhr)

Muhr, Adolph
1893(C)—Denver
48 King Block

Murphy, A.C.
1891-1899(C)—Evergreen

Muybridge, Edward
(T),(S & B), (W)

N

Nast, Charles A. (C.B.) & Co.
1880-1881(D)—Denver
372 Larimer
1882(D)—Denver
(with H. Watson)
1883(D) — Denver
(with Chas. Weitfle)
1884(D) — Denver
(with C. C. Wright)
1885-1890(D) — Denver
(with A. E. Rinehart)
1891-1893(C)—Denver
1624 Curtis
1893-1896(C) — Harman
1897-1901(C) — Denver
1624 Curtis or 16th & Curtis

Nast, John E. (see also Needles & Nast)
1881-1882(C & D)—Denver
372 Larimer
1884(D)—Denver
(with H.W. Watson)

Nast Brothers
1882(C)—Denver
372 Larimer

National Gallery of Art
(see McKinney, Albert S.)

Neal, A.
— Morrison
(Two pictures at Colorado State Historical Society)

Needles (see Stone & Needles)

Needles, John T. & Co.
1881(LCor) — Leadville
116 East 4th
1881-1884(C)—Leadville
116 East 4th or
600-613 Harrison Avenue
1885-1886—not listed
1887(C)—Pueblo
229½ Union
1888-1891(C)—Pueblo
14 Holden Block

Needles & Nast
1888(C)—Pueblo
229½ Union

Neel, J.W.
1888(C)—Erie

Neel Brothers
1888(T)—Trinidad
1889(C)—Trinidad
(with Gregory)
1890—not listed
1891-1892(C)—Trinidad

Nelles (see Pollard & Nelles)

Nelson, Aaron
1890(C)—Central City
1891—not listed
1892-1893(C)—Central City

Nelson, L.E.
1900(C)—Boulder
1017 Pearl

Nelson, O.A.
1897-1898(C)—Leadville
219 Harrison

Nesbit, Carroll E. (see Sours & Co.)

Neville, David S.
1900-1901(CS & C) — Colorado Springs
111 South Tejon

New York Photograph Gallery
(see Abraham & Isaacs)

Newbury (see Faul & Newbury)

Newby, L. C. & Co.
1892-1895(C) — Aspen
1894 — not listed
1896-1898 — not listed
1899(C) — Victor, W of Hotel Victor

Newby, Mrs. M. W.
1881(D) — Denver
(with B. E. Hawkins)

Newby & Wilson
1900(C)—Victor
125 South 3rd

Newton, Howell Dewitt
1890-1901—Salida (1893—Dentist)

Nichols, George B.
1888(C)—Colorado City

Nilson, Carl
1881(D)—Denver

Nims, F.A.
1882(C)—Colorado Springs

Nims & Co. (see also Clark & Nims and Clarke & Nims)
1886(C) — Colorado Springs

Noble, Oliver D.
1887(D)—Denver
1888(D) (A.E. Rinehart)

1890(D) (with C.H. Wells)

Nockin (see Oiler & Nockin)

Nockin Photo Co. (Edward)
1899-1901(C)—Denver
1617 Champa

Nofts, Robert W.
1896(C)—Goldfield

Nonpareil Portrait & Publishing Company
1898(CS)—Colorado Springs
24-26 East Bijou Street
1899(C)—Denver
1625 Welton
1899(D)—Denver
1615 Arapahoe

Northwestern Portrait Co.
1899(C)—Denver
20 Tabor Block

Nott, Victor E.
1890(D)—Denver
(with E.S. Marshall)

Nutt, James W.
1885(D) — Denver
(with E. S. Marshall)
1885(C) — Alma
(see also Miller and Nutt)
(Photo)

Nye, Willis A. (see also Bates & Nye)
1880(L Cor) — Leadville
141 West 2nd

O

Ogden, John T. & Co.
1889-1890(C & D)—Denver
14 Braisie Block
1890 — 523 & 525 Charles Building; 15th, corner Curtis

Ogden & Irish
1891(C)—Denver
525 Charles Block

Oiler's Photograph Gallery (Frank E.)
1896-1897(C & D)—Denver
Riche Block, 16th & Curtis
1898—see below
1899(D)—Denver
1615 Arapahoe

Oiler, N.R. Photo Co.
1899-1900(D)—Denver

Oiler & Nockin
1898(C)—Denver
1617 Champa

O'Keefe, C. Frank
1892-1893(L & C)—Leadville
425 Harrison

O'Keefe, M.T.
1885(C)—Leadville
503 Harrison

O'Keefe (C.F.) & Stockdorf
1894-1897(L & C) — Leadville
5th & Harrison

Oldroyd, L. K.
1873-1876 — Colorado Springs (bought Eugene Brandt's business in 1876)
1877 — not listed
1878-1882(C) — Colorado Springs

O'Neal, L.
1892(C) — Grand Junction

Opie & Kerr
1891(C)—Aspen

Orr, J.E. (Orris, Ore)
1895-1901(C)—Rocky Ford

O'Sullivan, Timothy H.
1871, 1873-1874 — Wheeler Surveys

Owen, George
1895-1899(C)—Wray

P

Page Camera Co.
1895(C)—Denver

Painter, Orrin C.

1886(D)—Denver
(with W.H. Jackson)

Palace Art Studio
1901(C)—Denver
1113-16th

Palmer, Charles H.
1890(D)—Denver

Paris (see Rankin, Paris & Allyn)

Park, H.S.
1889(D)—Denver

Parks, Arthur L.
1889(D)—Denver
(with H. Rothberg)
1890(D)—Denver

Parks & Childs
1878
1881(L)—Leadville
103 East 5th

Parks & Van Horn
1882(L)—Leadville
424 Harrison

Pascoe (see Stephan & Pascoe)

Pascoe, Elmer E.
1888(D)—Denver
1889(D)—Denver
16th southeast corner Court Place
1891-1892—Creede

Pasamore, William G.
1896-1901(C)—Colorado City
623 Colorado

Payne (D. R.) & Stockdorf (Fred)
1887(L) — Leadville
613 Harrison
1888-1889(C)—Leadville
613 Harrison

Peers, O.L. (see also Martin & Peers)
1880(C)—Central City

Peirson & Co. (H. F., Howard F. or Howard T.)
1894(D) — Denver
1609 Arapahoe
1895-1896(C)—Denver
1615 Arapahoe
1897-1899(C)—Denver
Opera House Block
1900(C)—Denver
1617 Lawrence

Perry (Charles M.) & Bohm
1872-1875—Denver

Perry, O.H.
1901(C)—Boulder
2028-14th

Peters, George
1901(C)—Cripple Creek
3rd and Carr

Peters, Ottis
1881(D)—Denver

Peterson, Charles
(S & B)

Peterson, Fountain L.
1866 — Fort Collins
Mumey — "The Saga of 'Auntie' Stone" pp. 51, 91, 93

Peterson, John F.
1879(L)—Leadville
Main Street near Harrison
1880(L.Cor)—Leadville
119 East 3rd
1883(D)—Denver
326 Larimer

Phillips (see Mealey & Phillips)

Phillips, E.F. (E.T.)
1893-1895(C)—Sterling

Phillips, H.M. (see also Clegg & Phillips)
1897(C)—Victor

Phillips, L.R.
1888(C)—Saguache
1889-1896—not listed
1897(C)—Pueblo

239 North Union

Phillips, Russell T.
1881(D) — Denver
(with J. Collier)

Phillips & Schedin
1899(C) — Cripple Creek
412 Bennett

Phillips & Smith
1899(C) — Grand Junction

Photo Novelty Co.
1899(C)—Denver
1624 Curtis

Plumbe, John (Ta)

Poley, Horace S. & Co.
(see also Sooy & Poley)
1892-1901(C) — Colorado Springs
713-715 North Tejon
1895—not listed

Pollard (R.M.) & Nelles (W.A.)
1889(D)—Denver
37 & 45 Steele Block

Porter, C.Y.
1890-1891(C)—Cockrell

Porter, George
Mt. Sneffels, Colorado

Porter, J.H.
1871—Georgetown
(with Eggleston Brothers)

Post, Frederick E.
1889-1891(C & D)—Denver
1459 Larimer
1892(C)—Denver
1759 Larimer
1893-1901(C & D)—Denver
1206-15th

Potter, C.T.
1889(C)—Cockrell

Powell, Clement
(Ta) — Powell Surveys

Powell, W.A.
1897(C)—Ouray

Power, Eustace B.
1892(D)—Denver

Powers, W.C.
1891-1900(C)—Holyoke

Price, N.B.
1900-1901(C)—Chromo

Prudden, T. Mitchell
(Del)

Pruden (see Sturtevant & Pruden)

Pywell, William R.
(Ta) (W)

Q

Quackenbush, Richard M.
1885(D) — Denver
Larimer northwest corner 27th

R

Randall, A. Frank
1890(D) — Denver
10, 16, 4, 5 Curtis
(S & B) (W)

Rankin & Co.
1861 — Central City

Rankin, Paris & Allyn
1861 — Denver

Rapin, A.
1892(CC & G) — Silver Plume

Ray, F.L.
1899-1901(C)—Salida

Read & Reed
1901(C)—Delta

Reall, John A.
1894(D)—Denver
1897-1898(C & D)—Denver
2330 Larimer

Reaves, H.D.P.
1889(C)—Ouray

397

Reed (see Read & Reed, Hopkins & Reed, Smith & Reed)

Reed and Kellum
1879—Colorado Springs

Reed, Melville
1884(C & L)—Leadville
103 East 5th
1885(C)—Leadville
Harrison & East 5th

Reed, S. E.
1897-1898(C)—Colorado Springs
425 South Tejon

Reed, William H.
1869—Central City
1870—Central City
(with McKenney)

Reed & McKenney
1871 1072—Denver
1873—Central City and Georgetown

Rees, C. E.& Co. (C. C.)
1894-1895(C)—Aspen
1896-1898—not listed
1899-1901—Creede

Reeve, H.D.P.
1888(C)—Pueblo
115 West 4th
1889—not listed
1890(C)—Ouray

Reichene(c)ker, W. C.
1872—Golden
1873(D)—Denver

Reiff & Elliot
(see Georgetown, Colorado, in Western History Department, Denver Public Library)

Reiman, Leroy
1890 1891(C)—Eads

Reistle, Frank
1889(D)—Denver and Steamboat Springs
1901(C)—Denver
1420-22 Lawrence

Reitze, George
1888(D)—Denver
(with W.H. Jackson)

Richardson, Mrs. Mary
1900-1901(C)—Durango

Rich, V.E.(Riche)
1896-1897(C)—Walden

Richmond, E.O.
1899(C)—Durango

Richard, Charles
1870—Pueblo
1871—Canon City

Richard, E.S.
1893-1894(C)—Rocky Ford

Riddle, J. R.
1881-1890's—Loveland
(RMN October 21, 1881, p. 4, c. 6)

Rienhart, E.W.
1901(C)—Florence

Rinehart, Alfred Evans
1876(D)—(with G. W. Kirkland)
1875-1880—Denver
(associated with Charles Bohm)
1880-1881—Denver
(Rinehart & W.H. Jackson)
1881-1886(C)—Denver
413 Larimer
1887(C)—Denver
(with William H. Rinehart)
1637 Larimer
1888(C)—Denver
1630 Arapahoe
1889(C)—Denver
Londoner Block
1890-1894(C)—Denver
1830 Arapahoe
1895-1897(C)—Denver
827-16th
1898-1901(C)—Denver
1630 Arapahoe

Rinehart, Frank A.
1879-1881(D)—(with Charles Bohm)

Rinehart, William H.
1883(D)—Denver
(with A.E. Rinehart)

Roberts, O.U.
1900(C)—Denver
710 Santa Fe

Robinson, Roland A.
(see also Shipler)
1874—Denver
372 Larimer

Roche, T.C.
(Ta)

Rocky Mountain Gallery of Art
(see Johnson, I.M.)

Rodstrom, E.
1900(C)—Craig

Rogers, Orlando
1897-1899(C)—Independence

Rogers, Thomas J.
1888(D)—Denver

Roloson
(see Whitney & Roloson)

Rood, Edgar H.
1884-1885(C & D)—Denver
9 Steele Block
1886(C)—Denver
291-16th
1887-1888(C & D)—Denver
1113-16th
1889-1890(C)—Denver
16th and Arapahoe
(1113-16th)

Rose, Charles E.
1888(D)—Denver
1893(D)—Denver
1232 Larimer
1894(D)—Denver
(with George W. McDonald)
1895(D)—Denver
(no address)
1896-1897(C & D)—Denver
1206 Larimer
1898-1899(D)—Denver
1740 Larimer
1900-1901(D)—Denver
(no address)

Rose & Company (John K. Rose and Benjamin S. Hopkins)
1886-1898(D)—Denver
Tabor Block

Rose & Hopkins (Landscape)
1896-1898(D)—Denver
Tabor Block
1899-1901(D)—Denver
Tabor Block
(No longer Rose & Co.)

Ross, H.E.
1882(McKBD)—Salida

Ross, J. Leask (see Clements & Rose)

Ross, John
1889(C)—Aspen

Rothberger, Henry (H. V.)
(Rothenberg, Henry)
1882(D)—Denver
(with H. W. Watson)
1883(D)—Denver
18th, northwest corner Larimer
1884-1887—not listed
1888(C)—Denver
910-16th
1889-1901(C)—Denver
1539 Arapahoe

Rouff, Henry
1888(D)—Denver

Rowley, M.V.
1888(D)—Denver

Royer (W.C.) & Moore
1893(D)—Denver
1645 Curtis

Rudasill, H.M.
1898(C)—Colorado Springs
25 South Weber

Rudy, W. Ira
1892(CS)—Colorado Springs
18 South Tejon

Rudy & Clinton
1889(C)—Colorado Springs

Runkle, Maud (Miss)
1889(D)—Denver
(with H. Rothberger)

Russel, Capt. A.J.
1868, UPRR, Wyoming (Ta)

Russell, Warren H.
1884-1885(D)—Denver
326 Larimer
1886—see below
1887(D)—Denver
1354 Lawrence
(see also Jennings & Russell)

Russell & Luke (Lake)
1874-1876—Colorado Springs

Russell Brothers (Frederick C. & Warren H.)
1885(D)—Denver
1886(D)—Denver
281 Larimer
1889(D)—Denver
(with Frank)

Ryan, D. J. (see also Van Tassell & Ryan)
1895-1898(C)—Denver
Cass & Graham Block, 16th & Curtis
1899(C)—Denver
913 16th

Ryan's Photograph Gallery
1900(C)—Denver
16th & Curtis

S

Sabine, James E.
(First photographer to set up business in gold fields)
1859

Saint, T.G.
1862(August)—Central City
(with Henry Faul)
1863—not found
1864—Central City
(with Henry Garbanati)
1865-1866—not found
1867—Denver
(with W.G. Chamberlain)
1867(September)—Central City

Samelson (A.J.) & Co.
1899-1901(C)—Denver
428-16th

Sanborn, G.B.
529 East 5th, Leadville, Colorado

Savage, Charles Roscoe
1874(Summer)—Colorado Springs

Savage, N. W. Jr.
1891(P)—Pueblo
229 South Union

Savage and Ottinger
1869(T)Mormons, UPRR

Savigny (see Mealey & Savigny)

Scarbrough, Charles W.
1900(L)—Leadville
219 Harrison Avenue

Schaffer
1878(D)—Denver
244—15th

Schawalter, Fred
1887(D)—Denver
(with W.H. Forman)

Schedin (see Phillips & Schedin)

Schedin & Lehman
1900-1901(C)—Cripple Creek
412 Bennett

Schumacher, C.E.
1888-1889(D)—Denver
(with H. Rothberger)

Schindler, A. Zeno
(T)

Schneider, R.
1877(C)—Parrott City

Scott, —
1900(C)—Pueblo
304 North Main

Scovill, Homer W.
1884(D)—Denver

Seavy, F. D.
1876(C)—Del Norte

Seckner (Sackner), S. H.
(see also Bunn & Seckner)
1892-1894(C)—Fort Collins
1895-1897 not listed
1898-1901(C)—Fort Collins

Sedgwick, S. J.
(Ta)

Segerberg, Bern
1890(D)—Denver
1891(C)—Denver
1213—19th

Seitz, Perry
1884(D) (with H.W. Watson)
1885-1886(C)—Denver
556 Larimer
1887-1890(C & D)—Denver
2100 Larimer

Seymour, James
1888(C)—Aspen
1889—not listed
1890(C)—Colorado Springs

Shaffner, C. H.
1882(C)—Georgetown

Shaver, J.C.
1900(C)—Georgetown

Shaw, J.W.
1892(C)—Pueblo
115 West 4th
1893-1895(C)—Pueblo
Santa Fe corner 6th
1894—Cripple Creek

Sheldon Photo Co.
1901(C)—Hotchkiss

Sherholtz, —
1880(D)—Denver

Shipler, James William
1872—Denver

Shipler (J. W.) & Co.
1880(D)—Denver
448 Larimer
1878(D)—Denver

Shipler & Chew
1875—Denver

Shipler & Robinson
1875—Denver
372 Larimer

Shipler & Williamson
1877—Denver
377 Larimer

Shirley, George A.
1897(D)—Denver
2052 Larimer

Silsbee, George M.
(see Danielson, Frank M.)

Simmons, Court J.
1886-1887(D)—Denver
Emerald Avenue corner 6th & Highland

Simpson, W.P.
1899(C & D)—Denver
(133 or 331) Symes
1900-1901(C)—Pueblo
205 North Main

Sinclair, Warren A.
1900(D)—Denver
24 South 11th Street

Skinner, C.E.
1893(C)—Salida
1894-1900—not listed
1901(C)—Salida

Skolas, Miss Julia
1899-1901(C)—Colorado Springs
222 South Tejon

Slack & Kurts
1889(C)—Boston & Springfield

Smallwood (William) & Ball (George)
1876(D)—Denver
275—8th

Smith, Albert P.
1896(C)—Green P.O.

Smith, James
1887-1888(C)—Denver
1439-18th
1889(D)—Denver
18th corner Holladay

Smith (Stephen S.) & Grove
1864-1866—Pueblo
(R. W. Cragin's notebook, vol. XVII, p. 9)
1867-1868—Pueblo
1871-1873—Pueblo

Smith-Hassell Co.
1899-1901(C & D)—Denver
437-17th
Studio—1644 Broadway

Smith & Reed
1868—Pueblo

Soderberg, Pont (artist)
Ca. 1885—Kokomo
(photo in WHD)

Solons, Anton
1888-1889(C)—Coal Creek

Sonnberger, —
1867—Georgetown

Sooy, Benjamin
1884(D)—(with C. Weitfle)

Sooy (Sovy), Ben F.
1888(C)—Boulder
1889—see below
1892(C)—Boulder

Sooy & Poley
1889-1891(C)—Colorado Springs
112 North Tejon

Soper, Roy W.
1900(D)—Denver
2323 West 30th Avenue

Soule, W.S.
(S & B) (W)

Sours, Charles W. & Co.
1889-1891(D)—Denver
1705 Champa
1892-1894—not listed
1895-1896(C & D)—Denver
906-15th
1899-1900(L & C)—Leadville
219 Harrison

Sours, Robert S. & Co.
1890-1892(C & D)—Denver
1705 Champa
1893-1894—not listed
1895(C)—Denver
2100 Larimer
1896—not listed
1897(C)—Cripple Creek
1898-1899(L & C)—Leadville
217 or 219 Harrison

Sours Brothers
1897(P)—Pueblo
407 Santa Fe

Spracklen & Ghormley
1880(C)—Trinidad

Stanley, J.M.
1853—U.S. Government Photographer

States, H.L.
1894-1895(C)—Delta
1896-1897—not listed
1898-1900(C)—New Castle

Steele, William C.
1886(D)—Denver
(with H.W. Watson)
1887(D) (with Wells & King)
1888(D)—Denver
1889(D)—Denver
1890(D)—Denver

Stein, R.
1897(C)—Denver
2617 Larimer
1898(C)—Denver
2207 Larimer

398

Stephan, George & Co.
1884(D)
1885-1886(C & D) — Denver
300 Larimer
1887-1889(C & D) — Denver
1226 & 1232 Larimer

Stephan & Co.
1891(C) — Denver
1232 Larimer

Stephan & Pascoe
1890(C) — Denver
1226 Larimer
1892(C) — Denver
1232 Larimer

Stephens, A.J. (Stevens)
1890(C) — Paonia
1891(C) — Montrose
1892-1896(C) — Paonia

Stevens, F.P.
1899-1901(C) — Colorado
Springs
24 East Bijou

Stevens, Lewis G.
1887(D) — Denver
1888(D) — Denver

Stevens Fotograferie
1900(CS) — Colorado Springs
24-26 East Bijou

Stevens (Stephens), Isaac N.
1873(D) — Denver
1874(D) — Denver

Stewart, William
1884(D) — Denver

Stiffler, George W.
1881(C) — Golden
1882 — not listed
1883(C) — South Pueblo
1884(C) — Longmont
1885-1886 — not listed
1886-1888 — see below
1889 — not listed
1890-1901(C) — Longmont
1892(BCo) — Longmont

Stiffler & Son
1887-1888(C) — Longmont

Stiles, H.L.
1899(C) — Colorado Springs
117 Pikes Peak
1900(C) — Colorado Springs
116 Pikes Peak
1901(C) — Colorado Springs
115 East Pikes Peak

Stimson, Charles (see Danielson, Frank M.)

Stivers, John O.
1889 — Colorado Springs
(Book in WHD)

Stockdorf, Frederick T.
(see also Payne & Stockdorf, O'Keefe & Stockdorf)
1897(L) — Leadville
501 Harrison

Stoll, George
1883(L) — Leadville
Chestnut southeast
corner Harrison
1884(C) — Leadville

Stoll, Mrs. Lottie N.
1884-1885(C,NM) — Leadville
105 East Chestnut

Stone & Needle(s)
1884-1886(C) — South Pueblo
Holden Block, or
39½ Union
1887 — not listed
1888(C) — South Pueblo
39½ Union

Stoneman, J.S.
1898(C) — Coal Creek

Storm(s), Frank D. (Francis D.)
1882(D) — Denver
359 Larimer northwest
corner 15th
1883(D) — Denver
361 Larimer
1884(D) — Denver
Lawrence southeast
corner 15th
1885-1886 — not listed
1887-1901(C) — Denver
Cass & Graham Block

Iron Building 906-15th
1893 — not listed

Storm Brothers
1881(C) — Arvada

Stormer & Co. (W.H. & H.W.)
1882(C) — Manitou Springs
1883 — not listed
1884(C) — Manitou Springs

Storms, F.D.
1882(C) — Denver

Stott, George
1884(C) — Leadville

Streeter, J.E.
1880-1882(C) — Boulder

Stringfellow, F. W.
Ca. 1898 — Anaconda

Strong (Mrs.) & Hargroves
1880(C) — Fort Collins

Studebaker, —
1900(C) — Colorado Springs
Oriel Block

Sturtevant, Joseph Bevier
(see also James & Sturtevant)
1887(C) — Boulder
1888 — not listed
1889 — see below
1890 — not listed
1891-1893(C) — Boulder
1894 — (see Meile & Sturtevant)
1895 — not listed
1896-1898(C & BCo) — Boulder (Sturtevant, J. B. & A.)
1899 — not listed
1900-1901(C) — Boulder
1761-12th

Sturtevant & Pruden
1889(C) — Boulder

Sullivan, Miss Mary
1879(D) — Denver
(with Hosier & Calhoun)

Swain Brothers (Swan)
1882(C) — Gunnison City
Irwin — Elk Mountain Pilot
May 18, 1882, p. 3, c. 1
June 8, 1882, p. 3, c. 1

Swan, Justus C.
1897-1899(C & D) — Denver
1206 Larimer
1900(C) — Denver
18th & California
1901(C) — Denver
1762 California

Swan Brothers
1886-1887(C) — Crested Butte

Swanson (see Chase & Swanson)

Swanson, Aaron
1888(C) — Denver
1740 Larimer

Swanson, John
1888(D) — Denver
1891-1892(C) — Central City

T

Talbert, Z.E.
1898(C) — Denver
14 Mack Block

Talbot, Chalmers W.
1874-1877 — Canon City

Talbot, Nathaniel H. (A.H.)
1873-1876 — Evans
1877-1879 — not listed
1880 — see below
1881(C) — Evans
1882-1885 — not listed
1886-1890(C) — Evans
1891-1892 — not listed
1893-1901(C) — Loveland
1894 — (Talbot's Photograph Gallery)

Talbot & Howe
1880(C) — Evans

Taylor (see Carpenter & Taylor)

Taylor, G.L.
1874 — Denver
372 Larimer (with W.H. Masters)

Taylor, Leve Miss
1889(D) — Denver
(with E.S. Marshall)
1890(D) — Denver

Teitzel, Louis
1899-1900(C) — Idaho Springs

Terington, J.P.
1877(D) — Denver
(with Charles Bohm)

Thayer, S.N.
1895-1896(C) — Leadville

Theilkuhl, Gustav
1900(CS) — Colorado Springs
25 South Weber

Thomas, A.M.
1900-1901(C) — Central City

Thomason, Mrs. Sophie
(may be same as Mrs. S. Thompson)
1882-1883(C) — Trinidad
1884 — see Thompson
1885(C) — Trinidad
1886(C) — Trinidad

Thompson (see Monroe-Thompson)

Thompson, Alvah B.
1895(D) — Denver
77 Barth Block,
16th corner Stout

Thompson, H.L.
Boulder (S & B)(W)

Thompson, Lawrence (H.L.)
1869-1874 — Boulder

Thompson, Mrs. S.
1881-1884(C) — Trinidad

Thompson, T.A.
1892-1893(C) — Denver
2200 Larimer

Thompson, Z.
1899 — Eldora

Throwbeck, Samuel J. O.
(Thorbeck, Throbeck)
1892(D) — Denver
Cass & Graham Block
1893-1896 — not listed
1897-1901(C) — Denver
827-16th

Thurlow, James
1874-1878 — Manitou
1879(C) — Manitou

Tittler, L.L.
1897(C) — Hotchkiss

Towner, Mrs. C.S.
1898-1901(C) — Buena Vista

Towner, Henry C.
1878(D) — Denver
322 Blake

Townsend (see Jamerson & Townsend)

Townsend & Hathaway
1892-1893(C) — Denver
6 McClelland Block,
15th & Lawrence

Tracht, William A.
1898-1901(C) — Manitou
Springs
999 Ruxton Avenue

Traeumer, George
1892-1893(C & D) — Denver
58 Skinner Block

Trager, G.E.
(S & B) (W)

Trask, Robert T. (see Minton & Trask)

Travis, W.R.
1899-1901(C) — Delta

Trendel, John A.
1891-1892(D) — Denver
1420 Larimer

Troutman, —
1871 — Boulder

Turner, J.E.
1901(C) — Boulder
14th & Pearl

Tweed, Miss A. M.
1896(CS) — Colorado Springs
322 North Nevada Avenue

U

Udell, A.A.
1885(D) — Denver

Ute Iron Springs Photo Gallery
(J. G. Hiestand)
Before 1891 — Ute Pass

V

Van Alstine, E.W.
1873(D) — Denver
(with A.S. McKenney)

Van Derman, Max
1883(D) — Denver
(with C. James)

Van Horn, John W. (see also Parks & Van Horn)
1883(L) — Leadville
103 East 5th

Van Tassell, Walter S.
(Frank M. Van Tassell)
1901(C) — Denver
931-16th

Van Tassell & Ryan
1900(C) — Denver
931-16th

Vance, Robert H.
1851(T) — San Francisco

Varney, Hiram
1880(D) — Denver
(Bates & Nye)
1887(D) — Denver
1889(D) — Denver
1890(D) — Denver
(with Beebe)

Velarde, Bartholomew
1872-1876 — Denver
F(15th) & Holladay
(Market)

Vila (Joseph) (see Barley & Vila)

Voice (Ulysses A.) & Co.
1890(D) — Denver
(with Stephan & Pascoe)
1891(C) — Denver
21st & Larimer

Voice & Comstock
1893(C) — Denver
2100 Larimer

Voice & Meile
1892(C) — Denver
21st & Larimer

Van Hofe, George D.
1882(D) — Denver
326 Larimer

Voorhees, Miss C.M.
1897 (C) — Alamosa

W

Wagner (see Wildhack & Wagner)

Wagner, F.S.
1899-1901(C) — Pueblo
233 South Union

Wakely, George D.
1859-1864 — Denver
1865-1878 — not listed
1879(L) — Leadville

Wakely & Clements
1880(L Cor) — Leadville
103 East 4th

Waldo, —
1861 — Central City
(with Henry Faul)

Walker, J.W.
1887(C) — Golden
1888-1891 — not listed
1892-1897(C) — Golden
1895 — not listed

Walker, William H.
1887(D) — Denver
1888(D) — Denver
1889-1890(C & D) — Denver
710 Santa Fe
1891(C) — Idaho Springs
1892(C) — Denver
710 Santa Fe
1893-1896 — not listed
1897(C) — Denver
710 Santa Fe

Wallihan, Allen Grant
1893-1894(C) — Craig
1894(C) — Lake City
1895(C) — Lay
1896(C) — Craig and Lay

Ward (see Longshore & Ward)

Warnky, F. C.
1876 — Fairplay
(Alma — Mount Lincoln News, September 2, 1876, p. 4)
1878 — Garland

Warrington Brothers
1901(C) — Montrose

Waters, F.E.
1890-1891(C) — Burlington
1892(C) — Denver
1645 Curtis

Watkins, C.E.
1860's (Ta),(N) California

Watson, Henry W.
1880(D) — Denver
274 — 16th
1881 — (Republican, April 4, p. 2, c. 2)
1881-1883(C & D) — Denver
300 Larimer
1882-1883(C) — Longmont
1883(C) — Golden
1884-1885(C) — Denver
300 Larimer
1886(C) — Denver
446 Larimer
1887-1894 — not listed
1889(D) — (with George Stephan & Co.)
1895(C) — Denver
1232 Larimer

Watson, O.T.
1881(C) — Golden

Webb, J.T. (see also Bates & Webb)
1885(C) — Denver
Tabor Block

Webb, John
1881(D) — Denver
(with Charles Bohm)

Webster, H. D. (see also below)
1899-1900(C) — Cripple Creek
3rd & Carr

Webster Brothers
1888-1889(C) — Greeley

Weitfle, Charles
1878-1885(C) — Central City
1883(D) — Denver
377 Larimer
1884(D) — Denver
448 Larimer

Weitfle, Paul
1883(D) — Denver
(with Charles Weitfle)
1884(D) — Denver
(with C.C. Wright)

Welch, —
1859 — Denver
(for Frank Leslie's Illustrated Newspaper)

Wells, Charles H. (see also below)
1886(D) — Denver
1890(D) — Denver
1894-1895(C) — Denver
1136 — 15th
Colorado Exchange Journal, October, 1889

Wells & King
1887-1893(C) — Denver
1136-15th, Evans Block

Westerman, Otto
1889-1901(C) — Breckenridge

Westlake, W.J.
1884-1885(C,NM)—Lakeside

Wheeler, C.L.
1884(C)—Colorado Springs

Wheeler, Danforth N. (& Co.)
(see also Barnhouse &
Wheeler, Luke & Wheeler
and Kuhn & Wheeler)
1885(C)—Colorado Springs
1886-1890—not listed
1891-1901(C)—Grand
Junction

Wheeler, Miss Una
Ca. 1899—Ouray

Wheeler & Chase
1878-1879(C)—Del Norte

Whitcombe & Co.
1888(C)—Fort Collins

White, A.D.
1882(McKBD)—South
Pueblo

White, Charles W.
1900(C)—Denver
1131-15th (McClelland
Block, 15th corner Law-
rence)

White, Martin
1882(McKBD)—Denver

White, P.C.
1886(D)—Denver

White, S.G.
1891(C)—Ouray

White, William A.

1880(CuC)—Rosita
1880-1881—Wet Mountain
Valley, Rosita, Querida,
Florence, Canon City
1882-1884(C & D)—Denver
571 Larimer

Whitney, W.H.
1887-1888(C)—Ouray

Whitney, William H.
1890(D)—Denver

Whitney & Roloson
1889—Ouray (picture in
WHD)

Whitney, J.E.
(W)

Whitter, Jacob (see McKirra-
han & Whitter)
1892-1897(D)—Denver
31 Corbett
1898-1899(D)—Denver
north-south Corbett be-
tween Stanton Avenue
& 22nd

Wilder, Edwin A.
1881—Rico
(Dolores News, July 23,
1881, p. 3, c. 1)
1882(C)—Rico
1883—not listed
1884-1885(C)—Durango
1886—not listed
1887-1889(C)—Durango

Wildhack, H. A.
1888—see below
1889-1896(C)—Meeker

Wildhack & Wagner
1888(C)—Meeker

Wilhem
Cripple Creek
219 Meyers
(had been 624 Madison
Avenue, New York)

Wilkins, E. I. & G. T.
1884-1885(C,NM)—Fort Col-
lins

Wilkins, G.T.
1881(C)-1882(McKBD)—Fort
Collins
1883-1885—not listed
1886-1899(C)—Fort Collins

Willett, C.G.
1890(CS)—Colorado Springs

Williams, H.G.
1900(C)—Walsenburg

Williams, W.L.
1887-1889(C)—Alamosa
1890—not listed
1891(C)—Antonito
1892—not listed
1893(C)—Alamosa
1894—not listed
1895-1897(C)—Pueblo
231 Union
1898(C)—Pueblo
Holden Block #2

Williams & Hansmans
1884-1885(C,NM)—Alamosa

Williams & McDonald
1867-1868—Denver

Williamson, Harry M. & Co.
1886(D)—Denver
Colorado Artotype Co.
439—16th, opposite Court-
house

1887—not listed
1888(D)—Denver
333-16th
1889(C)—Denver
329-16th
1890—see below

Williamson, M.A. (see Shipler
& Williamson)

Williamson & Curran (Thomas
J.)
1890(C & D)—Denver
16th & Tremont
329—16th, opposite Court-
house

Wilson (see Newby & Wilson)

Wilson, J.G.
1893—Cripple Creek

Wing's Photograph Gallery
1889-1890(L & C)—Leadville
506 Harrison

Wither, Mrs. Ada
1894(C)—Steamboat
Springs

Witter, Jacob
1882(D)—Denver

Wittick, Ben
(W)

Wolf, J.L.
1895-1896(C)—Alamosa

Wood, G.M.
before 1900—Georgetown,
Colorado

Woodbury, C.
1867—Central City

Wright, Charles C.
1885—Central City
(RMN December 25, 1885,
p. 8, c. 3)
1883-1886(C & D)—Denver
359 Larimer, northwest
corner Larimer & 15th
1887(C)—Denver
910-16th

Wright, Mrs. Charles C.
1887(D)—Denver
910-16th

Wright, G. Wallace
1881(C)—Greeley

Wright, William J.
1890(D)—Denver
1891(C)—Fort Collins

XYZ

Yale, D.B.
1888-1889(C)—Boulder

Yelton, E.A. (see also Webster & Yelton)
1899(C)—Cripple Creek
357 Bennett
1900(C)—Cripple Creek
127 West Eaton

Zahner, Jacob
1888(D)—Denver

Zeovy, Mrs.
1875(C)—Del Norte

Zerega, Clarence
1883-1884(C)—Breckenridge

Ziegler (see Boston & Ziegler)

INDEX

In the view above we see the library of the State Historical Society of Colorado as it looked during the year 1910.   SHSC

The owl of Minerva spreads her wings only with the
setting sun. This is an amateur print from the late
1890's.   SHSC

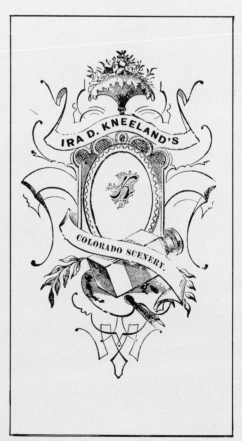